Advance Praise for *The Taming of the American Crowd*

"*The Taming of the American Crowd* offers a unique blend of popular culture and working class history—written with great flair. Sandine is one of the few scholars reckless and ambitious enough to take on a wide-ranging subject without sacrificing analytical rigor. If you've ever participated in a demonstration, gone crazy in the bleachers, or danced all night, you'll love this book."

—**BARBARA EHRENREICH**, author of *Nickel and Dimed*

"Sandine has given us a timely and indispensable book. *The Taming of the American Crowd* is not only a spirited tour through centuries of crowd action and crowd control but a searching meditation on today's consumer-crazy, politically passive Americans, who have squandered the power of the assembled populace to address enormous inequalities in power and wealth and to serve as an instrument for protest and change."

—**GARY B. NASH**, professor of history, UCLA; director of the National Center for History in the Schools; past president of the Organization of American Historians

"Riots and mobs, celebrations and demonstrations! An entertaining journey into American history that also manages to illuminate the soul of the country, its need for social protest and community as an antidote to despair and the key to a less predatory future."

—**ARIEL DORFMAN**, novelist, playwright, essayist; professor of literature and Latin American Studies, Duke University

"Al Sandine traces the rambunctious history of American crowds in a lively and erudite narrative that celebrates their power as a political tool of the masses. He issues a timely warning about the importance of the right of assembly and the simple fact that despite their advantages, online social media lack the political punch of people in the streets."

—**LINDA LUMSDEN**, assistant professor of journalism, University of Arizona

"Building on the tradition of European social historians E. P. Thompson, Eric Hobsbawm, and George Rude, Al Sandine, in this well-written and provocatively argued book, brings the crowd back to the center of U.S. historical and social analysis. In-so-doing, he makes innovative contributions to social movement analysis, and to urban and consumer sociology."

—**E. KAY TRIMBERGER**, visiting scholar at The Institute for the Study of Social change at the University of California, Berkeley; author of *The New Single Woman*

the TAMING *of th*

.MERICAN CROWD

From Stamp Riots to Shopping Sprees

By Al Sandine

MONTHLY REVIEW PRESS *New York*

Library of Congress Cataloging-in-Publication Data
Sandine, Al, 1938-
The taming of the American crowd : from stamp riots to shopping sprees / by Al Sandine.
p. cm.
Includes bibliographical references and index.
ISBN 978-1-58367-197-9 (pbk.) — ISBN 978-1-58367-198-6 (cloth)
1. United States—Social conditions. 2. Crowds—United States—History. 3. Social control—United States—History. 4. Collective behavior—United States—History. 5. Popular culture—United States—History. 6. Political culture—United States—History. 7. Mass society—History. 8. United States—Social life and customs. 9. United States—Politics and government. I. Title.
HN57.S26 2009
302.3'3—dc22

2009039802

Monthly Review Press
146 West 29th Street, Suite 6W
New York, NY 10001

5 4 3 2 1

For everyone who's had to summon courage
to join others in public protest

Acknowledgments

Just by expressing an interest in it, many people contributed to the project that became this book. Some did even more, and here I would like to thank Gary Handman of the University of California's Media Resources Center on the Berkeley campus for his help early on; my friend David Glick for serving as my initial guide to the world of shopping malls; Adrianne Aron for her critical readings of sections of my manuscript and for sharing her doctoral dissertation; and Sheryl Coryell for much needed technical assistance. I owe a special thanks to Elsa Johnson, and I am also grateful for the time or material provided by Rose Hauer, my sister Charlotte Holt, and my daughter-in-law Asea Sandine. Many thanks, as well, to Ariel Dorfman for his vital encouragement and to Michael Yates of Monthly Review Press for his adroit editing and continued backing. Finally, a big thank you to my partner Mary Bradford for her research assistance and her genial all-around support.

The author gratefully acknowledges use of material from *The St. Louis Veiled Prophet Celebration: Power on Parade, 1877–1995* by Thomas M. Spencer, by permission of the University of Missouri Press, copyright 2000 by the Curators of the University of Missouri; from Philip S. Foner, *May Day: A Short History of the International Workers' Holiday, 1886–1986,* by permission of International Publishers Co., New York; from *The New York City Draft Riots* by Iver Bernstein (1990), *The Decline of Popular Politics* by Michael McGerr (1986), and *American Mobbing* by David Grimsted (1998) by permission of Oxford University Press, Inc.; from *The Playful Crowd: Pleasure Places in the Twentieth Century* by Gary S. Cross and John K. Walton, copyright 2005 Columbia University Press, reprinted with permission of the publisher; from *The San Francisco Oracle 2: Youth Quake!*, reprinted with permission of Regent Press, publishers of the San Francisco oracle Digital Recreation, available at regentpress.net; and from *Do Americans Shop Too Much?* by Juliet Schor, copyright 2000 by Joshua Cohen and Joel Rogers, reprinted by permission of Beacon Press, Boston.

Contents

Introduction

A political commentator writes that "crowds of any sort . . . have almost disappeared from American public life."[1] "Of any sort"? How can that be, considering a recent Saturday afternoon in San Francisco when an estimated 65,000 people thronged Market Street to watch Lovefest, a parade of floats bearing electronic music partisans in strange, scanty costumes jerking their hips to a deafening techno-beat? Unconcernedly strolling through this crowd were some naked middle-aged men who had ventured up from the Folsom Street Fair, a seasonal gathering of what are usually leather-clad men, a few blocks away. Meanwhile, at Fort Mason, in another part of town, thousands were attending the annual blues festival. The following Saturday was another crowd-filled day, with thousands admiring the aerial acrobatics of the Blue Angels, the U.S. Navy's annual air show; many others attending events of Chinese National Day in Chinatown; and thousands flocking to North Beach for Italian Heritage Day. Not that events in San Francisco are typical of anything, but the suburbanites who clogged the freeways and filled the trains to attend were sufficiently representative of America that one must ask, What's going on? Clearly, home entertainment was an insufficient draw for the people who made up these crowds. In fact, Americans continue to be drawn to bustling sites.[2] The festive crowd, where it still exists, is a social magnet.

Yet the results of a simple experiment will show that at least some kinds of crowds "have almost disappeared from American public life." Leaf through a major American newspaper, any one on any day of the week, and you are almost certain to find at least one story in which a crowd figures prominently. Whether it consists of angry Nigerians stabbing and setting fire to bystanders, reacting to the suggestion of a local journalist that the Prophet Mohammed would have approved the Miss World beauty pageant scheduled to take place there,[3] or participants in a huge demonstration protesting an election result in the republic of Georgia, that crowd will not be sitting quietly watching a performance.[4] The newsworthy crowd has gone on a rampage, invaded an embassy, faced down a tank battalion, or battled with the police. But the point is, in all likelihood you will find such crowd items under international news. Despite a journalistic bias in favor of national and local events, American crowds are disproportionately underrepresented in the news.

One might supplement this newspaper test by consulting Elias Canetti's well-known *Crowds and Power*.[5] This, too, will confirm that crowds of a certain kind are generally missing from American life. Classifying crowds according to their underlying emotion, Canetti described the murderous "baiting crowd," the endangered "flight crowd," the mass panic, the "prohibition crowd" that might walk off the job, the "reversal crowd" of revolution, and many more. These are the kinds of crowds we seldom read about in the national or local news. What can it mean that American crowds seldom make the news? Does this signify that we have advanced to a higher level of civilization? In the 1970s, the only public gatherings permitted by the military dictatorships of Chile, Argentina, and Uruguay were those observing displays of military strength and those attending football matches.[6] If crowd participation in the United States is generally limited to watching, shopping, and traveling—and I will argue that it is—have we really advanced so far?

Much of the news of crowds in other parts of the world concerns disputed election results. America is different in this regard, as noted two hundred years ago by an observer of Thomas Jefferson's assumption of the presidency: "The changes in administration, which in every government and in every age have most generally been epochs of confusion, villainy and bloodshed, in this happy country take place without any species of distraction, or disorder."[7] Yes, but can an absence of "distraction, or disorder" serve as an occasion for national pride when the Supreme Court breaks a virtual tie for the American presidency by voting along party lines, as it notoriously did in 2000? Some people did take to the streets of Washington to protest George W. Bush's $40 million inauguration in January 2001, but the jeers and the signs that read "Hail to the Thief" fell far short of "confusion, villainy and bloodshed."

Easily forgotten, or perhaps a lesson never learned, is that throughout much of America's past (discussed in chapters 1 and 2), crowds have contributed plenty to the nation's history—or at least been in the news. Crowd actions powered the drive toward national independence. In the decades of the late nineteenth and early twentieth century, Americans came to see themselves as "inhabiting a culture of crowds."[8] This was mirrored in American literature (Jack London, Theodore Dreiser, John Steinbeck, and others) as well as in movies. Until the late 1940s, the typical Hollywood production with a contemporary setting would include at least one crowd scene. In some films—for example, King Vidor's *The Crowd* (1928) and Vincente Minnelli's *The Clock* (1945)—crowds were central to the action. What happened to these crowds is something that we will explore in chapter 7.

Canetti, Gustave Le Bon, and others who have written about crowds have tended to see their nature as fixed, though not necessarily by a single mold. The crowd that nearly beats Martellino to death in *The Decameron* is the crowd, some centuries removed, that chases down the unhappy protagonist of *The Bicycle Thief.* To the glancing eye of the busy passerby, knots of idlers remain. But the crowd that is characteristic of its time must change with changes in historic circumstances. American-style consumerism produces its own kind of crowds.

Before we begin we must say what constitutes a crowd. For some, the crowd is synonymous with the purposeful assembly, "a form of uninstitutionalized mobilization for action in order to modify one or more kinds of strains."[9] But what about the crowds of crowded sidewalks and packed aisles? What about the crowd in the stadium? Barbara Ehrenreich would distinguish between a crowd and an audience.[10] Such a distinction flies in the face of common usage. Reliance on it could make for some unlikely dialogue:

"Did many people go to the game?"
"Oh, yes, there was a big crowd."
"I assume you mean 'there was a big audience.'"

Mary Esteve's distinction between the "motivated" and the "unmotivated" crowd is more helpful.[11] For the latter, being numerous and near, like the people on a city's busiest streets at 5 p.m., is sufficient, whereas the "motivated" crowd acts as one, the most abhorrent example being the lynch mob. Every unmotivated crowd has the potential to become motivated by a riveting event, such as an accident, a robbery, or a dramatic announcement. The title of a Stephen Crane story nicely captures this relationship: "When a Man Falls a Crowd Gathers."[12] Such a crowd can only gather on a crowded street.

Another question: What is a mob and how does it differ from a crowd? I think that a "mob" is just a crowd engaged in some behavior of which the user of the term disapproves. For some it appears that a crowd becomes a mob simply by being numerous. But the crowd might be doing something so outrageous and contemptible as to make it a mob in almost anybody's mind.

Finally, how many people does it take to make up a crowd? That depends on the setting. Few rooms can hold as many people as a public plaza, but even an average living room is large enough to accommodate what most of us would describe as a crowd. And some plazas are so spacious that in them the kind of gathering that would fill a house to overflowing might be described as "a scattering of people." I will leave the etymology for chapter 1.

Americans have not formed crowds in a historical vacuum. With commentators on both the left and the right comparing American might and influence to that of imperial Rome, I have found it fruitful, at times, to compare our multitudes to those of the center of the ancient Occidental world. As for the Eurocentric nature of my other historical comparisons, I can justify them only on the basis of authorial convenience. Regarding the major contours of the territory ahead, chapter 1, "What Crowds Are For," describes the traditional functions of crowds. They acted to defend the community against outsiders, to obtain satisfaction of basic but unmet needs, and to engage in seasonal celebrations. In chapter 2, "When

Crowds Ruled," we see crowds flexing their muscles. The chapter gives ten examples of crowds that determined the course of historic events or, momentarily at least, held sway over a time and place.

But crowds, including American crowds, have at times engaged in horrendous abuses. Chapter 3, "Killer Crowds," denies that there is something in the social dynamic of the crowd itself which predisposes it to criminal acts. Chapter 4, "Crowd as Opportunity," shifts the focus to those outside the crowd—rulers, zealots, merchants, and others—for whom the crowd has been important. For them, the people who inhabited a crowded public space were (and remain) a resource to be awed, intimidated, converted, or marketed, though the would-be converts have sometimes gone on the attack. Besides being transit routes, America's major streets were a medium for communications when downtowns were thickly crowded places. Chapter 5,"Who Owns the Crowd?, examines how, from the paid-for crowds of the Roman Republic to today's metaphorical crowds of TV-watching celebrity hounds, the crowd may serve the interests of nonparticipants. In the age of consumer crowds, the colonized crowd has become the dominant type.

Chapter 6, "Regimes of Crowd Control," provides a historic sketch of crowd control in the United States. In the consumer society, official crowd control is generally reserved for non-consuming crowds of outdoor celebrants and demonstrations of political dissidents. With the spontaneous crowd becoming suspect, disaster victims are more likely to experience repression than to receive help. Witness New Orleans following Hurricane Katrina. Chapter 7, "Safe Crowds," describes the transformation of crowd space that has occurred since World War II, the hollowing out of downtowns and the population dispersal of suburbanization. Here we examine the compliant multitudes who occupy such spaces as the mall and stadium, the phantom crowds of freeways, and the harried transients of the airport.

The concluding chapter 8, "Who Needs Crowds," argues that hard-won assembly rights have not become irrelevant through disuse, nor have the virtual crowds of cyberspace made physical assemblages obsolete. With disasters looming and a tiny minority of the American population concentrating ever greater amounts of wealth and power in its own hands, the crowd remains a vital source of shelter and democratic leverage.

1. What Crowds Are For

Where there are many people, anything out of the ordinary may be enough to draw a crowd. But traditionally, crowds gathered to defend the community against outsiders who might otherwise impose their interests. Desperate people formed crowds to obtain satisfaction of basic unmet needs. In times of plenty, they would find one another again in the marketplace. Seasonal celebrations also included nearly everyone. Today such festive or purposeful crowds have almost vanished, at least in the United States. The bonds of community have dissolved under the influence of suburbanization, mass culture, home entertainment, distant employment, and the like. In addition, the desperate needs of the millions of Americans who have little or no share of our relative affluence as a nation are more likely to keep them isolated, angry, and ashamed than to bring them together. Can we agree that they, at least, would be better off as members of crowds? If they were to make physical use of their numbers to demand affordable housing, for example, they might eventually get it.

Consider the original meaning of the word. The English *crowd* seems to be derived from Old English and Medieval Dutch verbs meaning to press, push, or shove.[1] This capacity for physical turmoil, whether or not it gets played out in action, is one of the things that distinguishes a crowd from other groupings, such as a troupe of performers like a chorus or drill team. A crowd is potentially *turbulent,* and "turbulent" derives from the Latin *turba,* meaning both disorder or turmoil and a crowd or mob.

There is power in this turbulence, this "street heat." People who may never become members of a chorus or drill team, or even a work crew, may use their numbers physically and instrumentally to obtain satisfaction of basic human needs when individual efforts cannot.

The numerous poor of earlier times knew how to combine for political leverage. Livy, the great historian of the Roman republic, might have banished the commoners from his narrative altogether if they had not, on occasion, made some history of their own. For example, when the patricians tried to stifle land reform efforts with a military call-up, the people rioted. When the patricians tried to spread fear of foreign invasion one too many times, the people exited Rome *en masse*, leaving their betters to defend its walls. In Livy, patricians have names, reputations, and speech-making abilities. The people have only their numbers and the will to use them, if need be, to protect their mates from abduction and arbitrary arrest, and otherwise as mentioned.[2] In the later years of the republic, social polarization became so great that a crowd might kill anyone it met wearing gold rings or fine clothes.[3]

Although the near extinction of such dangerous crowds in our part of the world will certainly not elicit tears, perhaps we have lost something, too, even something of our nature. The turbulent multitude had a prominent role in human evolution. We know that other terrestrial primates, such as baboons, macaques, and chimpanzees, live in relatively large groups. Being numerous affords them some safety from predators. Once down from the refuge of trees and living on the African plains, our ancestors seem to have followed a similar strategy.[4] That there is safety in numbers remains generally sound advice. The visitor to a foreign city can usually feel secure on a crowded street. In ancient times the crowd could give a jolt to a Roman emperor's insular world of fawning courtiers and slaves, such as the time spectators cheered the rivals of Caligula's "favorites" (probably charioteers). "If only the Roman people had a single neck!" the emperor was heard to shout.[5] But the people had not one but many necks, far too many for even a psychopathic emperor to put to the ax. Still, the safety to be found in numbers is never absolute. In a fictional account of events leading up to the Tiananmen Square massacre, students keep assuring themselves that the state is powerless against a crowd.[6] We know how wrong they were. An imperial successor to

Caligula executed some who cheered against *his* favorites.[7] By moving to the exurbs, millions of Americans have lost the capacity even to become members of a crowd, except perhaps by driving to the nearest mall.

E. P. Thompson wrote that as recently as two hundred years ago in England and France, "the market remained a social as well as an economic nexus ... the place where the people, because they were numerous, felt for a moment that they were strong."[8] The focus of such presumptive strength was not the predatory beast that may have threatened their prehistoric ancestors but wealthy members of their own kind and their hired toughs. Absent the rise of a prominent middle class, such a polarity of rich and poor has been a prominent feature of almost every social landscape outside the tribal world. In fact, the power of the poor resides mainly in the assembled multitude. As the axiom has it, "We are many, you are few." But unless we, the many, come together bodily in our numbers we are powerless against the forces that wealth can buy.

In the United States today, the multitude has largely been dispersed. What crowds remain consist mostly of pacified consumers and distracted spectators. Do the impressive, near worshipful crowds drawn by Barack Obama during the 2008 presidential campaign represent the germ of a new era in crowd phenomena? The test will come if his administration fails to deliver the change in which he urged us to believe. Meanwhile, pacified and distracted, what need have we for the purposeful crowds of other times and other countries? This is to ask, what need have we for more influence over the decisions that affect us all? What need have we for the collective joy of traditional festivities? Might combining our numbers serve us well under certain easily imagined circumstances? As we gain a better sense of what has disappeared over the horizon of our history, the answers to these questions will become clear. We begin with a sketch of the historic role of rioting, proceed to public partying, and then see how the two are linked.

THE CITY MOB

In the centuries that followed the collapse of the Roman Empire and the disappearance of the kind of multitudes that had filled the capital's entertainment centers and public baths, slowly accumulating urban density reinvigorated European crowds. The preindustrial European city, especially if it were a capital, might include a district of potential rioters, a permanent mob consisting of "a combination of wage-earners, small property-owners and the unclassifiable urban poor."[9] Like the lowest of the low of Rome who worshipped Nero, this mob "lived in a sort of symbiosis" with its ruler, supporting and identifying with him and dependent on monarchic crumbs.[10] The ever-present crowds of eighteenth-century Parisian neighborhoods were expected to attend dozens of annual religious festivals, royal entrances to the city, royal marriage celebrations, occasions of state mourning, the cannon serenades of military victories, masses for royal births and illnesses, and public executions.[11] As Colin Lucas has written, "The crowd as assembled was a necessary but dangerous public for the state."[12] In return, the monarch tried to ensure that the capital got a steady supply of grain, often at the expense of the surrounding countryside. George Rudé has described similar crowd-mollifying measures in London.[13]

So long as the ruler met some minimal expectations of patronage and the ruler's actions clothed them in "vicarious glory," members of the city mob defended him or her enthusiastically.[14] But when the ruler disappointed them, they rioted, sending a message intended to restore things to their normal state. When not overly destructive, such violence was thought to be "socially functional."[15] The prototypical riot communicated a grievance by people without other effective means of vertical communication. As Martin Luther King Jr. put it, riots of protest speak "the language of the unheard."[16]

Eric Hobsbawm characterized the urban crowds of preindustrial Europe as "primitive rebels"—primitive because their rebellions did not attempt to overthrow the existing social order. Typically, the members of such crowds were only trying to get enough to eat. Another historian, Arlette Farge, has given us a vivid account of the "primitive rebels" who made the poorer neighborhoods of eighteenth-century Paris their home. "Crowds and gatherings were a regular part of the everyday scene," as they were in American cities of the time, though on a smaller scale.[17] In Paris, that scene might include a procession bearing the reliquary of a saint; the celebration of another saint's day with its own familiar rituals, feast, and pranks; fanatical harangues; an open-air version of the hiring hall; a purse-snatcher in a pillory; the agony of a woman giving birth; and a public hanging.[18] The latter was performed without benefit of the quick drop and speedy death by a broken neck.[19] Each such event would have its gathering. The crowd was the people's "natural organ" and representative, the enforcer of its traditional prerogatives, and—through derision, charivari, assault, and sometimes murder—its self-policing agent.

Police records show that rioting was also a part of ordinary, everyday Parisian life. In 1787 when Parlement called for public celebrations to mark the first successful challenge to royal authority (by nobles refusing to pay taxes) many of the poor took the opportunity to riot for a week.[20] Participation of the poor in the Revolution, when it came, "was a continuation in an extreme form of their everyday politics."[21] But the transition to revolution was not immediately clear. Still protesting as they always had, some of those who fought back against the Gardes françaises in the Faubourg St. Antoine in early 1789 were heard to shout, *"Vive le roi,"* while others were shouting, "*Vive le tiers état!*"[22]

PURPOSEFUL CROWDS IN THE UNITED STATES

American history is also dotted with spontaneous attempts to satisfy unmet needs and remedy grievances through collective action. During the early years of the Depression, for example, when over a hundred deaths by starvation were recorded and many more people perished of hunger-related illnesses, many responded as hungry people have for thousands of years, by banding together to obtain food.[23] Hundreds of farmers converged on the downtown of England, Arkansas, to demand food for their families in January 1931. Having received assurance from the Red Cross that they would be reimbursed, local merchants gave them food. An Oklahoma City crowd broke into a grocery store and was only dispersed by fire hoses and arrests.[24] Hundreds of people attacked a grocery and meat market in Minneapolis to grab what food they could through broken windows. When the store owner pulled a gun, they attacked him, too. It took a hundred police to restore order. In March 1931, over a thousand men waiting in a New York City bread line mobbed trucks delivering baked goods to a nearby hotel, perhaps inspiring the newspaper headline that appears in *Modern Times,* the Charlie Chaplin film classic of 1936, "Bread Line Broken by Unruly Mob."

Though most hunger riots went unreported for fear that such news could encourage additional acts of food vigilantism,[25] the "organized looting of food was a nationwide phenomenon."[26] Implicit in all such collective acts was the assertion of hungry Americans that they had a right to some minimal share of available food. Food riots got the poor of ancient Rome monthly allotments of free grain, distributed after 368 CE as bread. Americans got the Food Stamp program.

People also came together as unemployed workers during the Depression. They were often assaulted by the police.[27] Five hundred jobless men rioted for shelter in Detroit in 1931. In Indiana, 1,500 invaded a packing plant and demanded jobs.[28] A few months after that, jobless veterans and their families converged on the nation's capital to plead for pension payments due in 1945. Congress refused to act, and President Hoover loosed the army on them. The *Washington News* described the "pitiable spectacle" of "the great American Government, mightiest in the world, chasing men, women and children with Army tanks."[29] The soldiers killed two, injured thousands, and burned the camp of the "bonus marchers" to the ground.[30]

Sometimes organized by radicals, people also used their numbers to prevent evictions and obtain public relief. Tens of thousands of destitute residents were returned to their homes through the efforts of anti-eviction crowds, which would harass eviction teams, picket the process to draw larger crowds, and move ejected furniture back inside. A participant in one such action described an experience in a Chicago ghetto in 1931 that seems to have anticipated crowd tactics of thirty years hence. The police came on the scene and began to rain down blows with billy clubs and night sticks, while members of the anti-eviction crowd "stood like dumb beasts—no one ran, no one fought or offered resistance, [they] just stood, an immovable black mass."[31] There and elsewhere crowd pressure succeeded in forcing authorities to suspend evictions.[32]

Jobless crowds pushed into relief agencies to beleaguer bureaucrats and take up office space until their demands were met. Social workers were reluctant or unwilling to call the police, and the invading "committee" often had the outside backing of a neighborhood crowd. Success in obtaining food baskets increased the size and frequency of these efforts until the agitation for federal relief was irresistible.[33] But a continued clamor was required to get states to allocate the necessary funding to match that of Washington, under the formula of the Federal Emergency Relief Act of 1933. In Colorado in late 1934, mobs of the unemployed rioted at relief centers, looted food supplies, and drove panicked politicians from the state senate. Similar events occurred in other states.[34] A contemporary described the massive eruptions of the early Depression years as "a kind of spontaneous democracy expressing itself."[35]

Such spontaneity has often been associated with mass movements in the United States, but the deliberation and organizing required for large demonstrations and marches has also been a factor. Mass literacy meant that crowds could reach a much broader public with their messages than those who stopped to watch. As the suffragists discovered, if a gathering were sufficiently large and spectacular, newspapers would give it national and even international coverage.[36] "The enemy must be converted through his eyes," said suffragist Harriot Stanton Blatch.[37] She might have added, "and reading glasses." By contrast, the largest nonviolent demonstration of today becomes no more than a tiny blip on the screen of public awareness, if that. The massing of "activists" is nothing new.

Though they put the nonviolent demonstration to highly effective use, the suffragists did not invent it. Followers of John Wilkes, the English radical, were parading support for their hero "with flags flying and drums beating" in the 1760s.[38] They had counterparts in France before the American Revolution, too, and probably much earlier antecedents. For the long-term objective, a mere show of strength could be more effective than a riot. The observer of an early nineteenth-century demonstration described "a kind of discipline in disorder."[39] During the First World War, suffragists used their numbers to advance what Thoreau had called "civil disobedience," "pursuing peaceful means to achieve a violent reaction," which might include multiple arrests.[40]

Participants in the civil rights movement made broader and better known use of such tactics, hoping to gain federal intervention by provoking southern authorities to arrest them for peacefully demonstrating. Their tactics often brought brutal assaults by mobs. A major problem with this strategy was that the Democratic presidents to whom they appealed, Kennedy and Johnson, hoped to retain the support of segregationist Southern Democrats. Certainly President Kennedy did not want a repeat of what had happened when the government used federal officers to shield James Meredith's admission to the University of Mississippi in the fall of 1962. Substantiating the fact that in defending historic prerogatives the violent crowd is often an ugly obstruction to much needed change, an all-night riot of "beer cooler vigilantes" had ensued, resulting in the deaths of three bystanders and the wounding of 128 marshals.[41] Nonetheless, the goal of leaders of the Birmingham (Alabama) campaign was to so provoke southern extremism as to leave Kennedy no alternative but to intervene. The campaign was a spectacular success in terms of exposing racist violence, what with the police using clubs, dogs, and high-pressure water hoses on child marchers. The city buzzed with reporters from Europe and Japan, and the *New York Times* carried more stories on racial issues in two weeks than it had in the previous year. But it took a riot by blacks "wielding knives, overturning cars, hurling bricks and rocks at anyone who moved," following the bombing of King's brother's house and the motel headquarters of the Southern Christian Leadership Conference (SCLC), to get any federal troops sent to Birmingham.[42] Although the movement gained the moral high ground through nonviolent resistance, the federal government found it harder to ignore black rioters.

ROLLICKING IN THE STREETS

As children we learn to think of life in earlier times in terms of deprivation: no electricity, no central heating, no cars or planes. Physically, too, most people worked much harder in the past than we may care to imagine. But our ancestors had communal play to balance the rigors of work. Chinese villagers had numerous festivals.[43] Birth, initiations, marriage, and death were occasions for music and dance in Africa, but music and dancing might celebrate nothing more than the appearance of a full moon.[44] Central American villagers may still enjoy fireworks, dancing, drinking, feasting, and hilarious attempts by some to climb a greased pole, all of which figure in seasonal festivals. As for Europeans, consider the mass euphoria of traditional carnival. Historian Peter Burke has described this festival as "a huge play in which the main streets and squares became stages, the city became a theatre without walls and the inhabitants the actors and spectators."[45] As spectators, people would see a procession of floats; they would watch competitions such as races, tug-of-wars, and jousting over water; they might follow mock trials. They might also help celebrate the wedding of a bear and a man in a bridal dress. But no one was just a spectator. Many would wear costumes or masks and dance in the streets. Many would have sex with people they might never meet again or recognize if they did, though not to promote the fertility of the earth, the original purpose of such license.[46] Certainly, all would fill themselves with food and drink. As Mikhail Bakhtin wrote, "Everyone participates because [carnival's] very idea embraces all of the people"—and all of life, too, while it lasts.[47]

As in Saturnalia, the festival's ancient ancestor, rank and other hierarchical distinctions ceased to exist except to be mocked. The husband and wife exchanged roles, the poor gave alms to the rich, the judge was put in stocks: each familiar dyad was reversed,[48] as "all were considered equal during carnival."[49] In southern European towns, this fiesta could begin as early as late December and continue for several weeks until Lent.[50] Then, with the mock trial and execution of the figure personified as carnival (a laughing fat man adorned with hams, sausages, and other viands), the giant party would fizzle out, clearing the way for the lean time of Lent. Like the poor protagonist of the bittersweet Brazilian song,[51] participants were said to spend half the year remembering the last carnival and the other half preparing for the day when they could cast their vote for Dionysus once again.

Like rioting, the festival appears to have prehistoric roots. Some speculate that in a pre-patriarchal world, communal defense was succeeded or accompanied by communal hunting, which could have given rise to maenadism (the frenzies of female devotees of Dionysus) and its "very primordial form of festival."[52] The riot may be one descendant of such prehistoric practices and traditional festivals another. The ancestral line would include ancient vegetation rites of death and rebirth, especially (at least in the Aegean world) those of the mystery cults of Dionysus or Bacchus, whose celebrants would make music, engage in frenzied dancing, and consume immoderate amounts of wine, though their revelry might stop short of the ancient Cretan rite of tearing a bull to pieces with their teeth.[53] Early Christians shared elements of the Greek mystery cults and Rome's "Oriental" religions, such as ecstatic dancing. As late as the seventh century CE, the Church (the Council of Constantinople) condemned cross-dressing and invocations of Dionysus in winemaking. But going into the late Middle Ages, parishioners and priests still danced in church.[54] In medieval Germany, the Dionysian impulse "drove ever increasing crowds of people singing and dancing from place to place."[55] This according to Nietzsche, who added that with "the magic of the Dionysiac rite . . . [one] expresses himself through song and dance as the member of a higher community; he has forgotten how to walk, how to speak, and is on the brink of taking wing as he dances." One might gain an inkling of the ritual, he wrote, by imagining Beethoven's "Ode to Joy" as a painting.[56]

But there is no need to imagine a painting of collective joy. For that we have many examples, such as Pieter Brueghel the Elder's *The Wedding Dance* (1566) and *The Peasant Dance* (c. 1568), Pieter Brueghel the Younger's *Village Feast with a Theatre* (after 1616), and Petrus Paulus Rubens's *The Fair* or *Village Wedding* (c. 1635–38). We also have the banquet imagery of Rabelais.[57] For the crowds that filled the streets and squares of medieval and Renaissance European towns for carnival and other festivals, the holidays' indulgences and social summersaults "disclose[d] the potentiality of an entirely different world, of another order, another way of life" that stood in stark contrast to the austerity and fixed hierarchy of the official order, both clerical and secular.[58] Over the valley of lives filled with hard work, poverty, and want, the "Big Rock Candy Mountain" casts its glow. For the Levellers, Diggers, and other primitive communists of seventeenth-century England, as well as for their many intellectual successors, there would be an ultimate reversal followed by a lasting utopia. All hierarchies would then be relegated to the past and the earth become a "common treasury," to be equally enjoyed by all.[59] Or as May Day demonstrators chant in the streets of Berlin, "Everything for everyone and everything for free!"[60]

The slogan is reminiscent of another painting by Pieter Brueghel the Elder—*The Land of Cockaigne,* also known as *The Land of Milk and*

Honey (1567). Here a peasant, a cleric, and a soldier lie under a tree from which a table spills food and drink into the waiting mouth of one of them, while the others indulge in post-prandial slumber. A plucked chicken has put itself on a plate. An egg strolls by, ready to be eaten. Stuck in an obliging pig in the background is the knife that has already taken a slice out of its back. A kneeling knight waits for one of several pies to drop from a roof, and a man climbs into (or out of) a mountain of buckwheat. Clearly this fantasy of infantile orality was inspired by more than sympathy for hungry peasants. The goods of Brueghel's land of plenty satiate one and all alike, and do so without human effort.

The loaded shopping carts of most Americans, not to mention our pervasive weight problems, signify our occupation of a similar realm. But those goods do not fall into our shopping carts or leave the store by themselves. Overworked Americans of all ages and most income brackets, a great many of whom carry unsustainable debts, report growing dissatisfaction with the jobs that make high levels of food consumption individually possible.[61] Without the play of festival to balance work, there is only the food we eat, live and mediated spectacles, shopping, and occasionally, for some, the private party. The transition from recurrent periods of plenty for all to year-round overconsumption for most may represent the triumph of agricultural technology, but it does not seem to have left us any happier. And because markets do not distribute goods on the basis of need but only on the basis of ability to pay, many go hungry in spite of agricultural surpluses. Food pantries are having to contend with empty shelves as I write.

AMERICANS AT PLAY

Americans had no sooner gained national independence than they began acquiring holidays of their own, though they did not import the all-inclusiveness of Carnival. Typically, recurrent public events were experienced differently depending on gender, class, ingestion of alcohol, and one's cultural distance from the old country. Take the Fourth of July. John Adams thought that July 2 (the day in 1776 when the Continental Congress took a draft of the Declaration of Independence in hand to declare colonial independence) should be commemorated by "by solemn acts of devotion to God Almighty" and that it would be celebrated "by succeeding Generations, as the great anniversary Festival . . . to be solemnized with Pomp and Parade, with Shews, Games, Sports, Guns, Bells, Bonfires and Illuminations from one End of this Continent to the other."[62] On the original July 2, a sportive crowd in New York toppled a statue of George III on a horse, mutilated its face, and displayed the head on a flagpole.[63] But as the Fourth, and not the Second, gained recognition as the nation's birthday, many made good on other elements of Adams's prescription. For male members of Philadelphia's upper crust, it was a day of sermons, speeches, and military parades, followed by private dinners. A painting of July 4, 1819, depicting the celebration in that city's Central Square, includes in its crowded foreground a pair of elegantly uniformed militiamen, small boys with toy guns, women fixing picnic lunches, a dog, a violinist, and some men getting drunk.[64] Soon affluent Philadelphians were apt to go out of town on Independence Day, leaving it up to the sheriffs and watchmen of those pre-police days to control the "saturnalia of passion" that would tend to break out among working-class celebrants under the influence of alcohol, playing cards, and guns.[65] Many had to observe a one-day strike in order to participate in the saturnalia.

Around 1840, native-born Americans of Milwaukee attended Independence Day speeches that hammered home civic and moral themes, while the city's German-born Americans frolicked in beer gardens. Some Cincinnati workers paraded with the American flag. In 1837, a Rockdale, Pennsylvania, Sunday school's observance of the Fourth drew several hundred students and spectators, but the "rowdy men and women" of this industrial area generally celebrated the holiday by crowding local roads and attending "disorderly, political picnics."[66] In New York City, the Fourth was the occasion of an increase in the murder rate resulting from "drinking and group rowdiness." Christmas and New Year's were similarly riotous.[67]

These different ways of observing a common event can be explained, to some extent, by the fact that the immigrants who filled the country's newly industrialized cities of the nineteenth century were often members of a first generation of industrial workers, the first from their towns and villages to endure the discipline of the factory clock, men and women who had known and lost a life that balanced work with festival play. Until late in the century, having a job in their adopted land meant working for ten hours a day, six days a week. Whereas a member of the middle class would have a summer vacation, the industrial laborer's only break from the grinding succession of workdays came on Sunday and the infrequent holiday. As the original "labor day," the Fourth of July was especially important.

In late nineteenth-century Worcester, Massachusetts, the focus of Roy Rosenzweig's excellent study, members of the property-owning class would celebrate the Fourth with exclusive picnics or by socializing in their private clubs. They might also make social calls, attend musical recitals, or stay at home, wining and dining friends or playing croquet and lawn tennis.[68] The contrast with their immigrant workers could hardly have been more pronounced. For them, festivities began on the eve of the Fourth when crowds gathered downtown and in the streets of working-class neighborhoods as early as 8 p.m. "for an all-night carnival of noise-making and fireworks."[69] More rambunctious members of the crowd visited the homes of representatives of the local elite to unhinge their gates, overturn sheds, ring their doorbells, and so on, "in a muted form of class hostility."[70] Worcester was not unique: Independence Day "had a persistent underside of parody and burlesque" in other parts of the country, too.[71]

The Fourth itself was the occasion for a large outdoor gathering, with plenty of food, alcohol, and games—namely, foot races, tug-of-wars, and wrestling for cash prizes. Men engaged in spontaneous and numerous fistfights, and many chased after a greased pig. That was the experience of many of Worcester's Irish immigrants, at any rate. The Irish-Catholic temperance society attracted a less boisterous picnic crowd of about equal size, three to five thousand.[72] Worcester's generally more conservative Swedish immigrants were also split between rowdy and respectable celebrants.[73] The French Canadians, who made up Worcester's other large immigrant group in the late nineteenth century, also kept to themselves. Like Mexican-Americans with their *Cinco de Mayo*, they tended to celebrate St. Jean Baptiste Day (June 24), a holiday with roots in pre-Christian fertility rites, and to skip the Fourth.[74] The Nativist Order of United American Mechanics—an organization of native-born skilled workers, foremen, and clerks—held their own celebration of the Fourth.[75] The Italians, Poles, and Lithuanians who made up the next wave of immigrants to come to Worcester celebrated Independence Day as boisterously and separately as had their most intemperate predecessors.[76] Among the workers of this industrial city, ethnic events easily outdrew any multi-ethnic or interclass gatherings. The story of how such events were tamed and their celebrants brought together will be taken up in a later chapter.

Meanwhile, Sunday was regularly reserved "for the brawling, splashing, many-actioned, brilliant-colored crowd."[77] Its working-class constituents did not share middle-class longings to escape the multitude and the distractions of city life but sought instead "the sociable, often bibulous, sometimes violent, communal activities of their rural and preindustrial predecessors."[78] They found a reasonable semblance of such pursuits in the "'boss-less' crowds" of the private amusement parks that began to appear in the waning decades of the nineteenth century. Coney Island was easily the biggest of these, in terms of the crowds it drew on summer Sundays. Modeled on the popular entertainment sectors of the World's Fairs—for example, Philadelphia's (1876), Chicago's (1893), and St. Louis's (1904)—Coney offered thrill rides, spectacles, freak shows, exotic settings like Luna Park's "Streets of Delhi," animal acts, and a fine beach. For New Yorkers, it was only a subway ride away. In 1910, these attractions drew twenty million visitors, a higher proportion of the American population than the Disney theme parks would attract eighty years hence.[79]

With entrance fees, the proprietors of Coney's Luna Park, Dreamland, and Steeplechase Park could weed the crowd of undesirables, and with crowd energy diffused over multiple amusements—from peepshows to thrilling rides to immersion in the surf—the Coney experience fell well short of its sobriquet, "Sodom by the Sea." "Innocent play is a moral antiseptic," claimed Luna Park's Frederic Thompson.[80] Yet its "demographic" was young adults, not families. Luna Park even provided child care. Coney Island's grown-up patrons "may have acted like children, but they seldom burdened themselves with kids when they went to the parks."[81]

Coney Island was especially popular with recent immigrants. Like Worcester's Fourth of July celebrants, members of different European ethnicities gravitated to different bathhouses and different sections of the beach. Racist stall games—Kill the Coon and African Dodger—smoothed some such differences. But more important than homogenizing influences were the informality of the crowd and the leveling influence of the beach, where all wore swimming suits and all romped together in the surf, "exactly contrary to the manner of behavior anywhere else."[82] (Brought to mind are the baths of imperial Rome, which were "places of equalization in a highly stratified society.")[83] In addition, people were literally thrown together by some of the mechanical devices of the Coney Island parks. The Barrel of Love through which people entered Steeplechase Park, for instance, was a revolving drum that launched customers into one another's arms. The innocence of such involuntary embraces stands in contrast to the libidinal opportunities of the traditional festival, which would sometimes bump the birthrate up in nine months. Yet all in all, the mixing of genders, classes, and ethnicities of Coney's formative years was exceptional at the time.[84]

Coney Island attracted enormous pleasure-seeking crowds into the 1940s: 46 million passed through its turnstiles in 1943. Even three years later, when middle-class families were starting to take their leisure at sites that could only be accessed by car and Coney's stalls and rides had lost their glow, density at the beach reached 4,800 bathers per acre, meaning that each individual in this close-packed throng commanded, on average, nine square feet of sand.

THE FESTIVAL OF THE SIXTIES

Americans have not always deferred the experience of collective joy until the weekend or the arrival of an official holiday. Someone landing in San Francisco's Haight-Ashbury district on October 6, 1966, for example, might have run across a crowd of "Beautiful People ecstatically costumed and handing out flowers to friends and FBI agents" alike to celebrate their opposition to laws forbidding "chemical mysticism." The six hundred to a thousand people in the Panhandle on that sunny afternoon, "dancing with brave banners waving over their looney heads," had an audience consisting of cops, newsmen, and some real estate agents from a nearby conference. These men in suits stood "staring, simply transfixed, simply amazed [by the] flutes and finger cymbals, tinkle and toot, and all that long hair, short skirts, and laughter."[85] The *Oracle* article from which I have looted this account goes on to say that an FBI agent hid the flowers he had been given behind his back, and the real estate men "all stared at their shoes when a slim girl approached them with a juicy slice of watermelon. They were terrified that she intended to offer them a bite. 'Don't be afraid,' she said sweetly."[86] It seems that the antics of the "Beautiful People" needed the validation of witnesses with feet in the cultural mainstream.

Berkeley and San Francisco were at the epicenter of changes that, for those caught up in them, seemed to be coming from deep inside the earth. Free outdoor rock concerts were the order of the day. People danced at the slightest rhythmic provocation. Great music was in the air. So was the smell of hashish and incense. "We all wanted to be everything that was 'yes,'" a survivor says.[87] The lyrics of a song by Sly and the Family Stone, "Everybody Is a Star," had broad credibility: the stars in the rock-and-roll firmament included not only the onstage musicians but "the dancers with the face paint freaking freely in the crowd."[88] The early rock concerts seemed "beachheads of a new, ecstatic culture meant to replace the old repressive one."[89] And the counterculture taking root was a thing of crowds.

The local eruption sent sparks over a wide radius. Soon there were smoldering pieces of the cultural revolution's furniture scattered nearly everywhere across the land. A former student leader describes the 1970 shutdown of a midwestern university in these terms: "It was the original street party. . . . People were smoking dope on the streets. . . . We had our makeshift parades going down the street. Some guy with a Nixon mask on, it was a circus atmosphere . . . a lot of fun, nobody got hurt . . . everybody was everybody's friend."[90] To paraphrase what was said of France in May 1968, our party was a reprisal for a hundred and fifty years of ceremonial impoverishment.[91]

Was there any reason that this festival should not last throughout the year? The Calvinist ethic, which had made nonproductive use of one's time "the deadliest of sins," was made to turn cartwheels and stick out its tongue.[92] But political reaction to this cultural revolution followed closely on the run-down heels of youthful rebellion. Most Americans *were* afraid to take a bite of the watermelon. And the watermelon was not always sweet. Just as outrageous appearances need outraged witnesses, collective bliss would ultimately require something in the way of crowd control, to be discussed in chapter 6.

RIOTING FOR FUN

Back in the 1830s, civic leaders of both major parties, the Democrats and the Whigs, had invested heavily in the Bank of Maryland. Colluding with bank partners, they milked the bank of its capital by taking out loans and then closed it, using propaganda to persuade the public that the bank had gone broke and using Maryland law to avoid an audit or settlement.[93] But the bank had catered to people with scant savings. Its closure and the delay in settling accounts victimized widows, orphans, small tradesmen, and the like. On the other hand, the debtors and partners of the bank had "profited shamelessly."[94] By August 1835, a year and a half had gone by without a resolution. Handbills appeared that called for direct action by "Judge Lynch." Ten thousand people converged on a meeting site, but only to throw some rocks. Next evening, a citizens' guard, appointed by the mayor of Baltimore and armed with sticks, could not prevent a crowd from sacking the home of one of the partners of the bank. When the crowd turned on the citizens' guard, hurling stones and injuring several of them, the mayor okayed their use of guns. The guard then shot and killed twenty and wounded dozens. Next day, a Sunday, hundreds participated in the destruction of the mayor's home and those of four bankers, throwing furnishings out the door, where they fed the flames of bonfires as several thousand looked on.[95]

Large crowds, accompanied by a fife and drum, cheered on the Baltimore bank rioters. The rioters responded by making a show of burning the law library of an attorney of the bank, emptying his wine cellar, and ceremonially breaking his plates in the street. The rioting was "a saturnalia where social man's usual restraints could be shucked."[96] Just as the traditional festival would sometimes lead to rioting and even revolution, festivity has often broken out in the midst of a riot. Residents of

Watts, a predominantly black neighborhood of Los Angeles, joined the rioting there in 1965 "with a camaraderie and jubilation usually reserved for festive occasions."[97] "A spirit of carefree nihilism was taking hold" during Detroit's ghetto riot of 1967.[98] An observer reported that young rioters appeared to be "dancing amidst the flames."[99] The narrator of a fictional account of that event says that he had never before seen people so happy, despite the burning buildings and the bodies lying in the streets.[100]

If revelry and riot were born together in the need of our human ancestors to set up a hullabaloo to scare off savage predators, as some have suggested, it should not be surprising that riot and revelry occupy neighboring points on a continuum of communal possibilities.[101] Their social proximity goes some way to explain the tendency of police officials to overreact at times when confronted with festive gatherings. But such overreaction often *provokes* rioting; indeed, the recreational riot of the spring break seems to require it. On the other hand, maybe this link between riot and festivity is just a matter of too much testosterone. In reference to the singing, reciting, food sharing, and social breaks included in suffrage movement assemblies, Harriot Stanton Blatch declared that men's "democracy grew by riots, revolutions, wars. Women conquered in peace and quiet, with some fun."[102]

The question is, what has become of such crowd-determined behavior in the United States? The range of possibilities for collective action includes some that are clearly abhorrent. Yet without the self-directed crowd, we cannot respond to what may be a pressing need for collective action. We also lose the experience of collective euphoria. Here in America something as old as the city in human history is on the verge of becoming extinct. What remains of the crowd are agglutinations of individuals—shoppers, drivers, spectators—crowds whose constituents are individually distinct, competitive, and mutually obstructive. By describing various crowds that once held sway, the next chapter will give a better sense of the exceptional nature of this development.

2. When Crowds Ruled

How easy it is to forget that crowds made history in the past. Although they did not get to write that history themselves, their actions inspired historians to record their deeds—though perhaps more of their misdeeds. Crowd exploits have otherwise been lost to collective memory, making it all too easy to conclude that crowds have never done much of anything worth noting. For unlike the architecture of earlier ages, which continues on display in older cities, crowds of a certain kind have almost disappeared in the United States. Now, the best of surviving artistic creations of the past can generally be found in museums. What if there were a museum of empowered crowds? Surely some of the following would serve as prime exhibits:

- The crowds that governed a leading city of the ancient world for two hundred years. It is to them that we owe the ideal of democracy.

- The crowds whose actions served as dynamite to blow away eight centuries of arbitrary rule, clearing the way for a republic based on principles of individual liberty and social equality.

- The American crowds that pushed colonial protest toward a struggle for national independence.

- The crowds that helped free slaves before emancipation became the law of the land.

- The crowds that shut down industry in a major American city and did so without bloodshed.

- The crowds that backed up workers bringing rail traffic to a halt in the late nineteenth century and the crowds that supported workers struggling to win collective bargaining rights in the twentieth.

- The crowds of ghetto dwellers that inspired what civil rights tactics could not: white fear.

- The members of a crowd that sat as one to spark what would in time become the antiwar movement of the 1960s.

Let us examine each of these crowd regimes in turn.

CROWD RULE IN THE ANCIENT WORLD

Anyone who has read the early dialogues of Plato knows that a crowd—actually a 501-member jury—condemned Socrates. That jury was part of the larger crowd that governed ancient Athens. The legislative branch of this political system that "institutionalized the crowd" was the Assembly.[1] The Athenian Assembly met in the open air about forty times a year in a space that could hold about six thousand, which was the attendance figure needed for a quorum. Determinations ranging from decrees and denunciations to important trials in this "controlling body of the state" were made on the basis of majority rule—by a show of hands, at first, and later by ballot.[2] Anyone attending could ask for a recount and anyone who had the nerve could speak. Those making a momentous decision, such as a resolution to go to war, would be expected to carry it out themselves (along with absent others). But there were many absent others: attendance was limited to adult male citizens, which excluded a good part of the population of the state—women, slaves, minors, and foreigners.[3]

On an equal footing with the Assembly was the People's Court, which had both administrative and judicial functions. Jurors were selected daily by lot from an annual pool of six thousand citizens, also selected by lot. Here familiar practices end, as the People's Court excluded professionals and experts. In other words, Athens' legal system operated without attorneys, judges, bailiffs, or court reporters. A jury of hundreds would try a case brought by a citizen (or citizens), with the parties representing themselves.[4] Whether the outcome of the trial of Socrates is sufficient to condemn this ancient institution is a determination that should not be made solely on the basis of reading Plato. The Athenian jurors would have known Socrates as the cultish charlatan of Aristophanes' *The Clouds* and other comedies. They would have known of his friendship with anti-democrats. They would not have read the early dialogues of Plato.

Administrators, too, were selected by lot, 1,100 of them every year from a pool of volunteers. These officeholders were term-limited to one year. Such citizen-magistrates included a Council of five hundred that met daily, preparing the agenda for the Assembly meetings, providing someone to preside over those meetings, carrying out some financial and diplomatic responsibilities, and generally implementing the decisions of the Assembly. Historian John Thorley thinks that the requirement of an annual turnover and daily selection by lot made domination of Athenian politics by the Council "virtually impossible."[5]

This political system of 2,500 years ago remains the leading example of direct democracy—that is, institutionalized crowd rule. Government by the *demos* (democracy) meant government by the people, but allowing for the significant exclusions cited above, there is a question of who was included under that heading. For those devoted to popular governance, the *demos* meant everyone. For the anti-democrat, typically a wealthy aristocrat, the *demos* referred to the commonality—that is, people without real property.[6] Similar shifts in meaning attach themselves to our use of "the people."

The success of Athens' rule by the many required an informed and involved citizenry. They could look to no one else to spare them the need to be concerned with politics: there were no professional politicians. Before taking up an important issue in the Assembly, Athenians would discuss it in their shops, their taverns, their homes, and in the *agora* (market).[7] As we might read a newspaper or visit a familiar Web site, the active Athenian might make frequent stops at the Monument of the Eponymous Heroes to read the Assembly agenda, legislative motions, military call-up lists, and the like, posted on its podium.[8] The difference between him and most of us is that he would anticipate *acting* on the basis of such public information. As Pericles declared in his Funeral Oration, Athenians regarded the citizen who took no part in public affairs "not as unambitious but as useless."[9]

Like every ruling system, Athens' government by the people was far from perfect. Some of its actions, such as the decision to attack Syracuse and the conviction *en masse* of six generals for dereliction of duty, left the city open to the charge of mob rule. But the Athenians learned from their mistakes, and their democracy ultimately fell victim to Macedonian invasion, not domestic dissatisfaction.[10] Government by the many, however, will never please exponents of rule by the best (aristocracy) or by the wealthy few (oligarchy). Political philosophy got its start in opposition to the crowd power of Athenian democracy. Plato found the give-and-take of Athens' politics, its contention, turbulence, and impromptu solutions to lasting issues "a contradiction of every canon of order." Order required "subordination of the lower to the higher"—in other words, a hierarchy.[11] The philosopher king who would preside over Plato's ideal polity would rule on the basis of his arcane knowledge of metaphysical and unchanging values—the Good, Order, Beauty, etc.—which gave all things of the illusory world of the senses their distinguishing qualities. Presumably, the noisy crowd of the Athenian Assembly would be permanently consigned to the marketplace. In traditional political thought, "Being antithetical to crowd power was what institutionalized power was *for*."[12]

CROWDS MAKE A REVOLUTION

Parisian crowds rejoiced in September 1791 when a chastened Louis XVI (falsely) swore to accept the new constitution and govern through the elected assembly.[13] Fifteen months later, his most energetic defender would answer the many charges brought against the former monarch, which included deploying troops against the people, by asking members of the National Convention what *they* would do "if . . . an excited and armed crowd were marching against you with no respect for your character as sacred legislators?"[14]

When organized, the people from the poorer neighborhoods provided the revolution with its "main striking-force," though whether they would have turned out to risk (and often lose) their lives in the absence of spiraling food prices is highly questionable.[15] Excepting the attack on the Bastille, the crowd's search for weapons was also a search for grain. The crowd's destruction of the customs posts was a matter of direct action by consumers: custom duties (taxes) added to the cost of food and wine. In October 1789, what began as bread riots became a fifteen-mile women's march on Versailles, with "fishwives seated on the cannon . . . wine barrels next to powder kegs . . . joy, shouting, clamor, gaiety,"[16] the object being to bring back "the baker, the baker's wife, and the baker's little boy" —that is, the King, the Queen, and the Dauphin.[17] Even their chants announced that it was food that people had in mind.

The revolution waxed fullest when rural uprisings joined urban radicalism. Coinciding with the fall of the Bastille, there were grain riots in Pontoise, Poissy, Saint-Germain-en-Laye (where a miller was killed), as well as in Flanders and Verdun.[18] While capitalist penetration of the countryside was forcing the peasantry of England off the land, in France such modernizing tendencies merely heaped additional burdens on the peasants, who reacted by rebelling, leaving burning châteaux behind.[19] Rural famine, when it came, led to a proliferation of marches of peasants and craftsmen bearing pitchforks, drums, and banners, moving from village to village and town to town to impose a ceiling on the price of grains, eggs, butter, wood, iron, and coal.[20] Their English counterparts engaged in similar acts of vigilante price control, both before and after the revolution in France. As E. P. Thompson pointed out, such efforts to undo market imperatives were essentially conservative. They belonged to a paternalistic tradition that was deeply rooted in the past.[21]

In Paris, meanwhile, unemployment and "famine prices" continued to impose a regime of desperation. And the crowds continued to engage in "price control by riot"—for example, in the sugar riots of 1792. In February 1793, crowds responded to a bread crisis by stripping hundreds of stores of their supplies. The disorders continued over four days, prompting dozens of arrests. Moderates among the revolution's middle-class leaders, Girondins and others, charged that the crowds were not representative of "the people," that they were merely a mob and puppet of the revolution's aristocratic enemies.[22] The bourgeois leaders had no realistic answer to the unmet needs of the impoverished many. They were committed to market solutions, for which "any interference with the free circulation of supplies seemed a negation of the 'liberties' that the Revolution had proclaimed."[23]

But the revolutionary crowds of the summer of 1789 and beyond did more than burn châteaux and break into warehouses and grocery shops. They attacked any real or supposed enemies of revolutionary change on whom they could lay their hands. The assault on the Bastille included the murder of the Dean of the Paris Guild and the prison governor. An unemployed cook killed the latter by running past the laundryman who was trying to protect him.[24] A few days after that historic moment, a crowd attacked the Intendant of Paris and his father-in-law, tearing them to bits. The crowd that marched on Versailles in October 1789 and brought the royal family back to Paris displayed the heads of the queen's guards at the front of their procession.[25] The insurgents of August 1792 who ended the monarchy for good chased down and lynched the Swiss Guards. A few days after that, people intercepted a coach full of suspected royalists headed for a prison. An altercation with a priest became a riot, and crowds then entered the prisons to defend the revolution from the many prisoners who were thought to be its enemies.[26] French rebellion was no longer "primitive." Discussion of the September Massacres that followed will be picked up in the following chapter.

AMERICA'S REVOLUTIONARY CROWDS

The riotous actions that advanced the movement toward American national independence, though shockingly destructive by today's standards, were benign compared to the kind of events (touched on above) that would soon electrify France. Colonial massacres were reserved for natives. We begin the story of mass turbulence in 1763 when, through a series of laws—the Revenue Act (or Sugar Act), the Currency Act, and the Stamp Act—the British crown sought to increase revenue from the American colonies, bind their economy more closely to Britain's, and curtail the smuggling by which colonial merchants tried to evade royal taxes on trade. For many Americans, the Stamp Act's requirement that every newspaper, pamphlet, legal document, college diploma, pack of cards, liquor license, etc., bear certain revenue stamps was the last straw. In August 1765, thousands of Bostonians prevented the sheriff from stripping a tree of the unflattering effigies of Andrew Oliver, the recently appointed stamp distributor, and George Grenville, presumptive author of the hated act. The crowd then carried Oliver's effigy through the streets in a mock funeral march; tore down the brick office intended to serve as stamp distribution center; used the timbers of that building to fuel a bonfire at Oliver's luxurious home; destroyed his stable, coach, and chaise; routed Lieutenant Governor Thomas Hutchinson and the sheriff with a barrage of stones when they arrived on the scene; and demolished the interior of Oliver's house, as well as his garden.[27] All this "in accordance with the tradition of crowd action against outsiders breaking economic norms of the community," a practice that, locally, went back at least as far as 1710, when a crowd had cut the rudder of a grain exporter's ship during a time of local food shortages.[28] As for national independence, that was not even a glimmer in a Stamp Act rioter's eye.

Less than two weeks after the demolition of the Oliver residence, angry Bostonians who had recently assaulted the homes of a vice admiralty court official and the comptroller of customs attacked Thomas Hutchinson's mansion. They set about systematically splintering his fine furniture, stripping the walls until his house became a "hollow shell," drinking his wine, trashing his garden, and looting his house of cash and valuables. Note the crowd's targets: except for the cash, all were symbols of aristocratic refinement. But emulation of the European aristocracy by those with the means and motivation to purchase symbols of social superiority would not end with departure of America's colonial administrators and inauguration of the new republic's egalitarian ideology.[29] Some think that middle-class emulation of the purchasing patterns of upscale consumers is what fills America's shopping malls with customers today (but more on this in chapter 7).

The genius of Sam Adams and other emerging leaders of what became the American Revolution was that they were able to harness some of the riotous energy of the most aggrieved members of colonial society and then stand aside as it crashed against the ramparts of the colonial regime. Such men did not own the furious multitudes, which were led by men of their own kind like Boston shoemaker Ebenezer MacIntosh. American crowds were as self-directed as their European counterparts. After the Revolution, when riotous explosions were of no further use to members of the emerging political class, Adams would participate in the drafting of a Massachusetts Riot Act and a resolution suspending habeas corpus.[30]

In November 1765, half of Boston's adult males marched in a driving rain in the annual Pope's Day parade, leading Andrew Oliver—the man himself and not his effigy—through the streets to the Liberty Tree, where an enormous crowd cheered the would-be stamp distributor's humiliating declaration that he would always be happy "to serve this people."[31] Not to be outdone, a Newport, Rhode Island, crowd hung effigies of that town's stamp distributor and two notorious local conservatives. Some merchants led the burning of their likenesses. As Canetti wrote, "The destruction of representational images is the destruction of a hierarchy which is no longer recognized."[32] But what about the iconoclasts' own hierarchy? In this case, the crowd shook off control by its merchant organizers to march to the homes of the flesh-and-blood originals of their enemies, destroying their houses including floors, fences, and trees. With the arrest of their leader, crowd members threatened the homes of some of the Sons of Liberty who had urged Stamp Act resistance but balked at residential demolition.[33]

Meanwhile, in New York City, a compact between merchants not to import British goods until the Stamp Act was withdrawn did not go nearly far enough for thousands of members of the "lower orders," who embarked on a four-day rampage by assaulting the home of the super-rich colonial governor, parading his effigy through the streets, and then throwing his sleighs and coach onto a "monstrous bonfire."[34] Following what contemporaries called the "General Terror of November 1–4," in 1765, thousands gathered for a demonstration led by seamen outside Fort George, taunted its guards, and forced the governor to give over the detested stamps. Says historian Gary B. Nash, the patrician "Sons of Liberty had lost control of the city's masses" and had come to fear them.[35]

A crowd in Portsmouth, New Hampshire, stoned an effigy of the local stampmaster, thereby persuading him to resign. In Newburyport, New Hampshire, a crowd with a taste for the theatrical dropped the stampmaster's likeness into a flaming barrel of tar. A Maryland stampmaster fled the colony when members of a mob burned his warehouse. A North Carolina crowd dragged a stamp-man through the streets, forcing him to give up his commission, then trapped the governor of the colony in his own home. And so it went, as "up and down the coast, people who had never before voted or played any public role surged through the streets to participate in boisterous mock executions, defy royal authority, and initiate themselves in the rituals of revolution."[36] Those loyal to the colonial enterprise had significantly misjudged "the self-activating capacity of ordinary colonists," but so had well-to-do leaders of colonial protest.[37] Clearly, without such massive and riotous acts, members of Parliament would have had no reason to repeal the Stamp Act or even consider doing so.[38]

After 1765, New Yorkers held mass meetings and door-to-door canvasses to build opposition to the import of British goods. In New England, the non-importation movement mobilized additional first-time activists, eager to visit collective punishment on those suspected of informing on local smugglers like John Hancock.[39] Boston rioters stoned the homes of customs commissioners who had had the temerity to seize his sloop, the *Liberty*. The British responded by stationing two regiments of troops there. Soon, "harassment of the troops became a patriotic duty," an American version of the Intifada, similar to Hancock's non-compliance with the trade laws and to popular pressure put on merchants to go along with the non-importation pact.[40]

One bleak day in early 1770, an angry Boston crowd confronted one John Mein, who had exposed anti-Loyalist divisions by publishing the names of embarrassed Whig merchants who had reneged on their declared support for the non-importation agreement. Mein went into hiding, the non-importation agreement expired, and four days of mass meetings followed during which the shelves of boycott-compliant merchants remained bare. At this point, the mercurial William Molineux led a crowd of what might be called middle-class enforcers to the homes of Loyalist importers. These included the (presumably rebuilt) house of Thomas Hutchinson. Though the march was tightly controlled, "fringe elements" of farmers and youths chased some importers from their lodgings, threatened their friends, picketed their stores, harassed their customers, and threw mud and excrement on their houses.[41]

By now protest had reached such a pitch that schoolboys rioted every Thursday, when schools were closed for market day.[42] February 22 was such a day, but the rock-throwing crowd that attacked the home of Ebeneezer Richardson, a notorious informer, bit off more than it could easily digest. The irascible Richardson fired a musket into it, killing Christopher Snider, an eleven-year-old boy. Now the crowd had a martyr for its cause, which remained, at that point, continued colonial quasi-autonomy. "My eyes never beheld such a funeral," John Adams noted in his diary.[43] As for the killer, he might have been lynched had he not been rescued by merchant leaders, although the region's crowds seldom went beyond tarring and feathering when they meted out punishment.[44]

The King Street incident, better known as the Boston Massacre, took place a few days after Christopher Snider's massive funeral. A series of brawls between British troops and local rope workers had enlivened the interval. The behavior of the troops was often rude and arrogant, like that of any occupying force, and the rope-makers did not take kindly to foreign occupation. Amid multiple skirmishes, both sides were promising to settle scores on that snowy evening in early March when a crowd gathered outside the soldiers' barracks and threatened to burn it down. Someone rang the church bells, which doubled as the fire alarm. Bostonians converged on King Street and the Mainguard, where they found an isolated sentry who had earlier clubbed an apprentice for taunting an officer. Both sentry and crowd called for reinforcements.[45]

Apprentices flocked to King Street on news of the standoff. When a small party of British troops arrived with fixed bayonets, the crowd pelted them with snowballs and chunks of ice. As noted by the sophisticated American rioters, the troops lacked the required civilian authority (reading of the "riot act") to disperse them.[46] Accordingly, the crowd was able to do one of the things that angry crowds do best, which was to trap the rescue party in its midst. But members of the King Street crowd were divided. They did not act as Gustave Le Bon, a century later, would say crowds must.[47] Some, mostly sailors and "mechanics" (that is, skilled workmen), did everything they could to provoke the troops. Some, including King Street shopkeepers, held back as spectators. A few brave souls tried to make peace. At length, a British private, knocked down by someone wielding a stick, fired into the crowd. Amid cries from the rioters of "Fire! Fire!" other troops also fired what most people thought were blasts of powder. In fact, they were firing musket balls, which killed five of what John Adams called "the most obscure and inconsiderable [people] that could be found."[48]

FORGOTTEN RIOTERS AND OTHER CROWDS

Boston's patriotic rioters—"patriotic" in retrospect—had plenty of company. There were, for example, the crowds of rural Massachusetts that barred recently appointed colonial judges and magistrates from performing their duties, forcing them to squirm through gauntlets of hecklers and renounce their appointments. And there were plenty of others, including the crowd that assembled behind the Pennsylvania statehouse in May 1776. Its members resolved by acclamation to countermand a decision by Pennsylvania's legislature not to join the union that more rebellious colonies had formed.[49] Clearly *this* crowd wanted national independence. But they were no more typical of late eighteenth-century American crowds than were the Pennsylvania frontier farmers (the "Paxton Boys") who, finding themselves abandoned to face Pontiac's rebellion alone, marched on Philadelphia carrying clubs and pitchforks, slaughtering friendly natives en route.[50] This was on the eve of the Stamp Act crisis. Rhode Island rioters were animated as much by the opportunity to punish foreign-born aristocrats as by opposition to the Stamp Act.[51] The depredations of rebellious farmers in North Carolina's back country c. 1768—the so-called Regulators—included the destruction of some judges' homes and had nothing to do with a desire for American independence and everything to do with their unmet demands for tax relief, secret ballots, fiscal relaxation, and recognition of dissenting ministers.[52]

In brief, before, during, and after the years of war for independence, Americans were at least as divided by issues of power, privilege, and material inequality as they were united by a common political objective. From the revivalist meetings of the Great Awakening, with their challenge to social hierarchy, and beyond, these divisions were often expressed by the actions of crowds. These crowds did not become a governing institution like those of ancient Athens. They did not propel a social revolution forward like the crowds of Paris, although many of their class superiors feared that they might. But when pulled together by anger or the frustration of unmet needs, these early Americans held unaccustomed power, however short-lived. Thus, when we read that in 1775 the streets of New York had fallen under "the sway of the mob," we should understand that ordinary New Yorkers dominated some areas of public space and were not under the sway of the more affluent Liberty Boys or their peers.[53] As war commenced, militiamen of coastal Maryland and their impoverished civilian allies seized salt from the hoards of merchants and announced their readiness to defend the king. Service in the Continental Army, which was mainly borne by the poor and foreign-born, was resisted by individual deserters and by mass actions, such as those of club-wielding crowds in the Virginia interior that routed military recruiters. Thousands of others stormed the proceedings of draft lotteries. Mobs of draft resisters followed the British army, looting the abandoned homes of plantation owners in the wake of its forays in the Virginia countryside.[54] Tenant farmers in the Hudson Valley sided with the British against their aristocratic American landlords. In sum, "Instead of supporting the revolution, many of the most downtrodden members of society . . . opposed it."[55]

When ragged, unpaid soldiers surrounded the Philadelphia statehouse in June 1783, holding the Continental Congress hostage to their demands, thousands of onlookers chanted, "Stand for your rights!"[56] Disrupting the economy, the war brought inevitable hardship to civilians. Food riots were frequent occurrences throughout the former colonies but especially in the Boston area, where many women became rioters by necessity. At Longmeadow, Massachusetts, for example, a crowd pressured a merchant into lowering his prices on molasses, sugar, salt, and rum. When another merchant proved recalcitrant, a thinly disguised band of "Indians" raided his store, putting his liberated sugar, molasses, etc., in the hands of the town clerk, who sold it at affordable prices. The stubborn merchant was not allowed to refuse the proceeds of the sale, either. Confronting a crowd of angry women at his warehouse and refusing them entry, a third merchant was grabbed by the neck and thrown into a cart. The women then took his keys and helped themselves to his coffee supplies.[57] When occurring in eighteenth-century France, such actions were called *taxation populaire*, but these strong-armed New England women anticipated the women's march on Versailles by a dozen years. Temporarily, at least, the revolution "fueled a revival of the idea of a moral economy."[58] The pseudonymous "Mobility" drew on this tradition when he (or she) reminded merchants in a Philadelphia newspaper of 1778 that the people of Britain and France "have always done themselves justice when the scarcity of bread has arisen from the avarice of forestallers" (hoarding speculators, that is).[59]

These many examples of crowd action may suggest that eighteenth-century Americans were more violent than today's. They were probably not, and certainly their violence was less deadly. But they were far more ready than we to act collectively. After all, they inhabited a tight-knit, preindustrial social world. Not only riots but barn-raisings, harvests, ship launchings, fire suppression, the posse comitatus, and peaceful protests were among the kinds of collective action in which most male residents were expected to participate. We know from *The Scarlet Letter*, if nothing else, that a crowd of the earliest New Englanders might serve as a kind of morality police. Such joint efforts were as important to the community as any riot, but they were not the kind of gatherings that made history by being noted in journals, written up in news accounts, etc. They were more a matter of self-help than of self-rule.

But rioting *was* commonplace. There were "rescue riots," usually sparked by an unpopular verdict in a criminal case, and riots over the price of food; anti-tax riots, tenants' and other riots over land; "press riots," when men violently resisted abduction into the British navy (impressment); and factional riots, such as occurred between fishers and farmers over access to streams.[60] Crowd actions often blurred such categories, however, as in New Jersey in 1745 when 150 farmers armed with axes, clubs, and crowbars demanded that the Newark sheriff release one Samuel Baldwin, who had been arrested for cutting down trees on land claimed by Governor Lewis Morris, a man of immense wealth. When the sheriff refused, the crowd overpowered him and tore the door of the jail off its hinges to free Baldwin. Fourteen weeks after that, a club-bearing force of three hundred farmers brushed aside thirty militiamen to free some of their companions who had been jailed for participating in the earlier incident. A similar event occurred two years later. A woman, Magdalene Valleau, led the largest of New Jersey's land dispute riots during this period.[61] Some said that New Jersey's farmer-occupiers of land claimed by their social betters had their own tax system, militia, courts, and jail, "back in the woods."[62] The Hudson River Valley was the site of similar happenings.

In this first American frontier, social solidarity easily outweighed rugged individualism. If crowd turbulence now seems a primitive means of addressing unmet needs, consider the alternatives. What does a person do when he or she cannot afford to pay the rent or a hospital or heating bill, make a car payment, buy groceries, or pay for necessary car repairs? Individual answers may range from the benign but easily abused possibility of borrowing from a friend or family member all the way to robbing a gas station or a bank. Without social solidarity and the possibilities it affords, we are on our own with any desperate needs that we may have and our potentially desperate remedies. Yet we may be only a common disaster away from badly needing to take collective action. Would we know how?

HUMAN RIGHTS MELEES AND ANTI-IMMIGRANT RIOTING

In 1851, a crowd in Syracuse, New York, attacked a courthouse with crowbars and a battering ram to gain access to a black man who was awaiting trial. Contrary to what this scenario usually meant, the crowd was bent on freeing the man, not hanging him, for the prisoner was a runaway slave.[63] The marshals present drew their guns, but they did not fire them. In the years leading up to regional war, some Americans took collective action to prevent the capture of runaway slaves and the enslavement of free blacks. Consider the mixed-race crowd of Philadelphians that intervened to free a woman falsely accused of being a runaway slave in 1834. Another such crowd attacked slave catchers who had captured a family of actual runaway slaves in Buffalo. The spectacle of an escaped slave being led through the streets in chains incited a mobbing of authorities in Albany, New York. Crowds of Northern blacks, with and without white allies, were sometimes able to quash attempts to return fugitive slaves to their Southern masters, too.

Though only forty-five slaves were directly freed by crowds, the fugitive slave crowds intimidated would-be slave catchers. Even when these mobbings turned violent, causing injury and death, Northern juries were often sympathetic, and penalties for such rioters were light.[64] In at least one case, abolitionists used a crowd as cover to free a captured slave.[65] These human rights affrays were significant for the high-mindedness and courage of their participants. After 1849, runaway slave rioters acted in defiance of the Fugitive Slave Act.

But the crowds that often ruled the streets of American cities before the Civil War seldom served liberal ideals. More often their reigns were brutal and malicious, however brief. Acts of slave liberation were easily outnumbered by the racist and anti-abolition riots to be discussed in chapter 5. The Philadelphia crowd mentioned above was succeeded within a few weeks by a Philadelphia mob's attack on blacks. One issue that ignited continuing conflict was immigration, for even before the potato famine in Ireland (1845–49) and the smashing of liberal revolution in Germany (1848), large numbers of immigrants from those and other countries of northern and central Europe had been coming to the United States. Although the typical German immigrant might have had enough money or salable work skills to move beyond the port of entry and head west to ply his trade, Irish immigrants, forced off their native soil by English cattle barons and later by starvation, typically arrived without such advantages. They tended to pile up in ghettos in the cities where they landed. What baggage they had often included Old World feuds. Philadelphia's most serious riot of the early nineteenth century occurred when disembarking Irish Catholics and Protestants began to brawl when setting foot on the dock.[66] Irish immigrants battled one another in two of New York City's riots of 1835 as well. They were targets of rioting in Maine that year, and in upstate New York an Irish gang attacked some native-born Americans.

As today, the arrival of so many immigrants provoked a nativist reaction. Rumors began circulating as early as the 1830s that England and Germany were dumping their poor and their criminals on the United States. Such immigrants were represented in disproportionate numbers in alms-houses, asylums, prisons, and charity hospitals.[67] In 1844, when members of the Nativist Party held a rally in a predominantly Irish neighborhood of Philadelphia, gunfire from an "Irish firehouse" (that is, one staffed by immigrant beneficiaries of Democratic patronage) killed three of them. Ten more Nativists and an Irishman died in subsequent rioting. Nativists retaliated by destroying Irish homes and Catholic properties.[68]

In the 1850s, animosity between Nativists and Irish immigrants got acted out in additional urban brawls, some of which were sparked by anti-Catholic street preachers. Immigration opponents formed secret societies, which coalesced into the American Party, or Know-Nothings, so-called because of the canned answer members gave to questions about their secret societies, not their supposed ignorance. Like many aspirants for national office today, American Party candidates ran as outsiders against the corruption of politicians and the existing political system. Sometimes allying themselves with Whigs, they enjoyed immediate electoral success. This ignited fierce opposition from the Democrats, who accused the Know-Nothings of being abolitionists, which they were not. Having eagerly traded their votes for jobs, money, whiskey, and the like, immigrants were among the Democrats' most ardent constituents, and the rise of an anti-immigrant party touched off major political riots. David Grimsted has counted twenty-two affrays which, in one way or another, involved the American Party. They resulted in seventy-seven deaths, the vast majority of which occurred in the South.[69]

Anticipating today's citizen border patrols, Know-Nothings would challenge prospective voters in immigrant neighborhoods, asking to see their citizenship papers. In Brooklyn in 1854, a crowd beat to death an election official who was handling such challenges. A mob led by a Mrs. Murphy then turned on the deputies sent to protect American Party voters, killing two and maiming several.[70] In St. Louis that same year, an Irishman stabbed a boy when turned away at the polls for lack of proper documents. The crowd that chased him into an Irish neighborhood sacked twenty homes and taverns, some of which had been the source of gunfire. Next day a mob, abetted by Irish cops, went on a rampage of retaliation, killing ten and badly wounding thirty.[71]

In New Orleans, public impatience with the corruption of the Democrats, their Irish police, and their Irish and Sicilian supporters allowed a reform coalition of Whig and Know-Nothing activists to capture the reins of municipal government. When the Democrats formed a vigilante force, supposedly to restore law and order, the reformers countered with the appointment of "special police." People gathered on rooftops and in parks to watch the promised showdown, but the flames of battle were doused when the Democrats' law-and-order strongman misfired the cannon he had intended to use on opponents, killing four and wounding nine of his vigilante followers with a single shot.[72]

In Louisville in 1854, Know-Nothings traded election-day shootings with German and Irish immigrants, leaving twenty-two dead, most of them "foreigners," and many Irish homes destroyed by fire. The American Party won the local and state elections, but Louisville's "Bloody Monday" left the organization discredited nationally. There were similar battles with similar outcomes in Baltimore that year, when Democratic and Know-Nothing gangs contended to influence the fall election. An effort by Maryland's governor to put the voting under military control drew minimal local support. After all, "the violence was largely confined to the young men who enjoyed it."[73]

Chicago had a "beer riot" in 1855 when temperance interests, aligned with Nativists, pushed through a 600 percent increase in saloon license fees. German immigrants then led a battle in which police and members of an angry crowd exchanged shots, killing one rioter and badly wounding two on each side. Most of those prosecuted were Irish immigrants.[74]

Refined for popular consumption, reduced to a patriotic melee or two (the Boston Massacre, the famous tea party), the riotous underside of American history is like an ingredient in a food product known only by its inclusion in the tiny print on the side of a can or carton. A riot is something that occurs elsewhere in today's world, or it is associated, in the minds of many Americans, with ghetto-dwelling blacks. The word itself is likely to be preceded by "laugh." Responsibility for this lies partly with the kind of advances made in crowd control, which I will discuss. Rioting was formerly tolerated to a much greater extent. No wonder, for, as we will see, the riot often served powerful interests. Indeed, representatives of those interests sometimes put themselves at the head of a destructive mob. Only when rioters consisted of representatives of the commonality attempting to advance their own interests at the expense of the established order, as in the Bank of Maryland mobbing, were they likely to encounter forceful repression.

The peaceful demonstration has done its part toward making rioting obsolete, also making the militarization of the nation's police departments expensively beside the point. That rioting has largely become a thing of the past in the United States may also have something to do with the fact that liquor is no longer "consumed by men, women, and children at all times of day and every sort of gathering," as it was in the nation's earliest years.[75] By the super-riotous era of Jacksonian democracy, however, alcohol consumption was, on a per capita basis, declining to something like present-day levels, thanks to increased religiosity and the influence of the temperance movement.[76] Maybe members of our society simply express emotions with less openness and intensity than our forebears did.[77]

The near extinction of the riot in America may have more to do with how we have learned to entertain ourselves. For example, in the Jacksonian era, a public debate on religion or politics could be counted on to draw a crowd.[78] Many members of such a crowd would probably arrive with antagonistic values or beliefs. In the past half-century, entertainment has largely become a private, often solitary experience. We are isolated by our work as well. The industrial settings of the past brought people together and politicized them by making them aware of their commonalities. Working in a cubicle or alone behind a service counter has an opposite effect. The customer can reasonably expect a degree of polite subservience. Solidarity with other workers becomes an even remoter possibility for those who work alone at home.[79]

As consumers, we are isolated with the objects of our desires and consumption. Our relationships with others are colored by critical comparisons and unacknowledged competition. Social stratification feeds on consumer distinctions. As we mutate "into the species best fitted to the capitalist world," the loss of collective approaches to common problems is ameliorated by a fading of collective antagonisms.[80] Most Americans no longer live in enclaves surrounded by their ethnic enemies. For most

Americans, social solidarity does not extend beyond the family. Streets have become the domain of drivers, crowds have become markets for retail and entertainment capital, and most of us can go about our daily lives without setting foot in a crowd of any kind.

However, although rioting has largely become a thing of America's past, our daily lives are not necessarily more immune to violent attack. Jacksonian era riots caused hundreds of deaths, but in the present era, when the blast of a car horn or even an unfriendly look can lead to a shooting death, a city like New York or Philadelphia will experience hundreds of murders every year, thought few if any of them attributable to rioting.[81] Violence today has become more deadly, more random, and more dispersed. We are fortunate indeed that "the general level of violence in a society does not trigger riots."[82]

THE ST. LOUIS GENERAL STRIKE

During the "Great Upheaval" of 1877, an eruption of strikes by railroad and other workers, crowds in St. Louis shut down the local economy in a three-day general strike, doing so without bloodshed and, excepting business losses, with negligible damage to property. But those three days were followed by a ninety-year reprisal (described in chapter 4).

The strike had its beginning on July 23 when leaders of the Workingmen's Party, an obscure and recently formed socialist organization whose membership consisted mostly of German immigrants, called for an open-air meeting as a follow-up to events in which railroad workers had paralyzed the transport hub of East St. Louis by going on strike. To the probable astonishment of Workingmen's Party organizers, a crowd of around ten thousand showed up to listen to German and English-speaking orators, including a black man, at three different speaker's stands.[83] Next day a procession of hundreds of workers led by torch, fife, and drum returned to the meeting site. With some carrying clubs, it was "an awfully suggestive spectacle," in the carefully chosen words of the St. Louis *Times*.[84] A representative of a hastily formed "Executive Committee" called for a general strike aimed at obtaining an eight-hour workday and an end to child labor. Throughout the day, workers visited the Workingmen's Party headquarters to request that a committee be sent to their workplaces to ask them to stop working. Members of the party had gladly obliged.[85]

The following days featured marches to targeted worksites throughout the city, where the "vast, impetuous, and perspiring mass of men" would call on those within to come outside and join them. [86] They were sufficiently successful that by July 26 the strike had "permeated pretty much every branch of trade in St. Louis."[87] Or, as the British consul complained to his London office, "Parades of the discontented were permitted on all principal streets without a show of countervailing force, and nightly mass meetings were held in the most public places, where thousands of the most ignorant and depraved in the community were made riotous by the incendiary speeches of their orators."[88]

Officially directing all this activity was the Executive Committee, but what *was* the Executive Committee and to what extent did it provide leadership? Evidently the committee consisted of whoever appeared at the Workingmen's Party headquarters and took part in the discussions. According to Morris Hillquit, a later leader of the American Socialist Party, its only plan was "tying up all the industries in the city."[89] Much of its energy was devoted to assuring members of the city's establishment of the workers' peaceful intent and dousing any sparks of "mob violence," though strikers engaged in at least one orderly procession without the committee's leadership or okay. At one point, the committee sent its own "militia" to guard a sugar refinery, having acceded to the owner's request to allow him continued operations in order to prevent spoilage. The committee also petitioned the mayor to provide food for strikers' families, so as "to avoid plunder, arson or violence by persons made desperate by destitution."[90] A member of the committee even recommended the arrest of an unauthorized speaker at a mass rally. committee speakers called for the nationalization of American industry but said nothing about taking over the operation of any of St. Louis's many factories. Nor did they present a plan that would have enabled strikers "to gain concrete benefits from the strike" or provide a tactical alternative to the violence they deplored.[91] Regarding this last point, though, bear in mind that the committee had little in the way of a historic model for successful, nonviolent mass action and that the striking crowds met almost no resistance, at least at first.

As for the temporarily triumphant multitude, both its restraint and its condition were signified by a loaf of bread stuck on a flagstaff at the head of a march. "That is what we are fighting for," said a marcher. The bread had not been taken from a bakery but purchased.[92] Behind it came a brass band, followed by six hundred factory workers and a company of railroad workers with coupling pins, red signal flags, brake rods, and other occupational implements. A vanguard of strike committees called on those still working to put down their tools and join them, which they did, deserting foundries, bagging companies, bakeries, flour mills, chemical plants, metal works, etc., to swell their ranks. A similar, though self-organized, march took place in nearby Carondolet, while women demonstrated their support for the strike by parading in East St. Louis.[93]

The city's right-wing newspapers pounced on minor incidents of looting and breakage, enlarging them to evidence of "anarchy." Their reports of racial tensions among the biracial crowds may have been a matter of wishful thinking on the part of the business class, but maybe not. Depending on their communal identity, workers interviewed later were quick to condemn the "Dutchmen," "naygurs," or Irish for the strike's unhappy denouement.[94]

By July 27, the last day of the strike, the city's prime representatives of law and order had readied a force of "citizen soldiery" to march on strike headquarters. They instructed the adult males of leading merchant families, lawyers, railroad executives, bankers, white-collar workers, and others who made up their ranks to disperse the mob with bayonets and summarily shoot suspected arsonists. Meanwhile, a split developed between anxious strikers and the official strike leadership. A delegation of the crowd outside Executive Committee headquarters invaded the private meeting taking place upstairs and demanded to know whether the inaction of their leaders had been paid for with bribes. They got no satisfactory response.[95]

Such leadership can only suffer in comparison with, say, that of the Czechs in 1989 when a series of meetings to discuss national liberation that began in the theater known as the Magic Lantern proliferated until, as Timothy Garton Ash has written, all Prague became the Magic Lantern.[96] Though protest "is not created by organizers and leaders," without something of the steely determination of a Lenin, the moral example of a César Chavez, or the tactical audacity of a Harry Bridges, mass protest will rarely be sustained until transmuted into political or economic gain.[97] On the other hand, St. Louis in 1877 was a long way from Petrograd in 1917 or any other capital. The opponents of the loosely organized strikers had arms, including artillery pieces, and an eagerness to use them, while the disparate members of St. Louis's unskilled working class had only their numbers and needs and rumors of rifles coming their way.

As it turned out, the police and "vigilance committee" members had only to make an appearance at strike headquarters to scatter the strikers and the strike's presumptive leadership, as well as the crowd of onlookers that had begun to gather the day before, drawn by the promise of a bloody showdown.[98] In the torpor of daily meetings and efforts to police the unwashed crowds outside its doors, the Executive Committee may have achieved the optimal result under the circumstances: nobody wounded and nobody killed. Elsewhere armed defenders of the existing order often fired bullets into such crowds.

MASS REBELLION IN THE INDUSTRIAL HEARTLAND

About a week before the onset of the St. Louis general strike, railroad workers in Martinsburg, West Virginia, had ignited widespread industrial turmoil by uncoupling train engines and refusing to allow trains to leave the rail yard. Their action was neither planned nor sanctioned by union higher-ups but inspired by the announcement of another wage cut by their employer, the Baltimore and Ohio Railroad (B & O). The crowd of strikers and their sympathizers, which confronted the detachment of state troopers that the West Virginia governor sent to Martinsburg to put down the strike, was so large that the troops took refuge in the local courthouse. The governor then sent a telegram to the president, asking for federal troops "to protect the law abiding people of the State against domestic violence, and to maintain supremacy of the law."[99] The strike was spreading throughout the region, and President Hayes complied as best he could. But federal troops were neither readily available nor eager to put down strikes in the industrial heartland in 1877 because they were battling native rebellions on the western frontier and because their payrolls had become a political pawn.[100] Federal troops sent to Keyser, West Virginia, could only watch "helplessly" as a mob forced strikebreakers off a freight train.[101]

In Pittsburgh, crowds had gathered at the city's main rail crossings to prevent passage of freights. Many state troopers sent there simply failed to show up. When less sympathetic (or perhaps less frightened) militiamen from Philadelphia began clearing the tracks with fixed bayonets, a crowd of six thousand attacked them with stones and possibly pistol shots. The troops fired at their tormentors, killing twenty including three children. This mobilized such additional support for Pittsburgh's strikers that the local populace began forming armed military units and holding drills.[102] Local authority had evaporated, and in a battle that lasted twenty-four hours and caused twenty-five more deaths, the crowd laid siege to a roundhouse where the Philadelphia militiamen were holed up, setting it ablaze under the cover of supportive fire from more than sympathetic Pittsburgh policemen. Next day hundreds of people looted freight cars and distributed their goods to the crowds with the help of local cops.

A crowd in Altoona, Pennsylvania, that same summer engulfed a train bound for Pittsburgh with five hundred National Guard troops aboard and talked them into giving up their arms and going home. Another military unit surrendered its weapons to a crowd in Harrisburg. On the other hand, when police or military troops intervened as directed during the Great Upheaval of 1877, they all too often created working-class martyrs by firing their weapons directly into crowds. They did so not only in Pittsburgh but also, for example, in Baltimore and Chicago. They did so again during the Lawrence, Massachusetts, textile workers' strike of 1912, and they resumed such deadly tactics during the Depression years.

EN MASSE STRIKE SUPPORT

Though Canetti cites the work stoppage as the best example of the "prohibition crowd," workers peacefully withholding their labor to shut down production and win demands would generally not be considered a crowd in action.[103] But the tactics of mass defiance by industrial workers have ranged from the orderly to the chaotic. When workers struggled to win the collective bargaining rights promised by Section 7a of the National Recovery Act in the early 1930s, successful campaigns usually combined a disruptive but orderly refusal to work with the disorderly potential of massive picketing or a general strike. When Depression-era workers occupied buildings—in this case, manufacturing plants—they were doing something that crowds have done again and again to advance their cause. In some of the most significant sit-down strikes, those inside the plant were supported and defended by crowds at the factory gates. The crucial component of all such successful efforts was the unified action made possible by large numbers of people acting in solidarity. Consider some examples.

Responding to their employer's announcement of its second wage cut of the year, the hundreds of workers of a North Carolina hosiery manufacturer who walked off the job in July 1932 would have jeered at the notion that they were engaged in "collective bargaining by riot," as their critics charged.[104] But they then marched through the area with jobless supporters, inducing the closure of a hundred other factories of various kinds. They also wrecked a motor to shut off power to the hosiery plant's locale. With intervention by the governor, their wage-level was restored. They also gained recognition for a locally based industrial union.[105]

In Toledo, Ohio, in 1934, workers at the Electric Auto-Lite Company, a supplier of Willys-Overland, the area's largest employer, became so frustrated in their efforts to obtain union recognition that they walked off the job. When the company reneged on a federally mediated agreement to negotiate with its employees, some walked off again, and Auto-Lite hired replacements. At this point, jobless workers, mobilized by A. J. Muste's Unemployed Leagues, joined pickets from the plant until police made some arrests and the employer obtained an injunction to limit picketing. This generated a tsunami of strike support. So many appeared at the manufacturer's gates that the crowd was able to trap the strikebreakers inside. The thousands of picketers managed not only to hold their own against the violence of specially deputized police (financed by the employer) but to pack the courtroom in which Auto-Lite sought additional remedies. When a contingent of the Ohio National Guard was summoned to rescue the strikebreakers, the crowd responded with a hail of bottles and bricks.

Guardsmen fired on the crowd, killing two and wounding many, and still the crowd maintained its mass. Strikers and their community supporters then threatened a general strike, at which point the company agreed to most of the workers' demands. But not until a crowd began to gather at the company's gates again did Auto-Lite fully act on these commitments.[106]

We might return to North Carolina in 1934 for something new in the combination of organized numbers and massive turbulence. Attracted by the region's low labor costs (as low as $5.00 plus dilapidated company housing for a 55-hour workweek), the textile industry had been moving operations there from New England for years. But then 65,000 of their miserably low-paid workers walked off the job and created a national sensation by forming "flying squadrons." These motorcades of two hundred to a thousand picketers each drove from one town to another in the region, stopping before the local mill to demand a work stoppage, with the strikers sometimes going inside to shut down its machinery. What text messaging and email are to organizing today, this fossil-fueled picketing was to the textile workers' cause in 1934. Employers and their law enforcement allies could not anticipate where the strikers might turn up next. "The growing mass character of the picketing operations is rapidly assuming the appearance of military efficiency," reported the *New York Times* in a page-one account that warned of the situation's "grave danger."[107] Unfortunately for the workers, it was they who faced the gravest danger in what became a massive textile strike that spread across the South and into mill towns in New England, where thousands battled National Guardsmen in the streets. Several workers were killed, many more injured, and yet many more experienced mass arrest, detention without charges, bayonet attacks while peacefully picketing, and (in the South) lasting enmity toward unions when the United Textile Workers' leadership called off the strike with virtually nothing to show for it, leaving many workers unemployed.[108]

In 1937 Chrysler obtained an eviction order against the workers who had occupied its plants for thirty days. When the evacuation deadline arrived, huge crowds of pickets gathered outside the plants, with as many as fifty thousand participating. This made forced eviction politically inexpedient for elected officials.[109] When the workers occupying GM's Fisher

No. 1 plant in Flint, Michigan, were threatened with eviction by National Guard troops, thousands of supporters poured into Flint to occupy the town and surround the occupied plant.[110] Those workers and their supporters could not have anticipated that their struggles were occurring on the threshold of a transformation of productive forces that would make such solidarity largely a thing of the past. Under market imperatives and advances in technology and transport, industrial production required the consumer society to head off a systemic replay of the sorcerer's apprentice, in the form of a pileup of unbought goods, followed by economic collapse. Baudrillard wrote that "having socialized the masses into a labor force, the industrial system had to go further in order to fulfill itself" by creating a "force of consumption."[111] This has made consumption "a function of production," the equivalent of "social labor."[112] But if consumption is really an extension of production, it is production without the solidarity of the manufacturer's shop floor. Its crowds are merely aggregates of isolated individuals.

GHETTO ERUPTIONS

A few decades into the twentieth century, the country's majority woke to the fact that its typical central city had become the nursery of a new kind of race riot. The initial event occurred in Harlem, where population density was almost twice that of the rest of Manhattan and thousands lived in verminous cellars. There on March 19, 1935, Lino Rivera, a sixteen-year-old boy, was caught stealing a knife in an S. H. Kress store. When a police officer arrived, the store manager said that he would not press charges, though the boy had bitten the hands of his captors. Nevertheless, a crowd began to form, and to avoid their curious eyes, the policeman took the boy downstairs and through the basement of the store to a rear exit. Members of the crowd decided that the officer had taken the boy downstairs to give him a beating. When an ambulance arrived to treat the bite wounds on the hands of Rivera's captors, and that was followed by a hearse that happened to park in front of the store, a group called the Young Liberators began to circulate a flyer headed, "CHILD BRUTALLY BEATEN... NEAR DEATH." The rumor quickly spread that the boy had been killed: "Soon all of Harlem was repeating the rumor that a Negro boy had been murdered in the basement of Kress's store."[113]

Adding to the crowd's resentment, the police arrested a pair of soapbox speakers who had been haranguing people outside the store. Harlem sidewalks were already clotted with the unemployed, and angry crowds began to form spontaneously, dissolving when approached by the police, coalescing again in their absence. According to the report of the Mayor's Commission that investigated the matter, "The screaming of sirens, the sound of pistol shots and the crashing of glass created in many a mood for destruction and excitement."[114] This linking of sounds to action approaches Canetti's: "The noise of destruction adds to its satisfaction; the banging of windows and the crashing of glass are the robust signs of fresh life, the cries of something new-born."[115]

Looting soon got under way, targeting the property of white merchants. The Mayor's Commission would later conclude that people took things of no possible use to them: "They acted as if there were a chance to seize what rightfully belonged to them but had long been withheld."[116] No doubt many looters would have agreed with this formulation. When the police displayed a photo of Lino Rivera posing with a black officer, the rumor spread that this was not Rivera but a ringer. Such deep and widespread incredulity does not exist without cause. This first of many urban ghetto riots inspired the fictional riot of Ralph Ellison's *Invisible Man* and provided the background of events in James Baldwin's *Go Tell It on the Mountain.*

Blacks who came north and west for jobs during the Second World War were often stranded in some regions without further employment at war's end. In the following decades, the nation's cities were increasingly filled with people who were drawn there not so much by job opportunities as the fact that they had nowhere else to go. They had arrived in the North as the baby boomers were entering the job market, as inner cities and their services were deteriorating, and as manufacturing plants and offices were starting to follow fleeing whites to the suburbs.[117] In effect, the South had exported a labor force made redundant by the mechanization of agriculture, thus transforming "a depressed southern rural peasantry . . . into a depressed urban proletariat,"[118] which was "largely useless to the modern world."[119]

The civil rights movement heroically confronted legal segregation and discriminatory local ordinances, but its energy and moral leverage could not alter the reality that even well-intentioned employers required fewer and fewer unskilled workers at jobs that paid a decent wage. Neither sit-ins nor Freedom Rides, nor children's marches, nor any other tactic of the movement could eliminate poverty or win economic equality for any but middle-class blacks, who constituted a distinct minority. As Martin Luther King Jr. conceded, "Jobs are harder and costlier to create than voting rolls."[120] Harlem blacks "who had voted for years still lived in rat-infested slums."[121] With the rest of the world, they had seen the images of the howling mobs that tried to prevent black children from attending Little Rock High School in 1957, the "spectacular riot" that attended James Meredith's effort to integrate the University of Mississippi in 1962, and Birmingham police using fire hoses, police dogs, and truncheons on peaceful demonstrators, including children, in 1963.[122] They knew of the killings and bombings of blacks in the South. By contrast, the violence of chronic unemployment and squalid housing of the Northern slum was invisible except to ghetto residents.

The new urban proletariat may have been depressed, but it was also volatile. When an off-duty cop shot and killed a fifteen-year-old Harlem youth in July 1964, blacks rioted, leaving one dead, 118 injured, 465 under arrest, and millions in property damage from looting and burning. Rioters called civil rights leader Bayard Rustin an Uncle Tom when he appealed for calm, and they heckled James Farmer of the Congress of Racial Equality (CORE). New York mayor Robert Wagner called on King to control "the undermuck of Harlem."[123] Similar riots occurred in Rochester, New York; Cambridge, Maryland; Philadelphia; Brooklyn; Elizabeth, Paterson, and Jersey City, New Jersey; and Chicago.[124] An FBI investigation of these upheavals identified a pattern in which, time after time, an all-white (or nearly so) police force took a hands-off stance in the early stages of rioting, then engaged in "military-style suppression." But only a heavily sanitized version of the FBI's report saw the light of day.[125]

In Los Angeles, eighty thousand blacks occupied a rundown area known as Watts, which had four times the population density of the rest of the city. Official unemployment stood at 30 percent, and restrictive housing covenants in the surrounding suburbs trapped even those

Watts residents who were economically successful. On August 11, 1965, a white highway patrolman stopped a young black man in Watts for drunk driving. The struggle that ensued between the patrolman, the youth, and the youth's mother drew a large crowd, as well as Los Angeles police officers. Clusters of the crowd dispersed to stone passing cars, attack white drivers, even threaten a police command post. Then, following thirty hours of relative calm, an outbreak of looting, arson, and assaults began. The police did not respond at first, and the looting spread. Firebombing targeted white-owned properties. There was a delay in activation of the National Guard. Once involved, National Guard troops and the police "made heavy use of firearms" in response to numerous reports of sniper fire, and several people were hit by stray bullets and shots fired in panic.[126] The rioting caused thirty-four deaths, over a thousand injuries, and $40 million in property damage.[127] The police arrested four thousand.[128]

There would be no loaves of patronage bread for the Los Angeles "primitive rebels." What they got instead was a whitewash. The controversial McCone Commission, appointed by the California governor, concluded that the riot was the work of about ten thousand unemployed, poorly educated, rootless young delinquents. A critique of the McCone Commission's report, based on an independent survey, suggested otherwise. Civil rights leader Bayard Rustin, Berkeley sociologist Robert Blauner, and UCLA political scientist Harry Scoble found that as many as fifty thousand participated in the riot, and they were not the "riffraff" of the black community. Most participants were permanent residents, employed, and better educated than non-participants, though they had the support of many who did not take part. Their experience of job insecurity, consumer exploitation, discrimination, and residential segregation was sufficiently grievous that, as Robert Fogelson pointed out, they could hurdle such ordinary barriers to rioting as fear of arrest, injury, or death.[129] Rioters of America's earlier ages did not always face such risks, enjoying as they often did the tacit support of the established order including the police.

There was a lot more violence to come, with eruptions of varying intensity in 1966 in the racial ghettos of Cleveland, Omaha, Dayton, Chicago, Los Angeles again, and elsewhere. ("Oakland's next" was often heard in the Bay Area.) With official unemployment among black youths hovering just below 35 percent, the following year brought the worst urban riots in American history.[130] The National Advisory Commission on Civil Disorders, appointed by President Johnson to determine what happened, why it happened, and what could be done to prevent its happening again, identified eight major riots, thirty-three "serious but not major" outbreaks, and 123 "minor" disorders, all in 1967.[131] The commission's report, known as the Kerner Report (after Illinois governor Otto Kerner, chairman of the commission), identified a pattern wherein a series of disturbing incidents became linked to ghetto residents' underlying grievances by a further incident, "often routine or trivial," which became the trigger of collective rage. Police actions figured in about half of the prior incidents, as well as half of the precipitating "final" incidents.[132] We may get a sense of the range of social eruptions that occurred during that long hot summer of over forty years ago by considering some particulars.

On June 11, 1967, a Tampa police officer cornered and shot a fleeing robbery suspect, who was black. He did so under compromising circumstances, as clinging to a cyclone fence, the fatally wounded suspect appeared to have been shot while surrendering. The police then did nothing to prevent a large, riotous crowd from forming, which began breaking into stores, setting fires, and engaging in other acts of destruction. At one point, a white couple exited a nearby freeway to determine the cause of smoke they had observed. Their car was set upon by a mob, the driver dragged out and beaten. His terrified spouse was about to be assaulted, too, when a nineteen-year-old black man physically intervened, at some risk to himself, to save the pair. Authorities were gradually able to bring the rioting under control by recruiting an indigenous force to serve as peacemakers in a youth patrol.[133] But perhaps the rioting had simply run its course.

At the same time, rioting broke out in Cincinnati where blacks, a significant minority of the population, faced systematic discrimination. The first spark took the form of selective enforcement, by the police, of an anti-loitering ordinance so as to suppress the message of a man who was using a sandwich board to protest a cousin's murder conviction and death sentence. This provoked a minor riot. A judge made matters worse by levying harsh penalties on the blacks involved. An angry crowd then confronted local police, attacking them with rocks and bottles and utilizing Molotov cocktails to start dozens of fires. The National Guard gradually restored order, but not before sixty-three people, mostly whites, had been injured, some seriously, and 404 people arrested.[134]

Blacks in Atlanta, who made up 44 percent of the population, were grossly underrepresented in the city's board rooms. In fact if not in law, Atlanta's neighborhoods and schools were racially segregated. A minor incident of June 17 drew a succession of gatherings of frustrated blacks. Then a speech by Stokely Carmichael, described as wearing a green Malcolm X sweatshirt, incited those attending a public meeting to pour into the streets, where they were joined by others, and some began throwing rocks and bottles at the police cars drawn up there. Officials responded as they had in Tampa, by recruiting members of a black youth patrol. Perhaps more important in defusing the situation, the city suddenly began to meet long-standing demands of black residents for playground equipment and the like.[135]

Though whites clung to political control in Newark, New Jersey, people of color composed a majority of the population following white flight to surrounding suburbs, which had left the city with a greatly weakened capacity for providing public services. Controversy simmered over Newark's plan to allocate 150 acres of the central city for the building of a medical and dental school. A second issue was the political establishment's determination to choose a white man over a seemingly more qualified black to head the school board. On the night of July 12, the arrest of a resisting black cab driver under the angry gaze of residents of a high-rise housing project brought people into the streets for a standoff with police. Eventually that crowd dispersed, but rumors contributed to mounting tension, token concessions angered many, and on the following night the police station at the site of the previous night's arrest came under attack. This was accompanied by looting of businesses in the general area and by acts of arson. State police and National Guard troops were rushed to the scene. Responding to rumors and, in some cases, the actuality of snipers, these panicky forces fired over thirteen thousand rounds of ammunition, killing eight non-participants, including two children, and firing on any shop displaying a "soul brother" sign. "Friendly fire" may have been responsible for the deaths of a fireman and policeman as well. Twenty-three people were killed, in all, and Newark suffered over $10 million in damage.[136]

Elsewhere during that riotous season, events sometimes followed a more genial course. Residents of Elizabeth, New Jersey, feared a blood-bath like that of nearby Newark because of conflict between local police and angry black youths. A crowd had gathered, which some members of the community were trying to pacify, when tension was defused by a chicken that fluttered out into the street through the broken window of a poultry market. One youth splattered gasoline on the bird, and another stomped on it as it lay on the ground. With a flurry of feathers, the bird suddenly darted up, at which the startled youth let out a scream, then slipped and fell against a tree. The crowd cracked up laughing, and many left for home.[137]

In New Brunswick, New Jersey, an emblematic exchange occurred when a towering black minister tried to reason with a column of young marchers. "Brothers!" he pleaded, "let me talk to you!" An undersized thirteen-year-old looked up at him: "Black power, baby!" he said.[138] That city probably avoided a major riot when its mayor answered the demands of an angry crowd by assuring them that people arrested the night before had already been released, even allowing representatives of the crowd to confirm this by inspecting the jail.[139]

Finally, Detroit. There urban renewal had transformed an integrated neighborhood into a crowded and impoverished black ghetto where reports of police brutality were commonplace. During the night of July 22, police raided an after-hours club where a party celebrating the return of some servicemen from Vietnam was in progress. Eighty-two arrests were made, and denizens of the area responded by looting local stores. The police took a hands-off approach initially, even joking with some of the people who were running in and out of stores. But the rumor of a police bayoneting spread with the speed of the windblown fires that were jumping from roof to roof. Firefighters were met with volleys of bottles and rocks, though a few people pitched in to help the crews. National Guard troops were activated. They began shooting looters and, panicked by rumors of snipers and finding no mobs to control, were soon firing at street lights, empty buildings, almost anything that moved, including non-participants framed by windows. The "snipers" were everywhere. Meanwhile, local police conducted "alley court," beating many of the 7,200 people arrested to obtain confessions and seriously injuring some. At length, a force of disciplined federal troops—paratroopers brought in by presidential order—began to take control of the chaotic situation. As the Kerner commissioners noted in a supplement to their report, "For some years, the Army has conducted the military planning and coordination necessary to control civil disorders."[140] But by the time order was restored, the police had killed at least twenty people, National Guardsmen another seven to nine, and the rioters two or three.[141]

The commission held white racism "essentially responsible for the explosive mixture which has been accumulating in our cities since the end of World War II." White institutions created and maintained the ghetto, they wrote, "and white society condones it."[142] The Commission's "Recommendations for National Action" in employment, education, housing, the welfare system, etc., as needed to bring about a "single society, in which every citizen [would be] free to live and work according to his capabilities and desires,"[143] were not translated into action, and the nation's ghettos remain explosive.

But it would be a mistake to conclude that the ghetto rioters of forty years ago achieved nothing. At the very least, blacks won white fear. To trivialize this victory is to ignore not only the brutality of slavery but an extensive history of mob depredations intended to overturn the outcome of the Civil War and to maintain a racial hierarchy throughout the United States via lynchings and pogroms. From the Memphis and New Orleans massacres of 1866[144] to frequent and well-attended central Texas lynchings,[145] the Colfax (Louisiana) Massacre of 1873, and the mobs that went on a "lynching bee" following heavyweight Jack Johnson's thrashing of James Jeffries (the "Great White Hope") in 1910,[146] America's ugly record of collective assaults on members of widely despised minorities puts us in some notorious company. This includes the mobs of Eastern and Central Europe that for centuries waged pogroms against Jews and Gypsies, the upper-caste assailants of Panchamas (Untouchables) in India, and various disreputable others. In the 1890s, a black person was lynched somewhere in America about once every two days, killed by rope or by fire with little or no provocation. Testifying against a white in court, trying to change jobs, using offensive language, failing to address a white man as "Mister," attempting to cast a vote, "being too prosperous," being accused of raping a white woman—any one of these might rouse a mob of whites to become judge, jury, torturer, and executioner. If the victim were a woman, she might be raped before being hanged.[147] Asian immigrants fared little better in the West. Mob attacks directed against people of color continued well into the twentieth century, with major incidents in East St. Louis in 1917, Chicago in 1919, Oklahoma in 1921, and Los Angeles (the "Zoot suit riots") and Detroit as late as 1943. A complete history would fill volumes.

Why did the violence of the collective hate crime wane as the new kind of race riot was beginning to erupt? One explanation is black migration from the rural South, which for the migrants meant an exchange of population dispersal and interracial "intimacy" for highly concentrated pockets of urban poverty. The breakdown of regional cultural differences through the homogenizing influence of mass media, especially television, has also been a factor, as has the success of the civil rights movement in proscribing overt racism. Nor should we forget the influence of the Cold War on official concern for the nation's image. But the willingness of blacks to go on a rampage contributed to this historic trade-off, too.

In the nation's most recent major uprising, that of April 1992, race did not entirely trump class. What started as a black reaction to the notorious verdict in the Rodney King police beating case became a massive transfer of goods from retail establishments to the commandeered shopping carts of black, brown, and even white looters. Over half of the first five thousand arrested were Latinos; 10 percent were whites.[148] A social critic described the process as "a race riot that had no border . . . a race riot without nationality."[149] A gang member may have had a better handle on it, saying of the nationally televised violence that it was "not a riot—it was a class struggle."[150] It was also a reminder of what A. Philip Randolph (head of the Sleeping-Car Porters Union) had predicted back in 1963: "The Negro's protest today is but the first rumbling of the 'under-class.' As the Negro has taken to the streets, so will the unemployed of all races take to the streets."[151] With the income gap between rich and poor presently rising to pre-Depression levels, it would probably be a mistake to assume that the L.A. explosion of 1992 will prove to be the last of its kind.

In any case, the (somewhat) advantageous use of the riot since the Second World War has not been confined to racial or ethnic minorities. The Stonewall riots became a landmark event in the struggle for gay liberation. And gender relations in the United States would never be quite the same following the feminist demonstration against and disruption of the 1968 Miss America Pageant in Atlantic City.[152]

WHEN EVERYONE SAT DOWN

The civil rights movement has had a lasting impact on the en masse tactics of political protesters. Many of the people who became leaders of the student movement of the 1960s cut their teeth (or had them broken) in voting rights and related campaigns in the South. In the San Francisco Bay Area there were mass sit-ins to protest racial discrimination in hiring by major employers, with college students providing most of the mass. These led to mass arrests. CORE cadre organized "shop-ins" at Lucky's food stores in which participants would pile goods into their shopping carts, wheel them up to the checkout counter, then change their minds about buying anything. Like many civil rights tactics, the shop-ins were both legal and highly disruptive. At San Francisco's classy Sheraton-Palace Hotel, demonstrators filtered into the lobby from a picket line outside until the entire line had moved inside, "singing, chanting, and clapping hands."[153] Pursuant to a legal injunction they dispersed, but a few days later, on March 6, 1964, thousands of students again converged on the hotel, this time to picket and move into the lobby for an overnight "sleep-in." "It was all very orderly," writes a participant, when next day row after row of protesters moved forward, then sat with arms linked until the police could drag them out of the hotel for their arrests. Those who declined arrest cleaned the lobby up before they left. The protests (and pressure on the mayor from the longshoremen's union) resulted in a nondiscriminatory hiring agreement by the Hotel Owners Association.[154]

Considerable recruiting for this and other Bay Area civil rights actions took place on college campuses. At the area's biggest school, the University of California (UC) at Berkeley, activists worked information tables from a twenty-six-foot-wide free-speech strip bordering the campus's busiest entrance. Political advocacy there was beyond the university's control. Or so it was thought until William Knowland—former U.S. senator, chair of the state's Goldwater for President campaign, and a major backer of an initiative that would repeal California's ban on housing discrimination—apparently responded to picketing of his *Oakland Tribune* by pointing out to UC administrators (or maybe the Board of Regents) that the advocacy strip was actually *on* campus property, and thus subject to the school's prohibition on unauthorized political speech. On September 21, the administration brought the free-speech strip under campus-wide limitations. This united Berkeley activists of every stripe.[155]

When some elected to defy the ban, an administrator summoned five for disciplinary action. Five hundred signed a petition of solidarity. Among those subsequently suspended was Mario Savio, a veteran of Mississippi Freedom Summer who had helped organize the petition. This was roughly the situation on October 1, 1964, when Jack Weinberg, manning a prohibited table with CORE literature regarding civil rights martyrs James Chaney and Michael Schwerner, refused to identify himself to an assistant dean, who summoned a police officer. The latter drove his patrol car into crowded Sproul Plaza to make the arrest, assuming that the students would allow his car and its unwilling passenger to exit the Plaza as he had entered it. But the students did not make a path for him. Instead they made a little history.

"A hundred people will tell you they were the first to sit down," wrote free speech movement archivist Michael Rossman. "Each is telling the truth; for it was a matter of collective impulse . . . in which we moved as one while acting independently."[156] "It seemed easy and appropriate to sit down on the ground with the other students," says another participant. "The police car . . . seemed tiny and helpless. . . . There was a sense of instant community and internal power."[157] Taking turns speaking from the roof of the car, pausing to vote on proposals of various kinds, "a thousand informed and independent minds [participated] in what the media, administrators, and even our professors could recognize only as a 'mob scene.'"[158] Though the account of Northern California's leading newspaper (in circulation) emphasized the divisions among those present—the hecklers and the fraternity boys who showed up late that night chanting, "Clear the car, clear the car" (and later, "We want beer, we want beer"), there was sufficient crowd cohesion for a detachment of five hundred or so to break away and occupy nearby Sproul Hall and for the larger crowd to maintain the sit-down around the police car and its prisoner for thirty-two hours.[159] Then, with hundreds of police officers ominously drawn up around them and Mario Savio recommending a dignified retreat, the students left the plaza on their own volition with a favorable truce agreement signed by UC president Clark Kerr in their collective pocket.

It was a victory for students' right to free speech achieved by the willingness of people to put their numerous bodies on the line, but it was far from the end of student protest, in Berkeley or elsewhere. For that it was a prototype.[160]

Though its expression may be tightly controlled, sublimated into harmless outlets, bought off, or otherwise diverted from challenges to the existing order, conflict is endemic to hierarchical society. But physical confrontations have been largely individualized in present-day America. The consumer society requires an orderly setting in which the only social obstacles are competing participants—other shoppers, other drivers, other spectators.

But what is this? No sooner have I closed and locked up our crowd museum than there comes a pounding on the door. The sound of something breaking outside also comes to me, accompanied by a burning smell. What is it they chant? The walls are thick, and I can barely make it out: "We want in too! We want in too!" Was there a "ruling crowd" that might have been left out?

3. Killer Crowds

At the end of the last chapter, what sounded like an angry mob had formed outside my crowd museum. It seemed to want to get inside. That crowd has not dispersed, and I can ignore its clamoring no longer. I open the museum door upon a raucous nighttime crowd. Prominent in the foreground are a pair of female adolescents who appear to be almost giddy with excitement. There is a woman who could be the mother of one of them, a diminutive older woman gazing off in another direction, and a tall youth with a gloating grin. A trio of older men appears in profile. They seem to be studying what they see. (One wears what appears to be the headgear of some lodge.) A short man with a hard stare and work-hardened arms is pointing redundantly at the bloodied bodies of two young black men, which hang above the crowd from the limbs of a tree. The mixed emotions on display do not include horror.

A spokesman for the crowd approaches. He says that they want to be included in the crowd museum, that they have a right to be admitted because they represent many similar crowds. The long list of examples he recites includes the mobs that surged through the streets of Manhattan in 1863 to protest the Conscription Act—burning, looting, and destroying lives. They include the murderous offshoot of that mob, the one that set fire to a black children's orphanage. They include the Memphis mob that murdered forty-six newly freed blacks and two white sympathizers in 1866, raping five women and burning ninety homes, twelve schools, and four churches for good measure. They include the Los Angeles mob that lynched sixteen Chinese men and a Chinese woman in 1871. They include the force responsible for the massacre of scores of prisoners in Louisiana in 1873, the festive crowd that applauded the public hanging of Jesse Jones in downtown Waco, Texas, in 1906, and the midday crowd of around fifteen thousand that gathered to watch the mutilation and agonizing murder of Jesse Washington next to Waco's city hall ten years later.[1] They say they represent every one of these powerful crowds and many, many more. On this basis, they insist, they have a much stronger claim to a place in the crowd museum than, say, that bunch of California delinquents that had nothing better to do that day in 1964 than interfere with a police car!

In considering this killing mob's application for a place in the museum of empowered crowds, the first thing that comes to mind, when the shock and horror begin to wear off, is the question of representation. Can a crowd represent something other than itself? Anyone can claim to represent a crowd, but the crowd itself, especially the angry and determined crowd, is that which others, under threat of harassment if not mob violence, hope to reduce to a few representatives. These others may range from a university president to the framers of a constitution for a new republic. Whether or not the lynch mob at the door can represent all the other mobs that have splattered American history with the blood of their victims, the more important question is whether the museum should be open only to the powerful and sometimes violent crowds we tend to like, such as those described in chapter 2. Republicans of the early modern era, such as Machiavelli, James Harrington, and Thomas Jefferson, would have said yes, the crowd is the source of popular sovereignty, a virtuous people sometimes armed, and that which needs to be enshrined.[2] The lynch mob is a perversion of this ideal, a criminal crowd. Prominent nineteenth-century theorists would have disagreed. For them the mobs so far excluded from the crowd museum run true to type. The crowd itself is criminal, they would say. These American mobs should be locked inside the museum with the rest, and we should throw away the key.

These opposing valuations of crowds are separated not only by ideology but by many historic events, including one in particular.

THE CROWD PATHOLOGIZED

In the previous chapter, we left not only what turned out to be a lynch mob at the door of the crowd museum but another mob of the Parisian poor at the gates of a prison, which they were about to invade to defend the revolution from its enemies within. Parisians were obsessed, at the time, with the approach of royalist armies under the Duke of Brunswick, who had vowed "delivering up [their city] to military execution, and total destruction."[3] The presence of hundreds of the revolution's presumptive enemies, imprisoned for now, seemed an intolerable added risk. The crowd gave the objects of these widespread fears impromptu trials. Some of these were pro forma, but others were extensive, resulting in acquittals and the freeing of hundreds of prisoners. Even at Abbaye, the first prison the crowds invaded, "the tribunals were genuinely concerned to determine an individual's guilt or innocence."[4] David Andress has written that the September Massacres, as the people's execution of prisoners was called, had become the stuff of legend while the blood of its victims still congealed in the prison yards.[5]

Certainly the killing of 1,100 prisoners added weight to the argument of all those who thought that collective violence had left the revolution's high-minded slogans trampled underfoot.[6] For conservatives who would later seek reasons to condemn what had happened in France, the revolution may as well have ended with the September Massacres, leaving as its emblem the picture Dickens planted in the minds of millions of readers of a "crowd of murderers struggling round the grindstone to sharpen their weapons before butchering the prisoners."[7] Critics found all the ammunition they needed there. But in September 1792 the revolution's most destructive phase still lay ahead. When it came, in the process known as the Terror, the crowds of Paris's poor could only stand and watch.

In 1793, amid serious food shortages in the capital, the Assembly's "Law of Suspects," also known as the Terror, imposed general price controls, enforceable by a Revolutionary Tribunal and a sans-culotte army (the *armée révolutionnaire*). The Tribunal was given the authority to execute anyone convicted of hoarding or of aiding foreign armies. Under a regime of "violence without disorder,"[8] the Terror replaced crowd violence with state violence, enabling the revolution to transcend the "galvanic, cathartic action" of crowds—acting with all the tumult Robespierre despised—to institutionalize "national vengeance."[9]

Use of the guillotine facilitated this "rationalization" process. Like the military technician who pushes a button to launch a missile, the executioner was only indirectly involved, severing a rope to end a life so quickly that the violence of the act would seem to disappear, unless one witnessed the result. The guillotine not only superseded crowd violence, its unremitting work turned the crowds of Paris into spectators again,[10] like those who massed along the route to the Place de la Révolution on October 16, 1793, to watch Marie Antoinette pass in an oxcart on the way to her death.[11] During the Terror, there were 17,000 official executions in fourteen months.[12]

In the end, the riotous Parisians who had been "the decisive revolutionary force" were betrayed by the Assembly, which controlled the army.[13] Thirty-six insurgents were executed, thirty-seven imprisoned or deported, 1,200 "terrorists" were arrested, the people were disarmed, and voting was made conditional on ownership of property. It was the moderates who consolidated the gains of revolution, riding on "a wave of anger, despair, and hope" borne by those who "did the dirty work of destruction."[14]

"After the experiences of the French Revolution," wrote Debord, "the efforts of all established powers to increase the means of maintaining order in the streets finally culminates in the suppression of the street."[15] Decades would pass before insurgent crowds would fill the streets of Paris again. When they did, in 1839, 1848, and 1871, it was not the commanders of the military regiments firing into these crowds who would become the objects of abiding aversion and widespread fear, even when their cannons slaughtered twenty thousand on May 23, 1871. Nor was it their political masters. It was the insurrectionary crowd. And the archetype of such crowds was the rioters cum revolutionaries of 1789–93. Those crowds carried, as we say, a lot of baggage, not only the baggage of their own bloody deeds but the additional burdens of epithets assigned them by conservative writers. Edmund Burke characterized the people who invaded the royal château following the women's march of October 1789 as "a band of cruel ruffians and assassins, reeking with . . . blood." H. A. Taine called the participants in the attack on the Bastille "bandits," "savages," and "ragamuffins."[16] More important, for our purposes, has been the lasting influence of the man who assigned responsibility for the Terror, not to Robespierre, Danton, and others of the cliques presiding over it, but to "the working of the soul of the masses."[17]

Popularizing the ideas of Taine, Scipio Sighele, Gabriel Tarde, and other practitioners of nineteenth-century social psychology, Gustave Le Bon wrote that "a sort of collective mind" takes possession of individuals who participate in a crowd, inducing them to "feel, think, and act in a manner quite different" from how they would act in isolation.[18] This collective mind is inferior to that of almost any isolated individual: "In crowds it is stupidity and not mother-wit that is accumulated." A gathering of distinguished but diverse specialists can make no better decisions of general interest than could "a gathering of imbeciles."[19] And this applies to "picked assemblies."[20] The dumbing down extends to anyone who joins a crowd: "From the moment that they form part of a crowd the learned man and the ignoramus are equally incapable of observation."[21] Clearly someone holding such views as these will have no use for democracy, either representative or direct. Better to have a monarch or general in charge than anything resembling an assemblage.

Aristotle took the opposite view, arguing that the collective ability of the crowd might surpass that of its individual constituents and even that of the "few best." He compared an outcome of the deliberations of the many to a potluck meal, which can excel the feast provided by an individual.[22] Following a century of revolution, however, middle-class readers wanted no part of such a spread. They had acquired a taste for the flavorings of M. Le Bon.

Here is Le Bon on the process by which the crowd mind works its spell: "The first suggestion formulated [by someone in the crowd, presumably its leader] . . . implants itself immediately by a process of contagion in the brains of all assembled, and the identical bent of the sentiments of the crowd is immediately an accomplished fact."[23] This "turning of feelings and ideas in an identical direction by means of suggestion and contagion" makes the individual in a crowd "an automaton who has ceased to be guided by his will."[24] Le Bon also compares the crowd man to a "hypnotised subject."[25] Though he compares crowds, in their volatility, to women, his crowds seem to consist only of men. Indeed, Le Bon's crowds resemble nothing so much as the "living dead" of the George Romero horror classics *Day of the Dead, Night of the Living Dead, Dawn of the Dead,* and the more recent *Land of the Dead.* "You can't have one zombie," says the author of the successful *Zombie Survival Guide: Complete Protection from the Living Dead,* "You've got to have millions of them."[26] The subtext of zombie fear is surely crowd fear, and Le Bon would have us fear crowds.

But for Le Bon, the crowd occupies only one side of the equation. On the other is its leader. When creatures gather, whether they are humans or animals, "they place themselves instinctively under the authority of a chief."[27] The most effective leaders are "unconscious psychologists" who can readily exploit the crowd's suggestibility, guiding it to acts that, though they appear to be murderous, are no more criminal than "the act of a tiger devouring a Hindoo."[28] It is simply what the crowd-tiger does. Their acts are likely to reflect the additional fact that crowds only give themselves to bullies and tyrants.[29] By implication, crowd control is inevitable, but who controls and for what purposes?

Still, the action of a crowd is not necessarily destructive. A crowd will sometimes sacrifice itself for ideals that its members hardly understand. As evidence, Le Bon cites the fact that the crowds participating in the September Massacres collected and accounted for the jewelry and other valuables of those they condemned instead of making off with these items as, presumably, a rational individual like Le Bon would have done.[30] His book, *The Crowd: A Study of the Popular Mind,* was a best-seller. It was reviewed in both scholarly and popular journals. It has been translated into at least seventeen languages.[31] And after more than a century, it remains in print. Freud, who thought the Paris street crowds he observed as a youth to be "possessed of a thousand demons,"[32] quoted Le Bon at length and praised "his brilliantly executed picture of the group mind," which resonated so well with his own description of unconscious processes.[33] He agreed that the group regresses "to an earlier stage" of mental development, comparable to that of children or savages.[34]

Hitler and Mussolini also found *The Crowd* intriguing. "The crowd loves strong men," pronounced the latter, paraphrasing Le Bon's "The crowd is like a woman."[35] Opponents of fascism also gave new life to the crowd mind concept. Jung wrote that "the psychology of a large crowd inevitably sinks to the level of mob psychology."[36] He cited Le Bon again in a discussion of "the mass psychosis" of Nazism.[37] But if Hitler's followers were temporarily psychotic, or if (as Freud thought) the individual in a crowd becomes a "horde animal . . . led by a chief" whose relationship to his followers is like that of a father to his children or a hypnotist to his subject, can they, the sleepwalking followers, be held responsible for their acts?[38]

The idea of a debased crowd mind remains part of the intellectual wardrobe of millions of people who know nothing of brown shirts and black shirts, people who would not be able to identify Le Bon if he appeared before them with a copy of his book. I suspect that most people would agree that

> a mob does not act intelligently. Those who make up a mob do not think independently. They do not think rationally. They are likely to do irrational things, including even turning on their leaders. Individually people in a mob are cowardly; only collectively, goaded by a leader, will a mob appear to act courageously. A mob is bloodthirsty.[39]

Such notions are commonplace. In this case, they trick a fictionalized Richard Nixon into mistaking a crowd of his supporters for a hostile mob. For anyone who has participated in many crowd events, Le Bon's pronouncements on crowd dynamics may seem laughable. But perhaps they have been the wrong crowds. Social scientists have determined that people participating in a group discussion, such as jury deliberations, tend to adopt more extreme positions than they would independently. But even higher levels of group polarization can occur among the scattered participants of online discussions.[40] We also know that a mass of political protestors or the like may grow dramatically larger when reaching a size threshold at which bystanders feel safe to join in. Such phenomena, however, fall far short of the crowd mind concept, as conceived by Le Bon. What kind of experience would make it plausible?

DISSECTING THE MURDEROUS CROWD'S MIND

My description above of the imaginary crowd that appeared at the door of the crowd museum is based on a famous photo labeled, "Marion, Ind., Aug. 1930."[41] For Gustave Le Bon, this photo could have struck a final note of vindication for everything he had written about crowds. He lived till 1931, and the photo appeared in newspapers all over the United States, everywhere but in Marion, Indiana.[42] Perhaps its circulation reached France. The recollections of some of the witnesses would have met with his approval, too. "Once you hear a mob like that, you never forget it. It was like wild animals," recalled Ruth Thomas, who was twelve years old at the time of the lynching.[43] Another "sensed a carnival air." Passing out pieces of one of the victim's pants as souvenirs, "people howled and milled around the lifeless bodies, their voices a mumbo jumbo of insane screams and giggles."[44] But this witness's impression may have been colored by the fact that he was an intended victim of the mob.

In some respects, what happened in Marion on the night of August 7, 1930, was a typical American lynching. A highly agitated crowd of whites broke into the county jail to seize three black youths accused of killing a white man and raping his date, also white. The mob met only token resistance from the police, and none of its members was ever punished. Such facts are all too familiar. It was the location and especially the notoriety of the lynching that made it exceptional. Prints of Lawrence Beitler's photo sold by the thousands. According to the photographer's daughter, the orders "started coming the next day."[45] As a result of Cynthia Carr's article in *The Village Voice* in 1994, the lynching got a second wave of publicity, and Marion "endured a media blitz."[46] Details of collective murders of an earlier era, like the gruesome demise of Francis McIntosh, who was roasted over a slow-burning fire with a crowd of two thousand looking on, were typically buried in the sand of local legend. We know of McIntosh's murder only because the onlookers, at a site near St. Louis, included an Illinois reporter.[47]

The Marion lynching was additionally exceptional in that one of the intended victims, James Cameron, though dragged from a jail cell, pummeled by adults, bitten by children, and collared with a noose, survived the incident to write a book about it and become the founder of the Black Holocaust Museum in Milwaukee.[48] He estimated that a mob of between twenty-five and fifty carried out the lynchings, while some thousands watched. (A former Marion mayor thought there might have been fifteen thousand people in the crowd.) In 1993, Cameron obtained a pardon from the governor of Indiana for his (still disputed) part in the events that led to the lynchings, was given the key to the city by the mayor of Marion, and announced he had forgiven Indiana.[49]

Contrary to local lore, as well as what the crowd mind theory would suggest, the Marion atrocity was not a spontaneous act. Sadie Pate, aged ninety when Carr interviewed her, recalled that the lynching was announced on flyers. Signs posted along the county roads outside of town advertised a "NECKTIE PARTY AT MARION." Ed Shelley remembered that on the day of the lynching men showed up to recruit participants at the paper plant where he worked. It was during the lunch break, and Claude Deeter, the shooting victim, was still alive in a hospital, although just barely. Walter Gunyon, then aged seven, reported that his father drove the entire family to the downtown lynching site, arriving hours early to get a good parking spot. Another witness remembered that men had closed the access streets and even taken the streetcars out of service. The lynching was announced over the PA system at a dance in another town.[50] (H. L. Mencken's description of lynchings as rural entertainment—standing in for "the theatre, the symphony orchestra, and other diversions common to larger communities"—was flippant but perhaps somewhat accurate.)[51] Clearly, most members of the Marion lynching crowd knew of the lynching before it occurred and decided before joining that crowd that they would attend. The collective murder in which they were participants was not a symptom of an infected crowd mind.

In seeking an understanding of what happened in Marion and many other sites throughout the United States, we might consider the diffusion of responsibility that can free individuals to participate in collective behavior that they would never consciously consider undertaking by themselves. Le Bon was on the right track in declaring that "a crowd being anonymous, and in consequence irresponsible, the sentiment of responsibility which always controls individuals disappears entirely."[52]

But he was on the wrong train: isolated individuals are quite capable of acting irresponsibly. Being in a crowd is neither necessary nor sufficient for one to collude in horrible deeds.

It is not only crowds, not even primarily crowds, that dice responsibility for collective acts into what may seem to be infinitesimal individual allotments. Adolf Hitler mobilized masses to great effect, but the Nazi bureaucracy served as his killing machine. It was this complex and multilayered bureaucracy, not a crowd, to which the Israeli judges in the trial of Nazi war criminal Adolf Eichmann referred when they wrote:

> these crimes were committed en masse, not only in regard to the number of victims, but also in regard to the numbers of those who perpetrated the crime, and the extent to which any of the many criminals was close to or remote from the actual killer of the victim means nothing, as far as the measure of his responsibility is concerned.[53]

We might seek further understanding of the Marion murders in that the Indiana outrage was committed under cover of darkness. "Any setting that cloaks people in anonymity reduces their sense of personal accountability and civic responsibility," writes Philip Zimbardo, designer of the famous Stanford Prison Experiment (SPE, a study of the psychological effects of becoming a prisoner or a prison guard).[54] His statement brings to mind the halfhearted disguises of the patriotic New England rioters and the unpatriotic whiskey rebels of the eighteenth century. But masked or not, the crowd is only one of many potential sites of anonymity. The events that Zimbardo writes about range from the real-life horrors of the Rwandan genocide and the outrages of Abu Ghraib Prison to numerous experiments in social psychology. The latter have shown that the potential for transgressive behavior mounts when those enjoying power over others are allowed to shield their identity, as did the "guards" in the SPE by donning uniforms and reflecting sunglasses.[55] In another experiment, anonymous participants thought they were administering electric shocks to test subjects, who feigned agony. Their shocks had twice the intended intensity of those given by participants wearing name tags.[56]

Marked difference in power—the most obvious example, considering the foregoing, would be that between a lynch mob and its victim—may also allow sadistic impulses to "slip out."[57] In addition, others become dehumanized in a social order that considers their kind—read race, religion, ethnicity, sexual preference—"to be excluded from the moral order of being a human person."[58] Their mistreatment can then be dismissed by saying, "Oh, they're only ________s." For example, a member of the Hutu militia during the Rwandan genocide later said, "We no longer saw a human being when we turned up a Tutsi in the swamps."[59] Racism and its evil cousins are not only wrong, they put some people at risk of terrible harm and diminish us all as moral agents.

We have a powerful need to fit in, to gain social approval through conformity. But conformity to what? Destructive behavior may be redefined to seem honorable, as happened in Nazi Germany and in lynching cultures of the United States. Hannah Arendt said of Adolf Eichmann that he did not have to ignore the voice of conscience because it spoke "with the voice of respectable society around him."[60] Texas's early history of white/Anglo contention for land against natives and Mexicans made heroes of Indian killers and martyrs of those slain in battle. Remember the Alamo? Such men were mythologized as the defenders of the (white/Anglo) community. Pogroms and ethnic cleansing became models for later crowd violence. The slave patrol further institutionalized the mob. As a result, a tradition of violent community action made "participation in a well-ordered lynch mob, for the region's Anglo Americans, a rite of passage, a public duty, and a source of prestige."[61]

Although Indiana's population was practically all white in 1930, the white supremacist values promoted by the Ku Klux Klan enjoyed a powerful and highly visible presence. The state had a "klavern" in every county; from 1915 to 1930, nearly 18 percent of white men were members. This is a conservative estimate. Klansmen occupied political offices at every level of government, including the gubernatorial.[62] In November 1922, a large crowd watched Klansmen parade around the Marion courthouse. Seven trumpeters, mounted and masked, led two Klan bands, as other Klansmen carried flaming crosses. But the local Klan held parades of around a thousand marchers and riders every month in its heyday in the 1920s.

Institutionalized racism was not confined by state borders or regional boundaries. *Birth of a Nation*, released in 1915, one of the biggest movie hits ever, glorified the role of the Klan as the defender of white women's virtue against black rapists in both the North and the South. Special trains brought rural residents into cities to see it. Times Square featured a gallant Klansman on a giant billboard. "'Ku Klux fever' gripped the nation," with Ku Klux clothes, Ku Klux parties, etc.[63]

This was the cultural context in which James Cameron and two older companions were charged with murder and the rape of a white woman (who may have been a prostitute colluding with robberies by Cameron's companions).[64] Augmenting this background and the shadowy organizing that preceded the lynching were such further incitements as the banner headline in the local newspaper, "SHOOT MAN, ASSAULT SWEETHEART." "Shot down in a valorous effort to save the honor of his sweetheart . . . " the front-page story began. There was also the bloody shirt of the shooting victim that was hung from a window of the Marion police station.[65] A local minister who preached against the lynching now sees his stance as "pretty radical." Cynthia Carr's investigation convinced her that "in 1930 most white residents of Grant County saw the lynching as an act of moral rectitude."[66] These were the practical and cultural ingredients of "crowd mind" at work in Marion, Indiana, on the night of August 7, 1930.

The *Marion Chronicle* editorialized, on the day after the lynching, that the mob consisted of "ordinary good citizens . . . stung to the quick by an atrocious crime."[67] The paper was outrageously wrong in its effort to exonerate mob justice, but its description of the murderers was probably an accurate generalization. Of course, there was no attempt to cull people with psychological disorders from the Marion mob, nothing like the screening process of the Stanford Prison Experiment. All participants in the SPE were normal, as determined by testing, yet within a few hours of the beginning of the study, those arbitrarily chosen to act as prison guards had begun to abuse the "prisoners," and the prisoners were becoming increasingly passive and compliant. The abuse increased, especially at night, but not one of the prisoners demanded that it stop or chose to quit the experiment. Zimbardo writes that at the beginning, "there were no differences between the two groups; less than a week later, there were no similarities."[68]

The point is that the behavior of normal people is largely shaped by the situation in which they find themselves. Fortunately, the general situation of Americans has changed sufficiently since 1930 that, absent dramatic and horrendous further changes, very few would see participation in a lynching "as an act of moral rectitude." Though racism appears to be far from dead, it has lost any vestige of respectability. The world has become too small, its dark corners too observable, for the collective hate crime to be carried off with impunity.

Opportunities for unaccountable actions yielded by the consumer society are trivial in comparison to the horrors discussed above. There is the anonymity of the driver, which permits him to curse other motorists without suffering a response; that of the shopper who may try on lots of clothes with no intention of buying anything; and the diffusion of responsibility among theatergoers who leave discarded cartons and cups for someone else to clean up. The crowd—the pseudo-crowd of consumer society—does not act as one, either for good or ill, because it lacks the glue of social solidarity.

No one would welcome a resurgence of American crowd justice, yet trailing in the wake of the dirty water of the racist mob may be some ancient assemblages that we should not want to become extinct. I have in mind the crowd of popular resistance and that of collective joy. Only the sufferer of clinical agoraphobia fears all crowds. For Le Bon, the physical gathering was just a symbol of what he saw as the real problem, which was the growing power of the masses. Eyes fixed on an horizon beyond late nineteenth-century Europe, Le Bon saw the advance of socialism—its ranks filled by those who intended "to utterly destroy society as it now exists"—as supplanting the natural aristocracy that had built up civilization over the centuries. Socialism would install in its stead the "primitive communism" of maximum work hours, the nationalization of major industries, the "equal distribution of all products, [and] the elimination of all the upper classes."[69]

In sum, the crowd as such does not exist. Thus when a journalist writes that "in white Los Angeles, there is an inbred fear of the crowd" that whites have even abandoned the parks and beaches frequented by the people of color who make up the city's majority, retreating to the "containerized" space of covered malls, corporate refuges, and upscale cultural oases, what he means is that white residents of L. A. are so afraid of aggregates of people of color that they retreat to crowd spaces of their own.[70]

With upheaval or disaster, the crowd "unleashes all kinds of agoraphobic stereotypes."[71] Few of us thought to doubt the stories of mobs splashing through the streets of New Orleans to engage in a frenzy of rape, murder, and mayhem following Hurricane Katrina. Although there was considerable looting (in the case of a Wal-Mart, looters followed the example of police, who had permission "to take what they needed from the store to survive"), in one instance after another the source of a report of violence had heard it had taken place elsewhere, in another part of town. Only two of the many people who failed to survive the collective misery and desperation of the Superdome and Convention Center died of gunshot wounds. As for the rapes, "I think it was an urban myth," a police lieutenant says. But fear of the mob delayed relief efforts considerably.[72] Instead of helping to evacuate people who had been flooded out, New Orleans police, National Guard troops, and private security contractors were preoccupied with stopping looters.[73] In a more recent allegation of mob violence, the Texas "mob" that beat a man to death after the car he was driving bumped a toddler turned out to consist of three or four individuals.[74]

Such reactions disclose "an underlying fear that the dominant class will be overthrown during a period of chaos," writes historian Philip Fradkin.[75] In *The Volcano Under the City,* a history of the New York draft riots of 1863 which was published some twenty years later, William Osborn Stoddard recommended that the city "fortify itself against an unseen working-class threat."[76] "These troops know how to shoot and kill," Louisiana's governor warned Katrina victims, echoing the order of a century earlier to kill anyone suspected of a crime in San Francisco as it was going up in flames. The ground had hardly stopped shaking when hundreds of ROTC cadets from the University of California were dispatched across the bay with rifles and five cartridges each to shoot looters.[77] But self-appointed militiamen were already on the scene. Though the city was remarkably free of crime at the time, many people were shot and killed.[78]

When an American city experiences a calamity, insecurities of class tend to be compounded by racial and ethnic fears, so that efforts to restore order fasten onto the mostly imagined crimes of minorities, such as the Germans in Chicago (1871); blacks in Galveston (1900), Los Angeles (1992), and New Orleans (2005); Chinese in San Francisco (1906), etc. At least the stories of "ghouls chewing earrings and rings from the ears and fingers of supine white women"—a medieval motif revived with the Chicago fire of 1871, the Galveston hurricane of 1900, and the San Francisco earthquake of 1906—did not resurface in New Orleans.[79]

The grain of truth in Le Bon's crowd mind concept is that crowds can be dangerous. But the dangerous crowd does not necessarily correspond to agoraphobic stereotypes. With the announcement of Japan's surrender and the end of the Second World War in August 1945, throngs of servicemen and civilians poured into San Francisco's Market Street to begin a wild celebration that would last two days and nights, beginning as a "mild riot" and becoming a giant orgy of drunken looting, destruction, and assorted mayhem. Twelve died, more than a thousand were injured, women were dragged into alleys and raped (the official count was six, but no one knows the actual number), nearly two thousand people were arrested, and considerable breakage occurred before the police could restore order.[80] Given that this was a patriotic celebration by men in uniform, authorities could summon no alternative to letting mass havoc run its course.

Again, no one would welcome resumption of the kind of crowd actions described in this chapter. These killer crowds often acted to maintain an oppressive racial hierarchy, as in Marion, Indiana. As we will discover in chapter 5, destructive and sometimes murderous crowds often advanced the interests of oppressive authorities and would not have done what they did without their leadership, or at least their tacit consent. But as we saw in chapter 2, the boisterous crowds of America's past included many that challenged an unjust social order. To the extent that such en masse challenges no longer occur, we the many become more vulnerable to the depredations—now clothed in legislation, tax codes, etc.—of the powerful few.

Finally, the "unmotivated" crowd—the crowd of disparate individuals at crowded sites—may also kill, but never intentionally. I am thinking of a recent "Black Friday" when a mass of shoppers in Long Island trampled a Wal-Mart worker in their frenzy to get inside the store and take advantage of reduced prices. Such incidents more often involve a panicked exit—from a burning nightclub or theater, for example. But the crowd of people who happen to occupy the same site is usually benign. Others may even see it as an opportunity to further their own objectives. This is the subject of the following chapter.

4. Crowd as Opportunity

For the ruler with a yearning to awe the populace, the zealot with a truth that everyone needs to hear, or the merchant with some goods to sell, the crowd is a valuable resource. It is worth seeking out or attracting. There is nothing new in this. John the Baptist may have begun his career as a voice in the wilderness, but eventually the crowds "went out to him [from] Jerusalem and all Judea, and all the region round about Jordan."[1] The hundreds of thousands of chariot racing fans composed a giant market for the merchants, caterers, pastry cooks, prostitutes, and astrologers who set up shop in Rome's enormous Circus Maximus.[2] What *is* new is that for the American president, evangelist, or corporate huckster of today, the crowd has been dispersed into millions of home-viewing sites. And the crowded thoroughfare, which was put to pedagogic uses in the past, has been given over almost entirely to motor vehicles.

POWER SHOWS

Traditionally, the existing regime would periodically put its power on display to thousands of people along the route of a procession. At times there were almost too many viewers. We know, for example, that papal officials inaugurated a new type of crowd control for the feast of Annunciation in Florence in 1436, erecting a thousand-foot-long gangway to enable the pope to advance unmolested and unimpeded, like the inhabitants of *Air Force One*, above the close-packed crowd. The gangway also allowed his entourage to dispense with the usual practice of flinging coins to scatter the people in his path.[3] Whether this new technology ever paid for itself is unknown.

Such a display would express the ethos of its time and place. For example, the Roman "triumph," which could be awarded a general for an outstanding military victory, exhibited the might of empire and marked the highest honor winnable by individual effort in the Roman world. The spectator would have stationed himself somewhere in the throng aligned along the route between the Campus Martius and the Capitol. Depending on his social status, he might have exulted in a sense of vicarious victory, rubbed his hands in anticipation of a share of the spoils, or experienced a paralyzing jolt of fear with the initial blare of horns. Such differences to the contrary, all but the most jaded would have felt a sense of awe at the approach of the lengthy display of spoils and trophies, which would include enchained prisoners heading for execution or slavery; the images of captured forts, cities, even parts of nature such as mountains and lakes; and, at last, the triumphant general (the so-called Imperator) in his special chariot with a public slave beside him holding a crown of gold above his head and repeatedly murmuring, "Remember that you are mortal."[4]

With the passage of a millennium, hierarchy in Europe assumed an altogether different mask. The medieval procession displayed the sublime surface of the feudal order, with a place for everyone and everyone in his or her place. Describing a procession he observed in Antwerp in the early sixteenth century, Albrecht Dürer described the rows of ranks and guilds, each with their sign and distinctive garb. There passed the pipes and drums, all "loudly and noisily blown and beaten"; "the Goldsmiths, the Painters, the Masons" and representatives of a dozen other medieval trades; then various other workers and merchants, shopkeepers, hunters, soldiers on foot and horse, and the Lord Magistrates. Interspersed with these were wagon-borne floats with Christian themes. Then, preceded by the distinctively robed ranks of various religious orders, "came a fine troop all in red, nobly and splendidly clad"; then the widows, "dressed from head to foot in white linen garments . . . very sorrowful to see"; and finally the clergy, scholars, and treasurers of the Church of Our Lady, with twenty people carrying the lavishly adorned image of the Virgin.[5] As the great procession turned a corner on its winding route, its participants could look back to become spectators. Order, eternal order, was the message that the procession conveyed: every estate a lasting estate because it was ordained by God.[6]

Actually, Antwerp stood on the threshold of great economic change and the social instability associated with a soaring cost of living. This culminated in two days of rioting in August 1566.[7] Future processions could not have accommodated every member of a growing class of unskilled, often unemployed laborers, except as spectators. As Guy Debord declared, the spectacle "is the diplomatic representation of hierarchic society to itself."[8] The keyword here is "diplomatic": society often manages a prettified self-image. As for the street display that expresses the ethos of America's time and place, I will get to that below.

AMERICA ON PARADE

As elsewhere, the main streets of America served not only as transport links but as media of communication, often carrying messages that made a political point. Preoccupied with traffic movement and land development, the nation's early city builders had seldom left space for public squares. As towns grew, spaces that were reserved for public purposes often gave way to houses and shops.[9] The layout of New York was fairly typical: "The 1811 adoption of the grid . . . reflected a view of the city as nothing more than a piece of real estate to be continuously developed. . . . No green spaces were provided for."[10] There and elsewhere, city streets became the public space most accessible to all.[11] Before they surrendered their arteries to motor vehicles, American cities seemed designed to accommodate processions and parades.

Early on, these ranged from a parade of "45 virgins" in New York in 1770, led by the (unnamed) wife of Alexander McDougall to protest his jailing,[12] to the skilled workers who carried their craft symbols and tools of trade as they marched with merchants and professionals in various American cities to celebrate adoption of the Constitution in 1788.[13] Serving as the nation's first capital, Philadelphia was the setting for the signing of the Declaration of Independence (1776), the Constitutional Convention (1787), Lafayette's post-Independence reception (1824), and the Bank War demonstrations (1834), each of which brought numerous people into the streets. But "a variety of less spectacular parades" enlivened everyday life.[14] In 1825 "grateful multitudes" lined the parade route for the Boston celebration of the groundbreaking for a memorial to the battle of Bunker Hill.[15] We might imagine people straining for a view of the revolutionary veterans' brigades, the dignitaries in their carriages, the children's contingents, and all the rest, watching them pass, then following the procession to the memorial site to hear, or try to hear, Daniel Webster's unamplified speech.

Giving his notebook a rest, Tocqueville marched in a Fourth of July parade in Albany, New York, c. 1832, "just ahead of a big float that featured a flag waving Goddess of Liberty, a bust of Benjamin Franklin, and a printing press that spewed out copies of the Declaration of Independence for the cheering crowd."[16] Nathaniel Hawthorne had the narrator of *The House of the Seven Gables* recommend watching a great procession from a solitary perch so as to see it "in its aggregate—as a mighty river of life."[17] In 1843, when the Bunker Hill monument finally got its dedication ceremony, there was another long parade through Boston's streets, and a crowd of perhaps a hundred thousand gathered to hear Webster speak again. [18]

Paraders in the nation's larger cities were assured of spectators. With their houses fronting closely on the street, residents had only to open their doors to enter the crowd of food vendors, beggars, hawkers, traders, children, animals, assorted members of the middle class, and others or to watch a passing procession.[19] As in Europe in ages past, "outside private life . . . everything happened in the street."[20]

COMPETING LESSON PLANS

Except in a military dictatorship or police state, the powerful do not enjoy exclusive use of the instruction and entertainment potential of the streets. Grandeur and pomp, for example, may inspire public mockery. In the Middle Ages, drunken clerics would perform a burlesque version of the mass for the annual Feast of Fools, using sausages for censers, burning shoes for incense, and gibberish for the Latin of the liturgy, all this under the direction of an all-clowns' pope or lord of revels. Then, young and naked, they would prance through the city streets, throwing clods of dung that may have sent people scattering with as much alacrity as papal coins.[21]

Parody found marchers in the New World as well. On July 4, 1778, for instance, closely following withdrawal of the British troops garrisoned in Philadelphia, a crowd mocked wealthy, fashion-conscious British sympathizers by parading an overdressed prostitute. In 1780, patriots pulled a papier-mâché image of Benedict Arnold through that city's streets to the tune of a fife-and-drum rendition of "The Rogue's March." Arnold had commanded the city during its occupation by British troops and married into a prominent Tory family.[22] Such comic processions (as well as instances of vigilante price control) drew inspiration from the ancestral world that had made a home for the Feast of Fools. The representative of upper-class pretensions and perceived injustices risked charivari, burlesque, tarring and feathering, and worse. In Philadelphia, such popular traditions gave birth to a parade character known as Colonel Pluck, dwarfed by the enormous plumes of a general's hat, who carried his rusty sword like a brilliant argument against the vastly unpopular militias of rich men's sons. Pluck's parody became "a national sensation."[23]

Before the regional loyalties of the Civil War and successive waves of immigration eroded class lines, American elites tried to pacify, eliminate, or otherwise control spontaneous gatherings. Philadelphia's gentry, for example, outlawed the public revels of blacks in 1770, banned tents and booths from the twice-a-year fairs in Central Square in 1823, campaigned against the public's use of State House Square, and eliminated the lure of public hangings by curtailing them.[24] They also sought to monopolize the didactic potential of city streets. The typical parade in preindustrial America did not consist of mummers and maskers but of affluent members of the private militias that had given life to Pluck. As a major medium of communication, the street was "contested terrain."[25]

With industrialization, working-class marchers shifted their aim from the antisocial behavior of wealthy patricians to the labor practices of owners of the many factories springing up. Angry workers paraded to protest unacceptable working conditions, the erosion of wages, and that long and arduous workdays failed to lighten the burden of poverty. In 1835, Philadelphia workers joined others throughout the United States in a strike led by Irish coal-wharf workers for increased wages and a ten-hour day. With fife and drums at their head, unions paraded their commitment to the campaign with banners calling for a workday "from 6 to 6" (including two hours for meals), as opposed to requirements that ranged up to sixteen hours a day in some settings. In Philadelphia, the effort won its demands in three weeks.[26] But workers themselves were divided, not only by ethnicity, religion, and race but by longings on the part of some to gain the respect of the establishment. Successful craftsmen and foremen paraded in orderly ranks, dressed in uniforms few factory workers could afford. The craftsmen turned their noses up at the "undue excitement" of their unskilled brothers and sisters.

Burlesque traditions, whose subtext was class difference, continued to enliven the streets of American cities well into the nineteenth century, but they did so less and less. By 1900, "the multivocal nature of the street had virtually disappeared."[27] This did not happen simply because bourgeois notions of respectability extinguished the bonfires of working-class culture, because the many voices of the street learned to speak with one accent, or because working-class crowds stood in awe of demonstrations of military might. Nor was the business establishment able to pacify members of the working class by giving them the opportunity to spend their hard-earned cash on affordable goods: the consumer society's "golden rule of internal peace" was a hundred years or so away.[28] Angry workers continued to parade and demonstrate in the streets, but members of the establishment seriously hampered such activity by requiring permission to do so, a permission the permit givers could deny, as they so often would for May Day march requests and the like. After about 1880, "spontaneous public displays were no longer allowed."[29] When it came to parades and other street displays, people were expected to limit themselves to standing, watching, and absorbing the message.

Having consolidated the power to determine who could make legitimate use of the propaganda potential of the public thoroughfare, civic leaders would put certain icons on display whenever it appeared that the social order might come apart at its seams. In the Midwest, for example, they employed the pioneer theme. The pioneer was a stand-in for patriotism. The flag and the nation's past defenders served the same end. Marching under American flags, 75,000 immigrants could parade through Cleveland's downtown streets on July 4, 1918. They were safe under those flags, and even safer for being *seen* under them. (Immigrant rights marchers, under media attack for flourishing Mexican flags in the spring of 2006, quickly switched to stars and stripes.) The flag, pioneers, veterans, place—by 1948 ethnic diversity could join this pantheon of middle-American parade values in a twelve-mile march through Madison, Wisconsin, to celebrate that state's centennial. [30]

Parades were used again in the 1960s to reassert such values as deference to established authority, unquestioning patriotism, and temperate behavior. Thousands celebrated Memorial Day in Carbondale, Illinois, in 1968 by watching a parade combining themes of covered wagons, industrial smokestacks, and the state capitol building—in other words, traditional values, jobs, and official benevolence. Arthur Godfrey was the featured speaker.[31] Four parades converged on an Indianapolis shopping center parking lot to hold a patriotic ceremony on the Fourth in 1970.[32] Patriotic shoppers had to park someplace else.

But American officials have not always confined themselves to symbolic displays. On Christmas Day1794, twenty thousand Philadelphians turned out to watch a parade of twenty captured whiskey rebels, who appeared emaciated and exhausted by the forced march over the Alleghenies they had endured.[33] During the Red Scare at the end of the First World War, officialdom showed its version of acceptable political theater by arresting five hundred alleged radicals, shackling them, and driving them through the streets of Boston.[34]

Although in 1886 the Michigan Supreme Court struck down a local ordinance that required the mayor's or the city council's consent to march or drive through a town with musical instruments, banners, flags, torches, or while singing or shouting (as Salvation Army marchers were wont to do), the court could see no legal barrier to a city's denying permission for a parade that could create a public disturbance or "threaten some tangible public or private mischief."[35] As the nation's streets became more and more the domain of fast-moving motor vehicles, the courts increasingly deferred to local denials of parade requests on the basis of the traffic problems they would create.[36] The question was, really, who shall instruct the crowd? But by around 1960, when a legal scholar could conclude that the right of people to march on public streets no longer enjoyed the same constitutional protection accorded other forms of assembly, such as meetings in public parks, the city street had become less and less the place to find a crowd.[37] A good part of the urban multitude had scattered to the suburbs (about which more in chapter 7). When venturing into the city, their descendents were using the streets for their own version of the chariot race. Despite such changes, officials will not hesitate to reroute traffic for parades with a non-controversial message and a constituency of potential viewers. Think of St. Patrick's Day and Veterans' Day. For the rest, the experience of an organizer of a recent immigrant rights march in South Carolina is generally representative: "There's so much red tape."[38]

DAZZLING THE MULTITUDE

St. Louis takes the prize for political use of street displays. We learned in chapter 2 that marching workers briefly occupied that city's streets in 1877 to advance a general strike. A counterrevolutionary force of middle-class volunteers then put them to flight. After destroying strike headquarters and seizing property as needed "on a scale far beyond anything the workers attempted," leaders of the city's property owners sought lasting inoculation against further class war from below by staging a "citizens' militia parade," amounting to "a simple show of armed power."[39] They also outlawed the people's right to demonstrate on public streets without a permit, thereafter routinely denying such permission to workers' organizations. But St. Louis's civic patrons wanted not only to frighten the city's underclass but to mystify its members with a spectacle. Looking to New Orleans for inspiration, they created a secret organization committed to putting on a nocturnal pageant of floats every year. This power show would feature a secretly chosen, anonymous, and "infallible" Veiled Prophet. (The illustration in Thomas Spencer's study of the Veiled Prophet—or VP—phenomenon shows a robed and masked figure with a conical cap, similar to the costume of the Ku Klux Klan.) Thus would they "instruct St. Louisans on respect for hierarchy."[40]

Actually, the identity of the first Veiled Prophet was known to one and all. It was the police commissioner credited with breaking the general strike. His props included a (seemingly) blood-drenched chopping block and ax. Establishment voices proclaimed him "king of St. Louis."[41] The commissioner's long line of successors remained cloaked in anonymity until 1972, when a civil rights activist tore the mask off the reigning Prophet at the VP Ball, revealing another VP, an executive vice president of the Monsanto Corporation.[42] One can imagine the commotion. Business cohorts in Memphis, Baltimore, Kansas City, and Omaha organized similar pageants, which had shorter lives than the St. Louis event.

Perhaps a bit embarrassed by their bloody props and no longer seeing a need for them, the St. Louis clubmen gave them up within a few years of the inaugural display in favor of allegorical themes intended to inculcate genteel values in working-class spectators, or at least to make the onlookers aware of them, and to teach loyalty to national and local leaders.[43] Intimidation was left to the St. Louis Police Department and its annual "riot gun" parade (1900–1920), which displayed the weapons used to kill striking streetcar workers in 1900, while the VP organizers served up cotton candy to the eager crowd.[44] By early in the twentieth century, they had adopted escapist and nostalgia-laden themes for the parade, such as "Childhood Memories," "The Circus," and "Mother Goose Tales." National crises brought back the didactic approach. With the Depression, spectators got to see "Traditions of the United States," with a cast of white male luminaries plus Betsy Ross (1930), and "The Romance of Commerce and Industry" (1931), an affair that had by then gone sour for many St. Louisans.[45]

Meanwhile, harassment of the VP parade had become a part of the tradition. Boys liked to knock the trolley poles off the lines that powered the floats. Whether or not they were aware of the symbolism of the act, they seemed to recognize the class enemy behind the disguise. Many shot peas and even threw rocks, forcing the VP and his coterie to adopt padding and protective masks.[46] And yet the throngs of mostly silent spectators increased, prompting the editor of a working-class newspaper to complain in 1930 "that workers . . . seemed so thoroughly under the annual celebration's spell."[47] Mystification had pretty much worked.

With the civil rights movement, the streets of St. Louis and other cities again became contested terrain, filled with people willing to face intimidation and worse for demanding racial equality and to risk arrest for demonstrating without a permit. A local organization (ACTION) targeted the exclusive VP club and its events, especially the annual VP Ball. One year activists went so far as to release tear gas into the ballroom.[48] Trying to jettison the racist baggage, VP organizers allowed a few black professionals into their club. In the 1990s the VP Fair, which had drawn heavy criticism for denying access to the mostly black residents of East St. Louis by closing a bridge, became Fair St. Louis, a large, peaceful, and racially integrated event, promoted as a way of bringing residents of the area together by offering "pure and simple entertainment."[49] Declared a prominent VP member, "People just didn't like other people flaunting their wealth and their position" anymore.[50]

WE INTERRUPT THIS MESSAGE

Marching dissenters are susceptible to super-patriotic attack, usually with the complicity if not the full cooperation of the police. The construction workers who assaulted antiwar demonstrators on Wall Street in 1970, a few weeks after the National Guard murders at Kent State, left some permanently injured. They had plenty of precedents. For example, Ohio opponents had thrown beer and sausages on nineteenth-century temperance marchers, and a Cleveland mob had sicced their dogs on them.[51] Suffragists who went over the heads of the police to get permission to hold a march in Washington, D.C., in 1913 had to force their way through the thousands of men who clogged their route. Their attackers spit on them, slapped them, pulled them off their floats, tore off articles of clothing, and caused dozens of injuries, as amused police stood by and watched. The incident created a wave of public sympathy for the suffragists, not only because of the abuse the women suffered but for their nonviolent resistance.[52]

On May Day, 1919, again in Cleveland, a few thousand marchers carrying red banners had to pass through a gauntlet of uniformed, armed veterans and jeering spectators. When an elderly man who had tried to grab one of the marchers' banners got knocked to the ground, police halted the procession and a fight broke out between marchers and spectators. This turned into a full-scale riot, with a truckload of club-swinging civilians joining hundreds of policemen in attacking marchers. An army tank was used to mop up what remained of the demonstration. Mobs then left the scene to attack Socialist Party headquarters. Forty people suffered serious injuries and an eighteen-year-old youth was killed. Police arrested 125 Socialists.[53]

Civil rights demonstrators suffered similar attacks and worse. Their commitment to nonviolent resistance precluded fighting back, in principle at least, if not always in practice. In St. Augustine, Florida, in June 1964, racists targeted various unresisting marchers, including Andrew Young, for assaults with blackjacks and kicks, but they could not reduce the disciplined activists to a crowd in flight. As Courtland Cox, a Student Nonviolent Coordinating Committee (SNCC) leader, declared, "To the extent that we think of our own lives, we are politically immobilized."[54]

For a particularly bizarre instance of vigilante violence against marchers, we might go to Berkeley, California, in October 1965, when sixteen members of the Hell's Angels Motorcycle Club surged through a police cordon to attack a procession of antiwar demonstrators who were heading for Oakland. Seizing their lead banner, the Angels began chanting, "America first—America for Americans!" Jerry Rubin and other organizers of the march had known, reportedly, that the police would allow the bikers to attack but had failed to warn the marchers. They assumed that the attack would turn the marchers into radicals, as if marching against America's Southeast Asian war in 1965 were an act of conformity.[55] Republicans paid the legal costs of an Angel who was booked for assaulting a police officer with a bottle.[56]

Generally accepted today is the principle that if an assembly qualifies for protection against government intrusion (by virtue of the fact that its aim is not violent or illegal, etc.), then officials are obligated to protect it against hostile groups.[57]

PARIAH PARADE

Sociologists Frances Fox Piven and Richard Cloward wrote that a local regime can generally "mobilize popular hatred against" dissidents if they are of "outcast status."[58] They might have added that a *national* regime can do the same and that turning dissidents into outcasts is part of the process. The fate of the May Day march is a perfect illustration. The marches began in 1890 as an international protest against industrial working conditions and a response to the execution by hanging of August Spies, Adolph Fisher, George Engel, and Albert Parsons, the prominent anarchists who with four others had been convicted of murder in connection with the May 4, 1886, bomb blast in Chicago's Haymarket Square,[59] which resulted in the deaths of seven policemen and the wounding of more than seventy.[60] None of the eight alleged murderers had been in a position to have thrown the bomb, but the prosecution had successfully argued that their speeches had influenced the unknown bomber and that anarchism in itself "constituted a conspiracy to commit murder."[61]

On this first observation of a post-Haymarket May Day, there were major demonstrations in Paris, Madrid, Barcelona, Lisbon, Copenhagen, Brussels, and Amsterdam, as well as in Cuba, Chile, Peru, and elsewhere.[62] Vienna was "peacefully ruled by the proletariat," despite fears of violence that had caused some middle-class families to flee. Over eighty thousand workers and peasants celebrated May Day in demonstrations throughout Hungary. Up to half a million Londoners turned out on May 4, a Sunday, in what the *Times* of London called the "greatest demonstration of modern times."[63] For fifty years after Haymarket, images of the martyred workers could be seen in May Day events over large parts of the world.[64] Thus did a tragic event in American history inspire an international workers' day.

Although Samuel Gompers soon withdrew American Federation of Labor (AFL) support, more progressive organizations continued to honor May Day in the United States for many years. In 1913, the *New York Times* reported that "some 50,000 organized workers, wearing the bright red of socialism as the worldwide bond of labor . . . marched through the streets of Manhattan . . . to celebrate the 1st of May, the international holiday of workers."[65] The *Times* mentioned similar demonstrations in other cities throughout the United States. The following May Day, however, the blood of demonstrators colored the scene when police attacked a rally of unionists and Socialists, leaving babies "crawling in the dust" to reach their fallen mothers.[66] But in 1916, over a hundred thousand turned out for a New York City march.[67]

Like other left institutions, May Day fell victim to the "red scare" that followed the First World War. Police and vigilantes attacked the 1919 march in Boston and demolished Socialist Party headquarters. Some of the 116 demonstrators who were arrested got prison terms of eighteen months, while their civilian attackers suffered no penalties. Troops staged an assault on the Russian People's House in New York and smashed the offices of the Socialist Party's daily paper.[68] "You can't even collect your thoughts without getting arrested for unlawful assemblage," declared Max Eastman.[69]

Following years of harassment of would-be May Day organizers, New York officials granted permission for a May Day parade in 1929 on the condition that marchers display the American flag and bear no "incendiary placards." Organizers complied, and New York had its first such event since 1916.[70] A year later, a crowd estimated at a hundred thousand showed up for a demonstration in New York's Union Square. Also appearing were hundreds of police with tear gas canisters at the ready and machine guns trained on the demonstrators. Undeterred, the red-clad marchers made "a vivid spectacle as they moved slowly around the square, singing as they walked."[71] There were May Day marches and demonstrations in Chicago and Philadelphia that year as well.

May Day, 1937, in New York saw a United Front Parade, "the largest and most peaceful of its kind."[72] Marchers' placards denounced fascist aggression and urged support for the Spanish Loyalists and for sit-down strikers in the United States. A photo shows white-clad marchers passing into Union Square through thousands of onlookers.[73] Chicago had a similar demonstration. Nine years later, in 1946, May Day was still a workers' holiday in New York, with an estimated fifty thousand participating in a march whose Communist Party contingent included five hundred Second World War veterans, defiantly (and illegally) wearing their uniforms.[74]

Newspapers had, from the beginning, contrasted the "European type" of May Day demonstrator with "the honest American workingman" who marched on Labor Day, the end-of-summer event adopted by Congress as a national holiday in 1894 and thereafter widely observed in the United States.[75] Although May Day was as American as apple pie, its place in the nation's diet approximated that of escargot. With the onset of the Cold War, May Day was all but banished from its country of origin. Executives of the AFL-CIO like Walter Reuther, James B. Carey, and Phillip Murray had become ardent anti-communists, and major media could easily characterize May 1 as Communist May Day. As Philip Foner dryly remarked, "In this atmosphere it became increasingly difficult to uphold the May Day tradition in the United States."[76] Some who tried to in New York in 1951 were pelted with "salvos of eggs."[77]

By 1953 the New York parade had again been banned. Would-be celebrants were limited to an hour and a half of evening use of Union Square on May Day, 1954. In 1955 New York authorities would only allow a May Day *meeting*, and that on April 29. Paul Robeson spoke to a determined audience.[78] When authorities felt secure enough to lift such restrictions in 1962, a new generation of left activists—soon to become civil rights and antiwar activists—had largely lost touch with the May Day tradition. Its rediscovery would require solidarity visits to other countries, such as El Salvador, where in April 1987 despite a brutal civil war workers were busily preparing posters and banners proclaiming solidarity with *los martires de Chicago* and organizing May Day marches that would require them to risk their lives for a made-in-America holiday that few in the United States knew anything about.

Still, some Americans remember the date. In 2007 May Day rallies were held in many cities and towns in the United States, including more than a hundred in California. Immigrant workers' rights was the leading theme.[79]

EVERY CORNER A CLASSROOM

Between around 1870 and 1925, in the "booming, bustling Downtown Age, . . . the crowds were six abreast on the sidewalks at high noon and all day Saturday."[80] Downtown Boston in the early 1890s was "jammed to suffocation with pedestrians," with people "elbowing each other off the sidewalk and into the gutter."[81] In the second decade of the twentieth century, people had to fight their way through the throngs at Fifth Avenue and 34th Street in New York, and it was "even more crowded at . . . Chicago's State and Madison streets."[82] Lower Manhattan was described as "one vast open air bazaar."[83] Filmmakers used approximations of such crowds as an intermittent backdrop for numerous Hollywood movies.

Under such conditions, every downtown street corner was a potential classroom for anyone with a burning message and a need to proselytize. Every downtown corner had a soapbox speaker every evening, before the advent of radio and television.[84] Even in a mid-sized city like Seattle, "the soapbox was the proletarian lecture platform, the street corner and the skid road the living school. . . . The workers listened, asked questions, bought pamphlets."[85] Whether the speaker was a socialist, a missionary, a politician, or a suffragist, people who gathered to hear what he or she had to say "were just the same kind of people you'd find if you had an auto accident on the corner. . . . Some of them went from one to another speaker, just to spend an evening listening to conversations. . . . That was the day of the soapbox."[86]

The novelty of suffragist street speakers can hardly be overstated. There were formidable cultural barriers to women speaking in public, all the more so on a public street. The social message of their sudden appearance on soapboxes in 1908, "forc[ing] the issue upon indifferent audiences," was more threatening than their political demands, writes historian Linda Lumsden.[87] By 1910 many of them had become participants on suffragist speaking tours. The women would write ahead for permission to speak, then make unannounced stops, setting up on a town's busiest street corner, often just outside a bar. While one would speak, others in the movement would hand out suffrage posters, sell "Votes for Women" buttons, and circulate petitions.[88] People attending demonstrations today do the same kind of things, but the soapboxers addressed their efforts to uncommitted members of a street crowd. Today's activists are far more likely to trade their flyers and political rhetoric with one another. "It was in the broadest spirit of democracy that we went out into the streets inviting all passersby to listen to our arguments and offer their objections or ask questions," said a soapbox pioneer.[89]

PARADE AS COMING OUT

Newspaper coverage of the women's suffrage movement's processions and parades expanded the observing crowd exponentially. This began in 1908 when six suffragists walked up New York City's Broadway. They led a crowd of over a thousand men and twenty-three women that had been invited to follow the half-dozen leaders to a meeting site after police prevented them from stopping to make a speech.[90] Two years later, thousands marched down Fifth Avenue behind ninety cars bearing suffrage movement leaders. A nighttime torchlight procession in 1912 was like a "river of fire" running down Fifth Avenue. Around a half-million people watched the twenty thousand marchers defy the stigma of women being out on public streets at night.[91] By 1917 around fifty thousand participated in the New York City parade, and there were suffrage marches in other cities and towns around the nation. "I never knew how necessary suffrage was until I saw the faces of the people who cheered for us and the faces of those who jeered," said a marcher.[92]

Spectators were generally dazzled by the women's color-coordinated costumes, hand-stitched banners of silk and velvet, "opulent" floats with their costumed riders, but also by the numbers and the dignity of the paraders. The stereotype of the suffragist as harridan was trampled under many feet.[93] "Suffragists never could have forced the public to consider votes for women if they had not taken their message to the streets," writes Lumsden.[94] Mother Jones employed an altogether different strategy, shaming opinion leaders and other middle-class citizens by bringing to the light of day the misshapen bodies and mutilated limbs of her marching mill children.[95]

The concluding decades of the twentieth century saw dramatic and quite public challenges to some other stereotypes. If we were to visit downtown San Francisco on the fourth Sunday in June of any year, we would join hundreds of thousands of others who come pouring out of public transit stations to climb onto utility poles and newspaper stands and press in behind those who have gotten there early to stake out a spot along the mile-plus route of the Pride Parade. What would we see? We would see the Women's Motorcycle Contingent (Dykes on Bikes), roaring by at the head of the parade with some of the riders flaunting bare breasts, and we would see the ever-popular contingent of Parents, Families and Friends of Lesbians and Gays (P-FLAG). We would watch the passage of dozens of floats, some bearing dancers, some perhaps precision marchers, some with people dressed in gender-bending garb, and some with people wearing not much of anything at all. In 2006 we would have watched performers on a Balloon Magic float dressed in "colorful inflated latex." That parade included cheerleaders, police officers, politicians, dancers, costumed men on stilts, toddlers in strollers, members of an HIV-awareness collective, teenagers from high school Gay-Straight Alliances, members of Old Lesbians Organizing for Change, representatives of various religious congregations including an evangelical church, and many colorful others.[96] Similar pride parades take place in other cities, wherever permitted, around the world. There were 140 in 2007, though none as big as San Francisco's, at least in the United States.[97]

Note that the Pride Parade is no longer exclusively a celebration of same-sex relationships. Marchers include gay men, lesbians, and bisexuals, as well as transgendered and intersex people and their allies. One cannot achieve greater visibility than by parading the kind of difference that could only be revealed at great personal risk just a few decades back. For many, the risk—of family ostracism, harassment, discrimination, or worse—remains. *Queer*—the word now used with pride was a homophobic epithet. So, yes, the parade is about pride, but for many it is mainly a festival, a chance to boogie to a disco beat before a vast audience. The many thousands of straight supporters who watch are also an important part of this community. But whether one looks on from the curb, joins the march, or mingles with the huge and close-packed crowd that collects at the parade's end, the Pride event is both joyous and safe. When people wearing nothing but feathers and beads are safe, everyone is safe.

The Pride Parade is also an opportunity for some to advertise corporate products and services. Putting on an event of this size is expensive, and years ago parade organizers began accepting corporate sponsorship. With corporate funding come corporate floats, such as Delta Airlines' in 2006. This makes for mixed messages, at the very least: "We're here and we're queer" and "Fly Delta." Some in the Queer community have found this intrusive and unacceptable. In San Francisco and elsewhere, thousands of women hold their own event on Pride Parade eve each year, the

Dyke March, with every year a new political theme. Celebrating the fifteenth anniversary of the event, the 2007 Dyke Marchers demanded health care for all. They neither ask for a parade permit nor accept corporate sponsorship: "Refusing to accept corporate funds ensures that the SF Dyke March annual exercise of free speech will remain just that," a 2004 Web site declares.[98] But a women-only event that attracts participants in the tens of thousands is a statement in itself.

Disneyland milked nostalgia for the traditional small-town parade with its daily Electric Parades down Main Street USA (1972–96), performed 3,600 times and viewed by seventy-five million.[99] But the traditional parade is not entirely a thing of the past. Residents of some small towns in the Midwest still turn out for the local high school's homecoming parade. Participants and spectators annually flock to Bristol, Rhode Island, for its Fourth of July parade, said to be the oldest "continuous" such event in the nation. And people come from all over the Bay Area to watch the marching bands, drill teams, dance teams, etc., of the Solano Stroll in Berkeley and Albany.

The loss of an oppositional culture on parade is also far from complete. North Carolina progressives employ satire and burlesque to make political statements in Greensboro's annual Fourth of July Parade and win prizes for their entries, too. They tweaked the theme of the 2004 event, "Celebrating the 50 States," for example, by sponsoring Ms. State of Denial, fifty-five-year-old Liz Seymour, who won a mock beauty pageant. Her white convertible bore the slogan, "Everything Is Under Control." Pulling it were people whose sashes identified them as "State of Despair," "State of Terror," "Police State," etc. Behind these beauties came a large mobile security camera, swiveling from side to side and reflecting the crowd in its mirrored lens. Emblazoned on its side was the question, "Do you feel safer?" Bringing up the rear of this contingent, clad in silver and black, was the Cackalack Radical Drum Corps, whose members chanted "Time for another revolution!" to the beat of their drums.[100]

In addition, some people are using Web sites, text messages, and mobile phones to organize the short-lived crowd stunts known as "flash mobs." A shaving-cream pie fight at a site usually filled with tourists, a downtown zombie walk, or a synchronized dance—anything goes. Such "free fun" offers what many seem to regard as an attractive and provocative alternative to "the dominant entertainment paradigm," letting people stake a short-lived claim on public space with a startling divertissement.[101]

DISSIDENT MARCHERS TODAY

With postwar dispersal of the downtown crowds of potential spectators (discussed in chapter 7) and the preemptive domination of streets by drivers, the powerful have found other media—newspapers, magazines, radio, TV, billboards, and the Internet—to convey their messages. For the most part, they have left use of the street as a would-be medium of mass persuasion to more or less marginalized political dissidents. Can we make good use of it to get our values and ideas across? With pedestrian flows thinned or almost nonexistent on all but a few busy commercial streets, demonstrators often play to an empty house. The crowd is elsewhere, in the mall perhaps, but the mall is not public space. Unless your state has adopted a broader interpretation of free speech rights, private property owners can impose a ban on political or other advocacy on their premises. Even in California, whose courts have given citizens some rights of political expression in shopping malls, mall management has the right to restrict such advocacy with rules as to time and place.[102] Ask for permission to hand out fliers in a California shopping mall and you will likely receive a five-page application with a notice that mall rules prohibit such activity during the holiday shopping season. Challenging such a position could entangle you in a drawn-out and expensive legal process. In short, the mall is a place for consumers, not citizens.

The irony is that from John Stuart Mill to more recent commentators, justification for the extension of speech and assembly rights to dissidents assumes that their views receive a hearing. Discussing the right of assembly, a scholar says that those who depend on it are often adherents of unpopular political or religious views who can ill afford to rent a private meeting hall and thus "must depend on collaring the casual passerby to acquire an audience."[103] And there is admitted value in the dissemination of unpopular views. Unless people are exposed to the diverse opinions expressed by street speakers and the like, their comfortable, conventional assumptions may never face a challenge. What happens when the casual passerby no longer passes by the political rally because she is at home, getting the same messages as everyone else who relies, consciously or not, on major media to provide an understanding of the world?

Confronted by empty sidewalks, today's marching dissidents try to use the medium of the streets to gain some attention by major electronic or print media and thereby capture the attention of descendants of the people who made up the crowds of formerly crowded sidewalks. But with few exceptions, today's dissidents have inherited the nonviolent legacy of the civil rights movement, and as even Martin Luther King Jr. acknowledged, "lack of resistance" by authorities—meaning on-camera beatings and arrests—makes nonviolence less effective.[104] Though urban police units continue to treat mass protest as a threat to public order (see chapter 6), they seldom act so foolishly as to facilitate expanded dissidence. Without visible, violent repression, peaceful tactics can gain neither a toehold on the moral high ground nor the attention of the media. As reporters will sometimes admit, if it doesn't bleed, it doesn't lead—or even make the news.[105] But any alternative to nonviolence—from breaking a window to battling with the police—will bring *unwanted* media coverage in which the broken window (or the like) upstages every other issue, besides risking a brutal response by the police and harsh sentences.

What is left for the nonviolent political crowd is the capacity to block normal flows of traffic and work, to disrupt business as usual. But if sitting down in a manufacturing plant or segregated restaurant was once a bold and effective tactic, sitting down to block a busy intersection has, by comparison, the tactical properties of a boomerang—unless the object is to compel the police to make mass arrests. For that protesters need only ignore an order to disperse, stand when ordered to, and volunteer their wrists for the plastic restraints now favored by the cops. Such watered-down tactics present an irresistible target to critics—like the author of a recent letter to the editor who chides a prominent local activist for courting "ceremonial" arrests, contrasting today's militants to Martin Luther King's "willingness to spend real time in real cells."[106] Small wonder that, having recently interviewed about a hundred grassroots organizers from across the United States, an antiwar activist concluded that they "felt weary of mass rallies and marches in this political moment."[107]

In sum, the public is indifferent, the major media jaded, and (though this is not a complaint) the police no longer fire bullets into crowds. Such trends have not precluded large demonstrations. In early 2003, people came out in huge numbers in many cities of the United States to voice their objections to the Bush II administration's impending attack on Iraq. The enormous marches of the spring of 2006 by immigrants who want to become fully documented Americans included, on May 1, what was said to be the largest turnout for a single day of protest in American history. For many evangelicals, the "end times" have arrived as crowd times. Their song lyrics differ from those of antiwar activists and other progressives, but their tactics are similar. A Florida crowd protesting the government's unwillingness to require reinsertion of Terri Schiavo's feeding tube was reportedly singing "Amazing Grace" and "Onward Christian Soldiers," as "one by one [they] stepped across the police line . . . and were taken into custody."[108]

Robert Putnam found these religious enthusiasts to be three to five times as active, civically, as the average American.[109] However, having captured the White House without, as yet, transforming society to accord with their beliefs, the evangelicals may have peaked as a highly visible social movement. And though a mass movement for immigrants' rights may yet be born, those marches of 2006 appear to represent false labor pains for now. As for progressives, none of these tactical dilemmas would be significant with dramatic and persistent growth in the number of people willing to join the existing core of activists in the streets to protest the government's disastrous wars, unresponsiveness to climate change, or the nation's increasingly skewed distribution of goods and burdens. With sufficient expansion of mass protest, anything might be possible. But at this point, no social movement of historic proportions, reminiscent of the 1930s and 1960s, appears to be in the offing.

Americans who do not engage in any kind of civic activity now compose a majority, and this represents the outcome of a long-term trend. Moreover, civic activities showing the slowest decline are those one can do alone, typically with a pen or keyboard.[110] Explaining why his organization makes no attempt to organize demonstrations, Eli Parisher, the international campaigns director of MoveOn.org, says, "Our members don't really consider themselves activists." He adds that "getting out in the street for them is a scary thought, but making contributions and helping pay for an ad is something they're only too willing to do." He sees MoveOn's electronic campaigning as "adding new tactics that haven't been available in the past to reach more mainstream audiences."[111] It appears that joining others in the streets is to explore an old and obscure tributary of the mainstream. (Chapter 8 has more on the virtual crowds of cyberspace.)

Insofar as they experience crowds only as consumers and patrons of spectacle, Americans are unlikely to consider collective action of the kind that takes place in the streets. The consumer society makes crowds—most crowds, anyway—its own. For individual consumers, massed others become obstacles or, at best, fellow fans. The model for the consumer crowd consists of atoms in random motion. With the help of major media, alternatives to customer aggregates become all but invisible. How could something be important if it isn't mentioned on the six o'clock news?

Thus, even when demonstrators manage to negotiate the permit process so successfully as to gain access to people on a crowded sidewalk, their message may be lost for lack of proper reception. The crowd is most likely to consist of downtown shoppers, who may pause for a moment to see what all the commotion is about, this body of marchers coming their way, waving their placards to the rhythm of their drums. They briefly stare, as if to say, "What's this? Why are you out in the street and why are you tying up all the police?" None forgo the realm of consumption to join the marchers. In fact, it appears that most people would rather just be left alone. As a recently observed bumper sticker jokes, "Stop Telling People What to Do."

PARADE AS HAPPY FACE

Like the power shows of ages past, the consumer society has its own emblematic pageant. The Macy's Thanksgiving Day Parade is rooted in the nineteenth century when Chamber of Commerce members came to see the crowd that a parade or festival could draw as an irresistible market. Roped off to vehicles, Main Street became an opportunity to use the pioneers or buccaneers of old to corral potential customers. Add sweetener to this mix, such as the coating of sugar that St. Louis's leading men applied to their domination of that city's streets when they felt secure enough to do so or the honey that Walt Disney daubed onto such ideals as progress, pioneers, and adventure to create a "narrative of American pseudo-history" at Disneyland, and we have come some way toward tracing the antecedents of the Macy's spectacle.[112] Around two and a half million spectators turn out every year to line Manhattan curbs for a view of Macy's Thanksgiving Day Parade.[113] The 2006 parade included something for every suburban-living, TV-watching American, especially the kids. There were dozens of giant balloons of animal and cartoon characters (Snoopie, Pikachu), most of them linked to familiar corporate entities; twenty-nine floats ("Barbie and 12 Dancing Princesses," "Paramount Pictures' Charlotte's Web"); eleven marching bands; several dance teams, choruses, and other performance groups; and a long list of celebrities from the sports and entertainment worlds, including celebrity cartoon characters and corporate icons. Images from the phantasmagoria of children's TV programming mingled freely with holiday reminders (Santa Claus, Macy's Tom Turkey) and the traditional marching bands, although the thirty-five casts of clowns of the 2004 spectacle suffered the pratfall of omission from the 2006 event.[114]

In 2007 the Macy's Parade featured Dolly Parton, pilgrims both as big balloons and as costumed actors, giant balloon characters from *Sesame Street*, an (apparently) all-black high school marching band from Georgia, an (apparently) all-white high school marching band from Utah, a Build-a-Bear float, Delta Airlines' replica of the Statue of Liberty, animated M&Ms representing characters from various Broadway shows, cheerleaders, an *Animal Planet* channel float, a McDonald's float, balloon heads of Ben Franklin and other "founders," etc., etc. One spectacular entry quickly following another and all were presented as icons of America. Parade organizers had not invented the promotion of commercial products through their association with iconic characters. This tradition goes back more than a century, drawing heavily on the "exceptionally icon-rich culture" of American entertainment media, including comic book imagery, film content, and radio/TV personalities, out of which have evolved the trademark characters that often appear on labels and are linked to various brands. Mickey Mouse blazed the way for Joe Camel. Crowded out by Disney's "culture of the cute" was the fascination with disaster and the supernatural of earlier generations of Americans.[115] As historians Gary Cross and John K. Walton have it, "The enchanted child [has] renewed the sated consumer."[116] Macy's annual parade puts the gamut of the cutesy culture on display.

There were also scenes from Broadway shows in 2007, performed for the TV cameras with the crowded sidewalk as backdrop. Indeed, watching the pageant on TV one became a member of its much larger and more important audience. At intervals of about six minutes, the viewer got a batch of commercials, many of them advertising the same shows and products just advertised on the street.

Left out of this heavy slice of Corporate Americana, with its frosting of tradition, was a lot of what was included in noncommercial predecessors. No workers were represented as workers, and in 2006 the nation's military establishment was reduced to the Air Force Academy Marching Band and a Toy Soldier giant balloon. This is understandable considering the major message that the Macy's Parade sought to deliver to its millions of adult viewers, at home and on the sidewalks of Manhattan—namely, "Time to buy things for your kids." (The message to the nation's children was something along the lines of "Here's what you should have.") Inclusion of tanks and marching troops could have dampened the intended shopping mood.

Given that their absence here could be excused, the question remains, what has become of our military parades? After all, the United States is not only the consumer society par excellence but the center of the greatest military empire in history, with nearly a thousand domestic military installations and another 737 bases in 130 foreign countries.[117] Is it only our armed forces' current preoccupation with the Middle East and the difficulties they have encountered there that deprive us of the spectacle of an American version of the Roman triumph? Are logistical problems or security concerns blocking our view of a sampling of America's jets, missiles, attack helicopters, artillery pieces, and the like, which our tax dollars are paying for? Americans got to view such martial pageants in the past. These days the ritualistic promotion of militarism is generally concentrated in the color guard before the ball game on the Fourth of July.[118]

As far as that goes, does the fact that our military prisoners (also known as "enemy combatants") are held incommunicado in various inaccessible locations rather than put on public display mean we are making progress in the realm of human rights? Although it is true that we have had no meaningful military victories to cheer in recent years, I suspect there is something else involved in this. Though the United States is responsible for over half the world's military expenditures (followed distantly by the UK, France, Japan, and China with 4 to 5 percent each), the Pentagon evidently sees no need to sell its bloated budget to American taxpayers.[119] And for good reason. If we did not rise up in the streets to demand a "peace dividend" at the end of the Cold War and the supposed rationale that it provided for forty years of high-level military spending, we are unlikely to object to such expenditures any time soon. We did not see demonstrations *against* a "peace dividend," at least. Besides using spectacles to seed opinions in the minds of passive viewers (as discussed above), elites have often furthered their interests by encouraging crowds to act on their behalf. The following chapter will treat this topic in some detail.

In any case, patriotism is no longer signified by doffing one's hat for the passing of the color guard. As the president made clear just after September 11, patriotism is now best expressed in shopping.

5. Who Owns the Crowd?

A common tactic of authorities who wish to discredit mass protest is to blame "outside agitators." The implication is that *our* people (students, workers, local citizens) are content. They would never rise in protest on their own. The crowd was manipulated, influenced by outsiders. Though often patently absurd, the charge is sometimes legitimate. Members of a crowd may be persuaded to take action that appears to be contrary or irrelevant to their objective interests. In fact, the politically potent crowds of the past were often bought outright.

The most obvious example comes from the Roman Republic of the ancient world. Scholars have often denied any semblance of popular sovereignty in the Republic. Sheldon Wolin, for example, thought that the appearance of political rivalry between the plebs and patricians boiled down to "contests between rival groups of the nobility . . . [which] never surrendered control of the game."[1] But the crowd in the Republic was not confined to watching, protesting, or disrupting the deliberations of the senate or the political maneuverings of the senatorial class: "It itself was the sovereign body, and as such exercised the legislative powers of the *populus Romanus.*"[2] With the support of the crowd, an individual could obtain a change of law.[3] Without it, a general would be denied his wish to lead an army. Well after the fall of the Republic, Juvenal (c. 55–138 CE) would contrast the devotion to bread and circuses of the Roman masses of his day to the crowds of this earlier era "when their plebiscite elected /

Generals, Heads of State, commanders of legions."[4] But "crowd rule" in the Republic refers to something quite specific—namely, the citizens present in the Forum, whoever happened to be there, voting out loud in the Republic's early years or by secret ballot later, to pass or reject legislation proposed by the senate and to elect tribunes and other officials. For an important legislative proposal, the Forum might be packed with twenty thousand people. The crowd could fill every temple commanding a view of the rostra.[5] Without its backhanded acknowledgment of the sovereignty of the Roman crowd, Shakespeare's *Coriolanus* would lose its central conflict.

Serious problems developed with the Roman plebiscite. For one, by the late Republic, Rome was no longer a city-state but a growing empire, and the Forum crowd was not representative of all citizens. The power of the Forum crowd was hugely disproportionate to its numbers and likely interests. Secondly, being in a Forum crowd was probably less like participating in a meeting than being in an audience. It meant listening to the harangues of speakers, including one's own elected leaders, though members of the crowd might intervene with shouts or enter into dialogue with the speaker. They could vote only when asked to do so by a presiding magistrate. Rather than wait for such an opportunity, some might drift away to find something else to do. Ultimately, politicians discovered that they could buy crowds of their own and bring them to the Forum to drown out the speeches of their rivals and intimidate the Forum's regulars.[6]

The Roman rent-a-crowd provides a lesson for democracy and its incompatibility with great economic inequality. Rome included individuals who could afford to hire a mass of others. For sufficient reward, these people were willing to risk their bodies and to jeopardize a popular institution of government, fomenting a riot in the Forum if need be. In our era of massive institutions and domesticated crowds, the powerful can fill the halls of Congress with their hired hordes of lobbyists. A powerful corporation may even pay people to hold seats until their employees can pack a public hearing.[7] The United States has the highest level of inequality as well as poverty among its economic peers in the Organization for Economic Cooperation and Development (OECD).[8] Under such conditions, it is doubtful that American democracy can consist of anything more than regularly scheduled elections.

BOUGHT CROWDS IN AMERICA

The crowds of America's past played an important role in the political process. For example, with the presidency of Andrew Jackson (elected in 1828), men whose political outlook had been most emphatically expressed by rioting gained the vote. They continued to riot, as we have seen, but they also became participants in a once-familiar seasonal phenomenon, recalled now only by historians. Where today's ideal voter sits at home, watching TV to weigh the relative merits of the two leading presidential brands, it was then the would-be officeholder, not the potential voter, who "concealed himself, his personality, his ambitions, and his emotions" in his home.[9] To enjoy electoral success, the political party of this cloistered candidate had to induce ordinary people to do his public campaigning. Tocqueville observed that the country's mostly peaceful citizens were "surrounded by the incessant agitation of parties, who attempt to gain their cooperation and support."[10] But he also noted that elections brought "a multitude of citizens permanently together who would otherwise always have remained unknown to one another."[11]

The parties obtained such participation and support not by promising reforms that might benefit the impoverished many at the expense of the prosperous few but by turning electioneering into festival and by stuffing political appointments down to the precinct level into the victory prize. With every election season from the Jacksonian era until well into the Gilded Age (1830s to 1890s), millions of people, many of them organized into clubs and companies, followed marching bands through the streets of northern cities and towns bearing torches or brooms toward a site where they would be treated to firework displays, free food, and fiery speeches. In the country, farmers drove their wagons into town for all-day rallies, which would end in the raising of the Liberty pole, if they were Whigs. Jacksonian Democrats had their own version of the politicized maypole in the "Hickory pole." These partisans might compete "to erect the highest pole in town," while their urban counterparts were worshipping the Goddess of Liberty.[12] By the 1860s the goddess would be represented by a live woman instead of a mockup on the horse-drawn float.[13]

The reminiscences of Ohioan Jesse Strawn about a procession that had awed him as a child in 1840 provide a more immediate sense of such partisan spectacles. There were, as he recalled, thirteen yoke of oxen pulling a wagon with a log cabin, which displayed a huge American flag, a stuffed eagle, coonskins, and a live raccoon. Inside the cabin were women dispensing drinks to the wagonloads of cheering men and boys that followed.[14] There was nothing incidental about the drinks. The parties provided so much alcohol during the 1840 electoral season that it became known as the "hard cider campaign." Taverns served as political forums: presence in the local saloon during voting season was regarded as a mark of civic virtue. What with mass banquets, parades, rallies, debates, barbecues, and feasts, all enlivened by the flow of liquor, "the two-party system provided an unbroken *party* system" (emphasis added) in the electoral season. "Voting days were American male holidays," says historian David Grimsted.[15] Eligible voters were so drawn into this "ritual of partisan display" that in effect they voted twice. In proportion to eligibility, Americans have never again cast ballots in such numbers.[16]

Electoral hoopla served the existing order by creating an artificial "community of interest" between the many who bore the torches, attended the orations, formed the glee clubs, and cheered the fireworks, and the candidates whose politics would advance the interests of business and financial elites.[17] Paraders serenaded their wealthy patron, named their organization after him, held marches in his honor, and bore his image through the streets like that of a patron saint. The saint himself was expected to pay for their uniforms, make himself available to lecture them, and otherwise show his generosity—for example, by standing them drinks. Michael McGerr characterizes the entire era as one of interclass "intimacy."[18] One thinks of the pickpocket's hasty embrace.

Farmers and wage-earners were not won over by the fireworks, liquor, and free lunch alone. As noted, party loyalists were often rewarded with city jobs. But mass politicization also taught people how to organize and gave them a sense of the power of their own mobilized numbers. The same era that made a fetish of loyalty to a major party produced radical alternatives in the Greenbackers, the Knights of Labor, the Populists, the Socialists, and others.[19] The People's Party (Populists), in particular, used the "smoke and noise and speeches" of the major parties for their own ends, organizing campaign clubs, parades, all-day rallies, singing, etc.[20] And political parties were not the only beneficiaries of these lessons in organizing mass events. Participants in the Woman's Temperance Crusade (1873–74) put on a "spectacular nineteenth-century version of street theater" as they marched to liquor stores in hundreds of towns to sing and pray.[21] Many nineteenth-century crowds were self-owned.

The partisan crowd did not necessarily disperse on election eve. In the period that ended in the Civil War, polling places were limited and votes were cast aloud. This encouraged both Democrats and Whigs to try to influence an election's outcome by surrounding voting sites with their partisans, especially young toughs, who would try to block and outshout would-be voters of the other party. The latter might send voters to a distant polling place, or might, as happened in St. Louis in 1838, dispatch its own band of partisans to the original site, like the Roman patricians who would send their hired mobs of voters to the Forum. With men making free use of fists, knives, clubs, and homemade blackjacks, would-be voters and anti-voters fought pitched battles which sometimes drew crowds of viewers. Such voting riots were the culmination of a process that might include, during the election season, partisan mobs attacking one another's speeches, meetings, symbols, and headquarters, as notoriously occurred in New York's voting riot of 1834. Grimsted counted seventy-two election-related brawls, resulting in 110 deaths and 341 serious injuries.[22]

Riotous attacks on abolitionists outnumbered every other category of collective violence in the super-riotous 1830s, and these usually had at least the tacit support of powerful partisan interests—that is, "outside agitators." The abolitionist movement was growing, its expansion fed by these violent attacks. Abolitionist literature was beginning to appear in the South, where its discovery among personal possessions could provoke a beating, a mob attack on the homes and businesses of blacks as occurred in Washington, D.C., in 1835, or even a lynching. Southerners regarded every anti-slavery pamphlet as an incitement to insurrection, though the intended readers were not illiterate slaves but slave owners with a guilty conscience. A clamorous chorus of Southern opinion leaders called on the North to repress the spread of abolitionist ideas.

In their efforts to placate the South and retain Southern votes, the Democrats and Whigs competed in denouncing abolitionists, dressing their verbal salvos in casual racist rhetoric. This no doubt contributed to collective violence, such as occurred in New York City in 1834, when newspapers magnified a scuffle between blacks and members of a music society over a scheduling mix-up at a meeting hall. Two nights later, a mob attacked an English actor, sacked the home of a wealthy abolitionist, and then attacked the churches and homes of anti-slavery ministers and black-owned properties, the latter suffering the "more serious destruction."[23] Additional mob attacks on abolitionists and blacks took place in New York and Philadelphia that year,[24] prompting Tocqueville to urge creation of a national police force (discussed in chapter 6).

In 1835, a New Hampshire mob destroyed a racially integrated school, and crowds in Philadelphia, Burlington, and Pittsburgh assaulted blacks. Business leaders organized anti-abolitionist mass meetings in Maine, Boston, New York, and elsewhere. Mobs led by Jacksonians and merchants attacked prominent abolitionists in Newport, Rhode Island, and in Vermont. Grimsted suggests that many of these flare-ups had symbolic value as quick and relatively cost-free responses to Southern demands and economic threats. A Jacksonian paper made sure that a newspaper clipping describing the New Hampshire mob's assault on the integrated school was sent to the South. The Boston mob that threatened to tar and feather William Lloyd Garrison refrained from doing so. A Jacksonian congressman led the attack that shut down a Utica meeting of the New York Anti-Slavery Society following the embarrassing outing, in the South, of a Utica newspaper that was both for Van Buren (Jackson's presumed heir) and against slavery.[25] Northern mobs beat abolitionists and sometimes tarred-and-feathered them, but most of the damage was done to presses, churches, meeting halls, and other properties.[26] In wooing the South, each national party was a suitor with a disturbing and recurrent dream of getting into bed with an abolitionist. Neither Democrats nor Whigs "dared do enough to satisfy the South."[27]

Certainly, the mobs of impoverished Irish immigrants who made "a bid to gain sway over an entire city" in New York City's anti-draft riots of 1863 were under nobody else's control.[28] Besides tormenting, shooting, burning, and hanging any blacks they came across, some demolished the furnishings of wealthy abolitionists in a manner that urges comparison with the destruction of the homes of Andrew Oliver and Thomas Hutchinson a century earlier. Still, the rioters' hatred of their betters was not indiscriminate. It was fixed on the same kind of people whom the newspapers and orators of New York's Peace Democrats (the "Copperheads") had long denounced as responsible for economic hard times and a misguided war—Republicans and the Lincoln administration. Especially targeted were Republican philanthropists, who typically were abolitionists.[29] Although rank-and-file abolitionists were drawn from every social and economic category in proportion to their numbers, it was the stereotype—a wealthy Protestant idler, more concerned about black orphans than impoverished white workers—that drew the wrath of rioters.[30] From Henry James's *The Bostonians* to Russell Banks's *Cloudsplitter,* members of the American Anti-Slavery Society and similar organizations were and still are depicted as well-heeled spinsters and eccentric ministers, long on talk but short on action. In addition, the antislavery movement, like the temperance crusade that served as its tactical model, thrust women into leadership roles. This could not have endeared it to its enemies, either.

Slavery and the abolitionist movement were central to collective violence in the antebellum South, which far exceeded that of the North in terms both of frequency and deadliness. Any deviation from the pro-slavery stance, any lack of enthusiasm for it, put one at risk of mob attack. That stance required contented slaves as an article of faith. But most southern whites had no slaves of their own. Thus the basis of white solidarity was a region-wide fear of a slave rebellion. Given the premise of slave contentment, rebellion could only be fomented by abolitionists.[31] During the Texas Panic of 1860, wrote a Southerner, "school boys have become so excited by the sport of hanging Abolitionists that the schools are completely deserted."[32] With civil war raging elsewhere in the nation, residents of Gainesville, Texas, lynched at least forty-four alleged Unionists in October 1862 alone.[33]

Like the Southern legal system it paralleled, mob justice favored wealth and privilege. For example, after brutalizing James Foster, a prominent Mississippi planter and probable wife killer, a mob threw him back into a cell from which he was allowed to escape.[34] Had he been a black man accused of killing a white, he might have been roasted alive.[35] In short, the Southern mob had to answer to class differences. They could act with impunity only insofar as their depredations posed no threat of economic loss to powerful local interests. Lynchings in central Texas were suspended for several years in the late nineteenth century following the unprecedented grand jury indictment of ten men who had brutally murdered a black field hand. Their crime was regarded "as an assault on the business rights" of the victim's employer. The victim and his companions, who fled the attack, had contracted to pick cotton more cheaply than others.[36]

CELEBRATION AS CULTURAL ENGINEERING, AD, AND MARKET

The powerful have often used the crowd-catching possibilities of festivity for their own purposes. In the age of Rome's empire, Saturnalia's mock king, who by ancient tradition was expected to die by his own hand at the end of his brief reign, had long been replaced by a Lord of Misrule, described by Frazer as a "feeble emasculated copy of the original."[37] The figs, plums, and candy that would rain from above on banqueting guests during the December festival when "all Rome went mad" were tokens of the imperial largesse which also paid for the feasting and entertainment ("buxom Lydian girls clapping hands," etc.).[38] Though it remained an exceptionally democratic kind of celebration—one table serving "every class alike, children, women, people, knights, and senators"—Saturnalia advertised the state's beneficence, as did every other popular assembly allowed in imperial Rome.[39] Even carnival, Saturnalia's successor and the people's holiday par excellence, served the existing order as social safety valve. As a clerical apologist wrote in a circular letter (the fifteenth-century's version of a Web site posting), "Wine barrels burst if from time to time we do not open them and let in some air."[40] Carnivalesque excess may have buttressed the existing order in other ways, too. An anthropologist remarks that "the lifting of normal taboos and restraints obviously serves to emphasize them."[41] Was not restoration of the status quo the point of killing carnival at the end of his reign?

By the eighteenth century, the "truly festive celebration" had become, at least in the enlightened minds of Europeans who recorded their opinions, "a thing of the past." What remained was an affront to genteel sensibilities: people blocking streets and squares, shooting birds, tearing geese apart, and "fighting over loaves of bread or sausages."[42] With revolution, festivity seemed to sail out of these doldrums, at least in France. Energy born of "terrified joy" animated crowds throughout that nation's crossroads and streets, and the revolution's bourgeois leaders sought to capture some of it.[43] Drawing what inspiration they could from the holidays of imperial Rome, they invented a series of public events intended to furnish the novel and exciting world that had fallen into their hands with a revolutionary culture. There was the Festival of Federation and the Festival of Republican Reunion, the Festival of Reason and the Festival of the Supreme Being, among other such public rituals. Like a new detergent applied to the nation, these were meant to cleanse society of all the layers of corruption that had built up over the monarchy's long reign. By their recurrence throughout the year, they would replace the Catholic ceremonies of the Christian calendar, exposing everyone to the religion of revolution.[44]

Let us take a closer look at one of these. The Festival of the Supreme Being, held in June 1794, displayed Robespierre's idea of liturgy for a republican religion. A choir of 2,400 children sang a "hymn to the Supreme Being," followed by a "hymn to divinity" sung by a chorus of blind children. An estimated 300,000 people then marched to the Champ de Mars where three years earlier Lafayette had ordered National Guard troops to open fire on demonstrators, which they had, killing around fifty.[45] There they watched the burning of an effigy of Atheism, revealing a monument to Wisdom inside. They also got to see Jacques David's papier-mâché statue of Hercules, standing fifty feet high. Certainly, this would not be the last time that the powerful set up an entertainment regime.

What the people of the poorer neighborhoods thought of these events is unclear. Regretful of a childhood that had no festivals,[46] Michelet had only high praise: he thought the revolutionary festivals expressed "a religion unaware of itself."[47] Others found them tedious. In the country, the typical revolutionary festival consisted of a public ceremony marking brotherhood between rival villages, after which the villagers might march to the nearest church and drag the pews out into the square. Paris tried to put its hands on these provincial happenings but without much success. In fact, the carnivalesque forms of two and a half centuries earlier began to reappear, as if carried by a recessive gene. In a revolution within the Revolution, the people gave rebirth to ancient themes of reversal and overturning. Women flogged statues of saints, nuns danced the carmagnole, royal and ecclesiastic ghosts were laid to rest with phony piety, and down the street came long processions of freakish effigies.[48] The Jacobins countered with a ban on cross-dressing and a frown on the revitalized maypole,[49] but as Mona Ozouf dryly concludes, the revolution was no longer "represented as a group of maidens dressed in white."[50] As Bataille wrote, festival is "sovereign by definition."[51]

The traditional festival was bowdlerized in America. Carnival, for example, became the summertime Carnival of Plenty at Coney Island, c. 1906, a mile-long parade of floats lit by electricity. Women, some dressed as "greenbacks," perched on outsized wineglasses and bottles, and the crowd bombarded them with confetti and drowned out the orchestras with the racket of their noisemakers. Though the vulgarity and rootlessness of the emerging mass culture evoked elite alarm, some saw that the popular "zest for amusement" provided both a social safety valve (like the traditional carnival) and an underpinning for the industrial work ethic.[52] Massive weekend leisure implied a productive workforce during the rest of the week. In any case, the Ferris wheel, roller coaster, and other rides, as well as the kaleidoscope of sensory inputs of the amusement park and the crowd itself, "offered thrills without the dangerous pleasures of commercial sex, gambling, and drink."[53]

As for the diverse celebrations of America's original "labor day," the Fourth of July, civic leaders and other representatives of the propertied classes condemned the excesses of working-class revels and tried to rein them in. Philadelphia's Muster Day was judged "the jubillee of general idleness."[54] The *Worcester Telegram* groused that Italian celebrants of Independence Day in 1907 "Couldn't Speak English but Could Fire Revolver Shots."[55] The existing order did not have to rely on editorializing news accounts in efforts to put down "mob rule of the downtown streets."[56] Its Worcester representatives passed ordinances to limit the use of fireworks, no doubt a legitimate concern of property owners. Hiring extra police for holidays, Worcester authorities also attempted to outlaw or control the all-night revelry that ushered in the Fourth. The crowds responded by moving their celebration to a nearby lake, where in 1906 a riot broke out over an arrest.[57]

Concurrent with official efforts to bring holiday celebrations under control, reformers were slowly turning up the heat under the melting pot by promoting "Americanism." This New World "ism" was intended as a counter to "foreign" ideologies, especially socialism.[58] Some differences, however, could not be boiled down. While members of various (European) ethnicities were marching in a long parade and attending speeches boosting patriotism, civic order, and anti-radicalism in Cleveland on July 4, 1894, unemployed men extolling none of these virtues were mounting a protest in the nation's capital.[59] The president had ordered the dispersal of Coxey's Army only two months earlier.

Frederic C. Howe, New York Port Commissioner of Immigration, urged that the Fourth of July become "Americanization Day." On that holiday in the wartime year of 1917, ten thousand people gathered at Worcester's City Hall for a "Ceremony of Citizenship" that included a pledge of cooperation between labor and management.[60] Such pronouncements to the contrary, for an unrepentant radical like the socialist orator Kate Sadler, the Fourth of July remained "the master's day . . . the day your masters set you free to celebrate."[61]

Like other city governments, Worcester's took on the task not only of policing but of entertaining local residents on the Fourth, providing a flag-raising ceremony, a military and civic parade, sports and games, and an official fireworks display.[62] A 1916 editorial in the local *Labor News* wondered, "Why is all the ginger taken out of our national holiday?"[63] Evidently ruling-class representatives were unwilling to tolerate the threat of working-class autonomy, even when it was expressed outside the factory gates in separate ethnic enclaves. An exception to the ginger-free celebration—ghetto dwellers setting off their own illegal fireworks displays—has recently prompted cancellation of one city's official Fourth of July show in order to free up enough police to snuff out these untamed spectacles.[64] For the rest, the midsummer holiday has gradually been transformed from something like a bacchanalia to a backyard barbecue where people make small talk and edge toward the gate when the host starts running low on ice. With the majority enjoying the Fourth, and Christmas too, as private family affairs, the rise in mortality rates that accompanies such holidays is now due to traffic accidents, not drunken brawls.[65] This development stands in some contrast to the annual celebration of Mexican independence by the enormous crowd that gathers in Mexico City's Zócalo, where as midnight starts to strike a raucous cry erupts from deep inside the gathering, which everyone takes up, "*¡Viva México! ¡Viva México! ¡Viva México!*"[66]

By the end of the nineteenth century, dominant commercial interests had turned expositions and memorials into "economic spectacles" like Philadelphia's centennial exposition of 1876, where Ulysses S. Grant appeared with a large military escort amid the patriotic rituals and history lessons.[67] Visitors were also entertained by a large model of George Washington, "rising from his tomb at regular intervals," though surely without the bloodlust usually associated with such feats.[68] Over a hundred million people attended such events as the Chicago World's Fair of 1893 (officially known as the World Columbian Exposition), Buffalo's PanAmerican Exposition in 1901, and the St. Louis World's Fair of 1904. In all of these extravaganzas, the past was presented as "essentially a story of enterprising individuals improving upon what they found."[69] Those individuals were the nation's great industrialists and entrepreneurs.

New York's World's Fair of 1939–40 commemorated the 150th anniversary of Washington's inauguration. In some respects, the so-called People's Fair was a hit: "Bands of strolling players—singers, dancers, acrobats, clowns, hired by management . . . [were] surrounded by crowds wherever they went."[70] For its organizers, however, the fair was a bust. They were pushing the sale of consumer goods and services, but the crowds failed to cooperate. They literally went their own way, consistently turning right at the entrance instead of using a ramp that would have brought them to an area of greater spending opportunities. (This was probably not an act of defiance. Recent research has determined that most people immediately turn right on entering a store.)[71] These fairgoers had yet to absorb the role of active consumers. They mistook this "place . . . of pilgrimage to the commodity fetish" for a cheap entertainment site.[72]

In any case, the Depression was lingering on in 1939 and 1940, and the credit card in every wallet was no more than a feverish fantasy of mass retailers and finance capitalists. Perhaps these fairgoers simply lacked the means for greater spending. Not shopping, intimidated by the pomp and ceremony, the crowd (as Warren Susman wrote) took greatest pleasure in itself.[73] They also seemed awed by the "vision of a technological future" that was on display, introducing them to television, plastics, and the freeways that would link their children's homes to distant jobs.[74] But the fairgoers already had some gadgets of their own. They had cars, many of them. They had telephones, some of them, and they had *radios*. With the world—at least some version of the world—available with the twist of a dial, there was a lot less need for entertainment en masse.[75] And if they did go out for entertainment, they had learned they would probably have to stand in line and buy a ticket. As pioneering patrons of commercialized recreation—attending the local amusement park; going to baseball games, football games, boxing matches, movies, and the nickelodeon—their parents and grandparents had taken "an important, but often unconscious, step away from the insular and restrictive world of . . . ethnic communities," to which the only ticket needed was cultural identity, into a "festival of consumption."[76]

As for the consumption of festival, the migration of middle-class families to the suburbs had already begun, leaving Coney Island and similar sites to more of a down-market crowd on which the proprietors of aging attractions could only lose money. People changed into their swimming suits at home or under the boardwalk, avoiding the bathhouse fees. They brought their own food and occupied the beach, ignoring the nearby rides, stalls, and other "amusements." Coney Island would enjoy an eventual last hurrah on the other side of the continent as a gentrified Coney replica, Paradise Pier of California Adventure Park, an outpost of the Disney theme park empire.[77]

In Disneyland, the initial colony of this empire, Walt Disney had selected various elements of the freak show, carnival, circus, amusement park, and diorama, altering each to accord with suburban sensibilities and accommodate middle-class anxieties. He addressed suburbanites' fear of working-class crowds by appealing to childlike wonder, the "strategy of the cute" now deployed by the organizers of the Macy's Thanksgiving Day Parade.[78] He did not invent this strategy. Luna Park had "presented visitors with the architecture of Fairy Picture-Books—Toy-Lands elaborated by adult hands."[79] Disney also provided a squeaky-clean setting for his crowd attractions, and he staffed his sites with clean-cut, friendly, middle-class employees. "Carnies" need not apply. The price of admission to the Disney theme parks alone excluded the poor: tickets now come to about $60 per person when purchased at the entrance to Disneyland (now Disneyland Park).

Disney capitalized on a social phenomenon that had begun to develop in Western Europe as early as the fifteenth century—namely, the child-centered family.[80] Thus "the child-centered play of families" replaced the interplay of young adults that had seasoned the Coney Island experience.[81] The basic units of the Disney crowds consisted of "intimate family groups," not individuals or clusters of friends.[82] Infantilization of the crowd was nudged further along by Disney's substitution of nostalgia for novelty and thrills—nostalgia for the small town that many of Disneyland's suburban patrons had never known (as in Main Street USA), ultimately a "self-referential nostalgia for . . . invented traditions."[83]

But the advent of the theme park was not the only transmutation of festival that could not have been predicted by World's Fair attendees in 1939. Within a quarter-century, the crowds of an official festival would draw opponents of the existing order. An anticipated automotive "stall-in" by civil rights activists, plus bad weather, reduced expected attendance for the opening of New York's 1964 World's Fair by several tens of thousands. The stall-in did not materialize, but "youthful pickets and sit-ins" disrupted the speech of President Johnson. Their shouts of "Freedom Now!" drowned him out at times. Pickets "seemed to be all over the fair," drawing mini-crowds of cops, photographers, and reporters, and forcing fairgoers to step on or over protesters to get to exhibits. One woman scolded her six-year-old for not stepping on demonstrators as she had instructed: "When I say step on them, step on them."[84] Student Nonviolent Coordinating Committee (SNCC) leader Bob Moses spoke with bitterness of the fair's vision of "slumless cities for the year 2000" at a time when more and more southern blacks were migrating into cities with vanishing opportunities for finding unskilled work.[85]

By the second half of the twentieth century, most rituals of public memory had become commercialized spectacles. For instance, Armistice Day, once celebrated by a parade of World War I veterans, had become a time of "gaiety"—that is, leisure and commercial entertainment. Fearing that people would otherwise not turn out, planners of Minnesota's statehood centennial in 1958 linked ceremonies of civic pride with speed skating, boxing, tennis, basketball, swimming, and other competitions, drawing 200,000 participants, the great majority of whom only came to watch. Memorial Day became Indianapolis 500 Day. The famous car race was then embellished with additional entertainment motifs, so that in 1969, for example, Indianapolis crowds of hundreds of thousands celebrated the International Fiesta, observing a float inspired by Polynesian surfing, another with a theme of deep-sea fishing, an exhibit on the history of aviation, etc.[86] The organizers might have taken their cue from Macchiavelli, who advised keeping "the people occupied with festivals and shows," except that the Florentine's object was princely power, not private enrichment.[87]

The praetorian guard of the cultural mainstream did not have to rely exclusively on legal repression to protect Americans from the youthful alternatives of the 1960s. Disneyland excluded freaks—that is, hippies—as well as freak shows. While the party was still in progress in the Haight and similar environments, civic planners began to counter it with sanitized events. On the Fourth of July 1970, Bob Hope presided over "Honor America Day" in Washington, D. C. For inspiration, the organizers could draw on more than a century of Americanized holidays.

For most who watch such events, the passing panorama is no longer a crowd experience but something that appears on a screen, within the privacy of the home. Festive participation has become, more and more, a thing of the past, replaced by *spectacle*, which had always been one of festival's major elements. Some would say that Americans never had it so good, and perhaps they would be right. But unless they can recall the experience of an older, more vernacular culture or the public enthusiasms that suffused the lives of Americans of an earlier day, how can they know?[88]

Today Disneyland and its cousins, uncles, and aunts represent the quintessentially American crowd space, and they are open year-round. Colonies of the Disney empire, as well as such major competitors as Marriott's Great America, the Dallas-based Six Flags (now nearing bankruptcy), Tampa's Busch Gardens, and MCA Universal Studios link TV, movies, toys, rides, etc., in a corporate production chain that has made the traveling carnival and fairground attractions of an earlier age seem like another country's small change. "Disneyfication" extends to Las Vegas and well beyond.[89] These days the nation has six hundred or so theme parks. They range from the artificial surf and falls of aquatic worlds to theme parks in shopping malls to biblical topics turned into roadside draws.[90] Together they attract around 320 million visitors annually. This exceeds the present population of the United States.[91] By 1990 Disney World had become the most powerful crowd magnet in the country, drawing 28.4 million visitors. Adapting to America's lower birth rates and conceding the development of a youth culture, Disney now offers "age-segmented, life-stage entertainment."[92]

We began this discussion of domesticated revelry by noting the official festivals of revolutionary France. The Festival of Federation in July 1790 marked the first anniversary of the fall of the Bastille. Thousands of people poured into Paris for the long military parade. But there was a breakdown of the order and solemnity intended by its organizers. Instead of returning home after the parade, people continued the celebration with their own parties, dances, and parodies. The revelry lasted for days, and similar festivities occurred throughout the nation.[93] Michelet described a "love-feast" in the town of Saint-Andéol, where "wine flowed in the streets, the tables were spread, provisions placed in common," and people joined hands in an enormous dance extending outward "into the fields [and] across the mountains of Ardèche."[94]

The point is that a kind of celebration—spontaneous, massive, and over the top—has been lost. We cannot recapture it by buying tickets to (let us suppose) a "French Village" where we might chuckle with our children or grandchildren over the antics of a cartoon mayor and his wife, village priest, schoolmaster, blacksmith, and other village characters. Certainly, we might feel comfortable in such a theme park crowd, might bask in the delight on our toddler's face. But this is not the same as feeling at one with a multitude and dancing together into the hills. A species of enjoyment has been lost and not even grieved.

MEDIA-DRIVEN CROWDS

In a society of the spectacle such as ours, to be seen by the many on a regular basis is the shortest path to fame. This was as true in imperial Rome as it is in the United States today. The victorious gladiator could rise from slavery to a status akin to that of a rock star. "The golden nose of Scorpius twinkled everywhere," wrote Martial of a famous charioteer.[95] Another was memorialized in Constantinople's hippodrome as a towering stone figure. Yet another had to share his burning funeral pyre with a distraught Roman fan.[96] Like today's superstars, Roman sports celebrities made fortunes and were not held accountable for their actions.[97] Juvenal warns the prospective teacher that he will only be paid as much at the end of the term "as a jockey / makes from a single race."[98] By late antiquity, the crowd would roar, "*Tu vincas!*" (You triumph!) on the appearance of either a famous charioteer or the emperor.[99]

Spectacular productions create superior beings, and the devotion accorded them by their admirers resembles nothing so much as worship. "He's a husband, he's a lover, he's a friend, he's everything," says a Barry Manilow fan.[100] The fact that many of the starstruck are not content with worship from afar but will attempt off-screen or offstage sightings of their gods underlies *The Day of the Locust,* Nathanael West's dark novel about Hollywood. West's "locusts" come to Southern California to die, but before dying they must seek relief from their profound boredom by frenzied efforts to glimpse one of the living symbols of the passion they lack. They get their glimpses, but their only possibility of direct emotional engagement comes in the riot at the Hollywood opening that provides the book's dénouement. The irony is that it took the spectacular possibilities of film to do this ending full justice. In director John Schlesinger's version of the chaotic scene, we see the bloodied Homer Simpson (the *original* Homer Simpson) crucified; notice someone nuzzling (if not buggering) the narcissistic ingenue; share the injured Todd's apocalyptic hallucinations amid flaming wreckage; and wince as the M.C. babbles maniacally about the roar of the rioting crowd being an homage to the opening's stars.[101]

One need no longer join a crowd outside a theater opening to catch a glimpse of real-life Hollywood stars, of course. The widespread hunger for a closer look, something to indicate what the gods and goddesses are like when off camera and off their guard, has created a celebrity-exposure industry in which paparazzi follow, block, and even ram the cars of the stars with their own.[102] One currently notorious female celebrity attracts three- or four-dozen paparazzi to the gates of her residence every night.[103] Anyone who has stood in line at a grocery checkout counter has seen the results of such encounters staring up from the covers of the celebrity tabloids. Despite what may seem an endless repetition of the famous faces' scandal du jour, starstruck fans cannot get enough. "Instead of reaching saturation, it seems that what all this stuff has done is created an even more ravenous appetite for more of it," says a professor of popular culture.[104]

Identification may seem too precarious for some unless supplemented by possession of a piece of the star: his signature, a photo, a cigarette butt, anything with prior celebrity contact will serve. In the case of a rock immortal (now deceased), even his toilet has become star-enhanced, thereby collectible.[105] Every baseball hit into the stands sets off a scramble for its possession. We also have a basketball hero "keeping with tradition" after his team's playoff win by giving up the shirt on his back. Literally. The star made his choice among a forest of imploring hands; "The [recipient] held the jersey high, then clutched it to his chest, the fans around him and the rest of the arena roaring all the way."[106] For those who attach value to that which is widely seen, vitality lies outside the self, embodied in the famous individual or widely represented object. Through sufficient fervor and fascination, we may bring a tiny share of it to earth to lodge in us.[107]

The ball that Barry Bonds hit into the stands one August night in 2007 to break the record for career home runs touched off a battle for possession in which people got bumped, bruised, and bloodied by fists and elbows in their efforts to lay hands on the precious spheroid. Couples were forced apart, seniors knocked to their knees, and children left to cower in fear. The man who ended up with the ball required a police escort to exit the stadium.[108] But this was not a struggle to acquire a prized souvenir, not directly anyway. Operating on the assumption that a rich collector would pay hundreds of thousands of dollars for the ball, the combatants were motivated by the prospect of instant wealth. In fact, a clothes designer subsequently bought the ball for just over $750,000.[109]

Emerging from theaters on March 31, 1957, members of the casts of Broadway shows were amazed to find the streets of midtown Manhattan nearly deserted. People were inside, watching the televised production of a "live," made-for-TV musical, Rodgers and Hammerstein's *Cinderella*, starring a young Julie Andrews. The CBS production was watched by 107 million Americans, then 60 percent of the population of the United States—and *Cinderella* was not even shown on the West Coast.[110] Entertainment in America had moved into the home as its top venue of choice.

In the Americanized Paris of *Playtime*, Jacque Tati's 1967 film fantasy, the viewer is positioned outside at night looking at silhouettes of people in adjoining apartments, all watching screens. By the 1970s, television had become the "chief common ground" of the large and heterogeneous land that is the United States.[111] Watching a performance not from a crowd but by yourself, an experience heretofore reserved for sultans and millionaires, had become possible for almost anyone, and people made the most of it. What we watch, increasingly we watch alone, immersed in a phantom crowd whose chatter and canned laughs provide us with "a false sense of companionship" and social engagement.[112]

This dispersal of the crowd into multitudinous private viewers is what mainly distinguishes our society of the spectacle from any predecessors. More than half of Americans tell researchers that watching television is their main form of entertainment; on average it takes up four hours of the day, roughly half of their free time.[113] We have more TV sets in our homes than people, and we spend more time watching television than anybody else in the world.[114] Is it merely coincidence that we also work more hours, on average, than people in countries with comparable levels of industrialization?[115] The seductive quality of the flickering screen and its addictive potential are well known, yet a third of our children under six have a set in their bedrooms, enabling other members of the family to watch their own shows.[116] But the television set is just one of the asocial devices of members of the dispersed crowd. Anyone who lives in a college town has grown accustomed to the sight of people clustered on the basis of presumed social ties, each in a separate conversation with an absent other via a mobile phone.

Less obvious is that devotion to televised images is creating new crowds. Some consist of people who seek closer contact with those who are "in the news." Many of these viewers became "political tourists" recently flocking to Iowa and New Hampshire for the presidential primaries, "merely to witness the spectacle of it all" directly. Celebrity sightings trumped evaluation of the candidates (something probably best achieved at some remove), as the iPhone-camera wielding visitors "wend[ed] their way through candidate events the way travelers traipse from cathedral to cathedral in Europe."[117] Coming into the proximity of Tim Russert, the late host of *Meet the Press*, an eighth grader got "the thrill of her life," according to her mom.[118]

"If your message isn't on TV," warns a letter to environmentalists, "to most Americans, it doesn't exist."[119] But if what exists is that which is on a screen, what are the implications for the viewer? Suppose that by dint of extraordinary effort and luck, she is one day able to win a place among the flickering events on view for everyone—as a guest of Dr. Phil, let's say. She is not going to tell the friends and relatives who missed the show, "I cried and exposed intimate details of my unhappy life to a nationwide audience." No, she will say, "I was on TV!"[120]

As for members of the studio audience of a popular TV show, one may assume that they ordered their tickets as much as a year in advance and then stood in line for at least two hours before the show. The tickets are free, but having one does not guarantee admission. Before the show begins, those lucky few admitted to the studio will rehearse displays of their enthusiasm. When, at last, the famous host appears and the show goes "on the air," a home recording will begin for almost every member of that audience so as to capture one's millisecond of celebrity as the studio camera pans the crowd. Asked why she and friends went to so much effort, the member of one such studio audience states the obvious: "We wanted to be on TV."[121]

RETROSPECTIVE APPROPRIATIONS

In the nation's infancy, the crowds of greatest value to nonparticipants conveyed political messages. The casualties of the King Street riot (or Boston Massacre), for example, were accorded near-immediate martyrdom. Thousands showed up for the next day's mass meeting, as well as for the funeral of the five whom John Adams had referred to so slightingly. With the wisdom of hindsight, he would conclude, "That night the foundation of American independence was laid."[122] That foundation was reinforced by cousin Samuel Adams's gloss on the King Street riot in a pamphlet beguilingly titled *Innocent Blood Crying to God from the Streets of Boston.* Absent other information, readers were left with the impression that the martyrs of the Boston "massacre" were victims of a British plot. Also widely circulated were prints of Paul Revere's engraving showing smirking British troops firing volleys into a peaceful crowd, some of whom lie wounded or dead as a woman wrings her hands.[123]

Although America has not experienced any martyr-producing riots recently, the demonstrations that characterized the 1960s and early 1970s have already become so culturally distant as to become museum specimens. Literally. A 2004 exhibit at the Oakland Museum of California, titled *What's Going On?—California and the Vietnam Era,* displayed giant photos of the embattled Veterans Day Committee march (October 15, 1965), the Stop the Draft Week demonstrations at the Oakland induction center, the riot at the Democratic National Convention in Chicago (1968), the Chicano Moratorium march before it was attacked by the police (August 29, 1970), the Asian-American-led march on the Ambassador Hotel in Los Angeles where Nguyen Cao Ky was scheduled to speak (unrecorded date), the Stop Our Ship march in San Francisco (1971), and several others.

Coinciding with this exhibit was a celebration at the University of California, Berkeley, of the fortieth anniversary of the event that sparked the formerly condemned, now honored Free Speech Movement. In a reenactment of the event, campus police volunteered a vehicle to represent the police car which thousands of students had trapped for thirty-two hours. Howard Dean served as proxy for the original long succession of speakers, though unlike the students in 1964 he kept his shoes *on*, mounting a wooden ramp that was put up to protect the car. From there he addressed the crowd of middle-aged former (and present) activists and curious students.[124] A critic cited the event as "an example of how opposition is domesticated and neutralized in this society," while "the political heirs of the *anti*-Free Speech Movement go about the business of running the world."[125]

Nostalgia for the demonstrations of yesteryear even bubbled over in the headline of a recent *New York Times* editorial: "There Is Silence in the Streets; Where Have All the Protesters Gone?"[126] Comparing the noisy presence of the "Vietnam generation" to the submissive silence of the "Iraq generation," the editorialist says that people these days see protesters as "vaguely embarrassing." Another op-ed writer dittoes this, calling political protest "an embarrassing relic from a different time . . . about as relevant as Civil War buffs or Trekkies."[127]

Embarrassing or not, mass protest did not end in 1975. The 1980s movement against the interventions of the United States in Central America staged dozens of demonstrations, some of them quite large. So many people were willing to engage in civil disobedience that veteran activists held weekly workshops on passive resistance, legal issues, jail solidarity, etc. In the run-up to the Persian Gulf War in 1990, an estimated 300,000 people turned out for marches in San Francisco on successive Saturdays. In March 2003, demonstrators "shut down" downtown San Francisco to protest the American assault on Iraq, resulting in over a thousand arrests. Large antiwar demonstrations continue intermittently to date, but the stifling embrace of past protestors by representatives of the existing establishment has the effect of reducing mass dissent to a fad whose time has long since passed.

WHO OWNS THE CONSUMER CROWD?

In the United States today, there are no buyers for the kind of crowds that once served powerful interests. No one rents a crowd to drown out the speech of an opponent, as in the Roman Republic. No one furnishes liquor, food, and pyrotechnics to partisan paraders, as politicians did in nineteenth-century America. And, thankfully, no one plays on the fears and hatreds of the majority to incite a riot or pogrom. Under a regime of consumer capitalism and unacknowledged empire, the crowd that acts as one has lost all value. What *is* valued is the aggregate spending potential of the numerous individual consumers who compose a market. If we would spend as much at home—via online shopping, for example—as we do when confronted by the vast array of goods in a big box store, there would be no need for consumer crowd spaces (discussed in chapter 7). Television coverage and high ticket prices have already scattered most of us as spectators. Whether as shoppers, spectators, or travelers, we are the ones who pay for our participation in crowds. What do we get in return?

As spectators we may be richly entertained. Membership in the commuting crowd (also known as the traffic jam) enables us to keep our jobs, so that we can find places in the after-work crowd of consumers, where we may buy much-needed, or at least desired, goods and services. In fact, we have to buy a lot of services because we don't have time to do a lot of the things that people used to do for themselves, such as yard work, cooking, and cleaning house. So we try to run just as fast as the consumer society's squirrel wheel spins, ever hoping to gain a little more time for leisure pursuits, and we have all these *things*.[128] Easy credit seems to offer limitless possibilities for travel, entertainment, and the acquisition of yet more things, but unless one pays the credit card balance down to zero every month, those things will cost much more than advertised. Working to pay for things acquired in the past is sometimes referred to as "debt peonage."

For a fan of consumer capitalism, "the market promotes a sense of freedom from constraint, an ultimate individuality through commodities."[129] The critic replies that if freedom has its postmodern home in consumption, why does status competition require acquisition of the same "socially visible" goods—the *dernier cri* in clothes, shoes, handbags, gadgets, vehicles, home décor?[130] If one *has to have* something, is she free *not* to have it? To the extent that we "use consumer goods to say things about ourselves," a lot of us are claiming the same identity.[131] But surely we *enjoy* the things we buy. Oh? If that were generally true, the United States would be the happiest place in the world. Statistics on suicides, murders, addictions, bankruptcies, abuse, etc., say that it is not. Enough to add that although consumption, along with voting, may convince the majority of Americans that they participate in the political and economic system, the prime beneficiaries of consumer society are not consumers at all but unseen investors—retail, financial, and manufacturing capitalists and moguls of the entertainment and travel industries.[132] They benefit not only by their returns on investments but by the production-consumption treadmill that leaves ordinary people without the time, energy, or inclination to engage in political activities. This has created a vacuum that the investor class has filled with crowds of its own to shape public policy along lines exemplified in recent times by globalization, deregulation, de-unionization, cutbacks in government spending for the poor, inaction on climate change, etc. Such policies have not only resulted in a greater concentration of power but in a redistribution of income from wages to capital that has left the wealthy in the well-padded driver's seat and leaves the rest of us stuck in commuter traffic, spending too much money at the mall, working at jobs we don't really like, trying to juggle bill payments to stay afloat, and collapsing in the evening in front of the tube.[133] Whether or not we mingle with others in the big box store or bigger stadium, we are pretty much alone in this.

6. Regimes of Crowd Control

For the crowd that will not be owned or at least heavily influenced by powerful others, there is crowd control. From rioters to demonstrators, from celebrants to spectators, and from the diverse throngs of urban streets in ages past to the disaster victims of today, all have necessitated crowd control in the eyes of local and national authorities. Only today is the typical crowd more likely to be regarded as a market than a threat to public order.

CROWDS AND THE CONSTITUTION

To start at the nation's beginning, the United States Constitution is obviously more than a blueprint for crowd control. Nevertheless, the framers were intent on blocking the capacity of ordinary people to come together in large numbers to confront and resist the power of moneyed interests. We have noted the readiness of early Americans to riot. Crowds were the face and strong right arm of popular power. This power sometimes served the interests of their social betters, as we have seen, but it was not something that they, their betters, could easily control.

With the winding down of the war for American independence and the signing of the Treaty of Paris, the poor continued to use their numbers as leverage for their grievances. Most of the former colonies were politically divided between indebted farmer-veterans and the people who had financed the war. The latter now sought payment on the bonds they had bought and loans they had made. In Massachusetts, for example, conservatives had managed to sidestep popular opposition to a state constitution that increased property requirements for voting and limited officeholding to men of great wealth. The state would now retire war debts by paying interest on notes at the rate in effect when they were issued, thus rewarding the speculators who had bought up the heavily discounted paper for a pittance. This would require a major tax increase.[1]

Adding to the frustration of heavily indebted farmers, many of whom had served the cause of independence in the war, the new Massachusetts legislature refused to expand the money supply by issuing paper currency. Facing imprisonment for debt and confiscation of their property, farmer-veterans in the western part of the state began holding extralegal town and county conventions and forcing the newly established courts to adjourn. In Hampshire County the sheriff called out a reluctant militia force of five hundred men to allow the courts to proceed toward judgments that could result in the seizure of cattle and farmland for unpaid debts. Confronted by 1,500 armed farmers, the courts adjourned.[2] A crowd led by a Revolutionary War captain rescued popular evangelist Samuel Ely and several debtors from a Springfield, Massachusetts, jail in 1782, then got into a "bone-bruising fracas" with troops, who took some hostages to secure the return of Ely. Subsequently, a crowd of six hundred freed the hostages from a Northampton jail.[3] Unopposed by sympathetic militiamen, armed farmers prevented courts from meeting at Worcester and Athol. A caravan of farmers with carts, wagons, horses, and oxen descended on Concord's town green to hold a county convention. The court was adjourned at the request of their spokesmen. At Great Barrington, a thousand militiamen faced off against protesting men and boys from nearby farms who filled a square. When the chief justice gave the troops a chance to express their loyalties, four-fifths sided with the farmers, and the court was adjourned. Samuel Adams blamed "British emissaries" for such disturbances.[4] Debtor uprisings also occurred in Maryland, New Hampshire, and elsewhere.[5]

Western Massachusetts' class war culminated in 1786 with events known as Shays's Rebellion. A veteran who had been wounded in action, resigned from the military for lack of pay, then found himself hauled into court for nonpayment of debts, Shays led seven hundred farmers to Springfield where they were met by nine hundred soldiers with a cannon. Granted permission to parade, Shays and company did so. Perhaps aroused by the sound of fifes and drums, bystanders including some militia members joined his force. The judges adjourned the court. Similar standoffs continued until winter when Shays led a thousand supporters toward Boston. They were stopped by a blizzard. Alarmed, Boston merchants financed "a special state army" to put down the rebellion,[6] which it did in January 1787, hanging several captured rebels.[7] The latter had acted on the power inherent in their numbers, but the men who opposed them could raise an army. Unless a rebellious multitude can win the support of soldiers sent to oppose it, as did crowds, for example, in Petrograd in 1917, Manila in 1986, and in America's industrial heartland in 1877, an army can usually subdue it without much difficulty.

Many Americans thought that the ideals for which they had fought against the British had been betrayed, but the "multiple radicalisms" spawned by revolution were not mutually supportive and did not coalesce into a single movement, nor have they since.[8] Nevertheless, energized as they were by their involvement in the drive toward national independence, ordinary Americans did not want to return to the status quo antebellum but to take part in the constitution-making and the new offices of government, at least at the local level.[9] As a clergyman marveled, "Even a large portion of that class of the community which is destined to daily labor" was closely following current events.[10] What the commonality favored in each state was a unicameral legislature, weak executive, and minimal if any property-owning requirements for voting and officeholding—in other words, a structure that would permit majority rule. This was just what elites were against. Future Yale president Timothy Dwight characterized the unicameral legislature as "no other than an organized mob. Its deliberations are necessarily tumultuous, violent and indecent."[11]

James Madison used similar language regarding democracy. In *Federalist* No. 10, the best-known section of the many arguments for ratification of the Constitution addressed to the people of the State of New York, he asserted that "turbulence and contention" made democracy "incompatible with personal security or the rights of property."[12] By "democracy," Madison meant *direct* democracy. No doubt he had in mind the institutionalized crowd that ruled ancient Athens, or something very similar. He contrasted this system with the republican form of government that would be created by the proposed Constitution. Madison also pointed out that the American Republic's "delegation of government" would allow the state to extend over a greater area and include more citizens than possible with a democracy.[13] The larger state envisioned by the framers of the Constitution would embrace more contending interests, reducing the likelihood of a majority "discover[ing] their own strength" and acting on it.[14] Checks and balances aside, the new republic's spatial extent would preclude the possibility of self-governance by a face-to-face society. Clearly, majority rule was not on the framers' agenda.

This was recognized at the time by careful readers. As one wrote, "Every man of reflection must see, that the change [from the Articles of Confederation] now proposed, is a transfer of power from the many to the few."[15] In contriving their system for minority rule, the framers of the Constitution were not operating in a vacuum or a space inhabited only by political abstractions. Madison revealed their fears in arguing for the antidemocratic features of the proposed Senate at the Constitutional Convention: "Symptoms of a leveling spirit . . . have sufficiently appeared in . . . certain quarters to give notice of the future danger."[16] *Federalist* No. 10 maintains that a republic, as opposed to a democracy, will disperse such dangers as "a rage for paper money, for an abolition of debts, for an equal division of property, or for any other improper or wicked project."[17] Madison would not have seen the first two of these as hypothetical threats. As noted above, heavily indebted farmers were clamoring for their states to boost the supply of currency and forgive their debts. The author of *Federalist* No. 6—assumed to be Alexander Hamilton—even cited Shays's Rebellion as an example of the danger that may flow "from domestic factions and convulsions" when not held in check.[18] Adoption of the Constitution would enervate the crowds of "rabble" that had brought these American Solons to power.

The pages of the *Federalist* evince much concern with "factions." About the time the reader decides that by "faction" the authors mean something like an interest group, he or she learns that a faction may consist of a *majority*.[19] All the more reason to support the defensive-minded government that the framers had conceived, for such a government would "break and control the violence of faction" and defeat "the superior force of an . . . overbearing majority."[20] Where these spokesmen of the framers say "faction," one can generally substitute "unruly crowd."

Once adopted, the Constitution enabled the new national government to serve its creditor constituency by functioning as the exclusive source of currency (Art. I, Sec. 10), by the right to levy taxes, and by the use of military force to put down insurrection (both under Art. I, Sec. 8). Its backers found an early opportunity to test these powers in the Whiskey Rebellion. For the settlers of the area of present-day Pittsburgh, the government's excise tax on whiskey went far beyond a tax on consumption, though admittedly the frontier folk consumed large quantities of the stuff. Whiskey was the region's most profitable export, given the difficulties of transporting any bulkier form of grain products east over the Allegheny Mountains to the only accessible markets. From the settlers' point of view, the new federal government stood in relation to them and their interests as Britain had to the thirteen colonies. Accordingly, some of them responded as American colonists had, by blackening their faces, tarring-and-feathering would-be whiskey tax collectors, posting warnings to anyone else who would violate the local community's economic norms, destroying the homes of non-compliant neighbors, and raising the liberty pole.[21] Their rebellion was put down by massive force under the command of Alexander Hamilton. Control by a majority over a local economy in defiance of federal imperatives would not be tolerated by the new national government, which had crushed such a rebellion as a demonstration of its might.

INVENTION OF THE POLICE

We may find it hard to imagine a world without police officers, but such a world existed here in the United States until around 150 years ago. Americans had inherited the constable and night watch system from the British, a mode of social control invented long ago by the Normans to maintain order in their newly conquered British territories. As a supplement to military control over conquered territory, the system worked well enough. But by the nineteenth century, the constable and night watch had become something of a joke, at least when it came to preventing or containing social explosions like the Baltimore bank riot of 1835. Fortuitously, the British had invented a more up-to-date model of social control. Young Robert Peel, a colonial administrator of Ireland in the early nineteenth century, had organized a uniformed bureaucracy there, "designed to control dissident and rebellious local populations by ethnically different conquerors."[22] This force could provide an alternative to frequent military interventions. (Think of "Vietnamization" and of today's efforts by the United States to train a force of native surrogates to bring order to Iraq.) Peel's model of colonial control inspired creation of the London Metropolitan Police, and London's "bobbies" caught the eye of American elites.

Adoption of this law enforcement innovation by one city after another was not a response to a surging rate of crime. What city fathers had begun to see as something requiring forceful intervention were the longstanding "problems of the streets—the fights, the crowds, the crime, the children," problems long ignored or taken for granted.[23] Tocqueville, whose *Democracy in America* would make him the most famous visitor to the United States in this era, thought that the volatile combination of free blacks and large numbers of destitute immigrants in America's largest cities "constitute[d] a rabble even more formidable" than that of European cities.[24] Unlike some areas of public space in European cities, the streets of America "belonged to everyone." Urchins, beggars, carters, woodcutters, and all the other members of the "vulgar multitude" mixed freely with those who aspired to be ladies and gentlemen: "No site was entirely secure."[25] Note that the object of upper-class concern at this point was not so much the purposeful crowds that had alarmed the framers of the Constitution, although the Bank of Maryland rioting had no doubt disturbed the sleep of some. What needed policing were the incipient crowds of crowded streets.

Because of such preoccupations on the part of their employers, "the uniformed police quickly inherited the burden of urban disorder and industrial poverty," becoming "agents of class control and social control in general."[26] To carry out this mandate under the guise of preventing crime, the police would have to focus on potential criminals, members of the "dangerous class"[27] that chafed the sensibilities of their genteel betters. This preoccupation was often obvious. In establishing a police department in the 1850s, Philadelphia's power holders staked out control of the city's central streets and refurbished public squares, using the men in uniform to enforce their own refined notions of respectability. They did so, among other things, by giving the police the discretion to arrest anyone deemed to be disturbing the peace. This was all the authority that police officers needed to eliminate maskers, beggars, and street-corner orators from the city's more genteel areas. Within a few years the city's leaders had even made it illegal for anyone to impersonate a politician.[28] Pluck died without so much as a funeral.

In 1880 over 60 percent of arrests in eighteen of the largest American cities were for behavior that challenged middle-class notions of propriety and public order: drunkenness, drunk and disorderly, "suspicion," vagrancy, "corner lounging"—it all added up to some people being on the wrong streets. Less than one arrest in a hundred was for murder or manslaughter.[29] These are the statistics of class war carried out by the police, warfare that is renewed whenever a city's commitment to tourism and retail trade seem to require gentrified sidewalks and streets. Consider the regime of Rudolph Giuliani as mayor of New York.

In some respects, the situation has gotten worse for people who spend a good part of their lives on the street. A century ago, the police would provide temporary housing for the poorest of the poor: bunks and breakfast. Their successors arrest homeless people for doing things in public that people with homes can easily do behind closed doors, such as using drugs and alcohol or relieving themselves. What some have called the criminalization of poverty may yet produce an American Jean Valjean. A man who had advertised his need for help while standing on a traffic median spent three days of 2004 in a jail cell for violating San Francisco's anti-panhandling ordinance.[30] Thus does one become a member of the "dangerous class."

In addition to keeping "undesirables" out of genteel neighborhoods, the police try to limit undesirable and illegal activities—that is, vice—to a special zone, usually designated as the "tenderloin."

Police responsibility for control over the social mix of crowded places has been eased in recent decades by the privatization of much of

America's crowd space. Take the shopping mall. The mall may now include a bank or two, a workout center, medical and dental offices, a movie multiplex, even a branch of the public library and an offshoot of city hall, just like a downtown. But the mall is private space, and it exists for shoppers. Though anyone who can pass for a potential shopper is at liberty to roam the big-box corridors, and adolescent "mall rats" may be tolerated as future (if not present) consumers, the mall is not really an appropriate space for people without disposable credit. The impecunious eccentric or freelance vendor will soon be shown the door to the parking lot, not by a police officer but by a private security guard. As a practical matter, the suburban location of most malls will preclude entry by anyone so poor as to have to get around without a private vehicle.

Similarly, the price of admission excludes most members of the "dangerous class" from admission to the sports arena. Few of the 25,000 flood victims, whose tax dollars had helped pay for New Orleans Superdome, had ever been inside the structure until forced into it by the devastation of Hurricane Katrina. Game tickets went for $90 in 2005.[31] The cost of flying obviously narrows the social mix in air terminal lounges, corridors, and waiting areas as well.

In short, the police are not much needed any longer to sift prime crowd spaces of undesirable social elements. However, officers played their traditional role in San Francisco recently with the gala opening, in the heart of downtown, of what was billed as the largest urban mall west of the Mississippi.[32] People clutching $25 gift certificates started lining up at 7 a.m. The first increment of 1,500 frenzied shoppers entered the Westfield San Francisco Centre two hours later, where they were greeted by musicians, acrobats, Bloomingdale's cheerleaders, and of course a wide array of goods. One awed shopper gushed that it was her "first time ever going into a Bloomingdale's."[33] At noon there was still a wait of at least an hour to get in.

But not everyone was made to feel welcome at the new mall. Guarding the entrance was a large force both of private security guards and San Francisco police. A news photo showed them shooing away a black man in a wheelchair. The area had already been cleansed of other regulars, like the sidewalk portrait artist who formerly made his living there. One of the policemen said that he thought the homeless people usually at the busy site had wanted to go "someplace else."[34] The author of yet another news item on the subject dispelled any mystery about their sudden flight, explaining that for such a retail venture to succeed, people must believe that shopping there is safe.[35] Suburbanites coming into the city via a Bay Area Rapid Transit (BART) train can visit the commercial complex without experiencing anything of the scary public realm, just by entering it directly from an underground stop.

In addition to social cleansing, the police were initially expected to put down riots like the Baltimore bank uprising. Any collective action that moves beyond the ridicule of privilege (a popular theme of street theater in the early nineteenth century, as we have seen) or demands for better working conditions to the destruction of property will set up a chorus of calls for more muscular law enforcement. Thus, even though the Baltimore riot was the only one of its kind and many riots of the riotous Jacksonian era served the needs of powerful interests, police departments were formed with riot control in mind. Trying to suppress a riot was no enviable task. In confronting and attempting to control a crowd by the use of force, the police would often become a stand-in for the preferred but absent target of collective wrath, thus becoming the crowd's antagonist.[36] In this they served their patrons well—and continue to do so to this day. Overprimed to maintain public order, the police will treat almost any outdoor public gathering outside the private spaces of consumption as potentially riotous.

From the mid-nineteenth century, when the uniform served as a patronage plum that embroiled the police in electoral and communal rioting of the kind discussed above, to the massive Chicago police riot of 1968 and beyond, the police have often proven better at fomenting riots than at putting them down. When confronting a purposeful mass, for instance, police officers will usually respond to an individual lawbreaker as though he were alone and not a member of a crowd, wading into the multitude to make an arrest. Such a response is almost certain to inflame the crowd.

America's industrial development gave the police an additional function, waning in importance in recent years. Members of the "dangerous class" were not always lounging on the street corners and stoops of their decrepit neighborhoods, after all. They spent most of their days working in the manufacturing plants that dominated nineteenth- and early twentieth-century cityscapes. Whenever this army of workers took direct action to improve their abysmal working conditions or, when unemployed, to demand relief, they faced an army of uniformed defenders of property. The latter had the backing not only of industrialists and their political allies but of home-grown xenophobes, who were galvanized by the fact that so many of the people who were agitating for better conditions were immigrants.[37] The police were backed by military force as well. The National Guard was used to intervene in labor disputes twenty-three times in 1892 alone. The bloody clashes between workers and the armed forces of capital caused an estimated six hundred deaths during the period of greatest strife, 1877 until around 1937.[38] These battles serve as ugly landmarks in the history of labor in the United States.

But as we saw in chapter 2, state and local forces often proved inadequate to the task, at least from the perspective of industrial capitalists. In any case, the latter could afford to hire their own strikebreaking troops, like the Pinkertons who opened fire on striking Carnegie Steel plant workers at Homestead, Pennsylvania, in 1892, and the Rockefellers' private troops who used machine guns on striking miners and their families in the "Ludlow [Colorado] Massacre" of 1914.[39] "The workers needed to be taught a lesson," Henry Clay Frick told his partner Andrew Carnegie, with regard to the bloody resolution of the Homestead strike.[40]

Automation and factory flight have taken a heavy toll by now on manufacturing and other industrial jobs in the United States. Postindustrial America features a service economy in which half the nation seems to be waiting on the other, more affluent half. Such service workers are notoriously hard to organize. Under the circumstances, the police are seldom called upon to take sides in a labor dispute, and ubiquitous security guards have taken the place of the robber barons' private armies. The former, though often unarmed, seem sufficient to maintain a sense of order in the consumer society's crowd spaces, and they easily outnumber police and sheriffs' department officers.[41]

EXPERIMENTS IN SELF-POLICING

"Do your own thing," the sixties' ethic, worked surprisingly well at the famous Woodstock gathering, overcoming problems that might elsewhere have produced a social disaster. Recall that the hundreds of thousands who were drawn there in August 1969 created an "instant city," third largest in the state of New York. Additional people trying to reach the thousand-acre site created a fifteen-mile backup of cars, making delivery of food and water to the crowd impossible and medical interventions difficult at best. Alternating heat and rain gave everyone a mud bath, compounded by overflow from the six hundred broken-down toilets that participants at the enormous gathering had to share. Yet in spite of many injuries and bad acid trips, three deaths, and universal use of drugs, there was no violence. The closest thing to it came when Abbie Hoffman grabbed a microphone to deliver a political message and one of the performers ran him off the stage. The crowd cheered.[42]

Order was maintained at Woodstock not by force but by the authority of "indigenous" hippies, members of a New Mexico commune known as the Hog Farmers. Thus "a gentleness and generosity prevailed," in which people shared what they had and left their belongings unattended, having established "a community safe for passivity because [it was] . . . bereft of aggression."[43] For three days and nights of living in a crowd, "the hippie dream of a passive, happy, turned on, thrill-filled life was possible."[44]

Four months after Woodstock, some 300,000 rock-and-roll fans converged on Altamont, a barren, windy pass about fifty miles east of San Francisco, to hear and see the Rolling Stones. Again, the backup of cars was such that many people never got within sight of the concert. A major east-west freeway was, literally, turned into a parking lot. But instead of bringing in indigenous hippies to police the event, the Stones hired members of the Hell's Angels Motorcycle Club. Living up to their reputation for violence, the Angels maintained order by brutalizing hundreds of people and thoroughly intimidating the crowd. While some watched in horror and Timothy Leary flashed peace signs, Angels stabbed an eighteen-year-old youth to death a few feet from the stage.[45]

Afterward, many blamed the Stones for the boy's death: they should not have retained such a violence-prone gang. Some even blamed the alignment of the stars.[46] Adrianne Aron argues that the real culprit was not violence but passivity, the hippie commitment to accept whatever might come. "The secret of the new community was passivity, and its vulnerability lay in the fact that it was easily exploited by wrongdoers," she says.[47] Altamont was not the only instance of hippie passivity being met with violence, but it was the most spectacular.[48]

No doubt the aggression of Altamont's leather-clad few and the passivity of the beaded many were augmented by their contrasting drug choices—alcohol versus marijuana and LSD. Dionysus, the god of wine, could not be expected to protect people smoking pot. Psychedelic drugs are generally not conducive to violence or even self-defense, whereas alcohol . . . well, the Stones paid for the Angels' services with $500 worth of beer.[49] Five hundred dollars could buy an awful lot of beer in 1969. Within another year or so, Seconal and heroin had replaced amphetamines and psychedelics as drugs of choice on many American streets. As Hunter Thompson wrote, "'Consciousness Expansion' went out with LBJ . . . downers came in with Nixon."[50] Woodstock's record of sustained nonviolence is unlikely to be met by another gathering of such size anytime soon, and there have been no further experiments in anarchist crowd control for massive events. At Burning Man, efforts of volunteers of a non-confrontational mediating group, the Black Rock Rangers, merely supplement the work of members of four law enforcement agencies, including a few in plain clothes, who respond as needed to reported crimes.[51]

CONTROLLING SPECTATORS

Crowds of spectators have often raised issues of control, at least in the minds of authorities. No sooner had people begun to gather in large numbers to watch sports and other spectacles than authorities responded with measures to maintain order and submissiveness. "Whip-bearers" and "truncheon-bearers" patrolled the crowd at the original Olympic games.[52] Plato applauded the well-behaved musical audiences of earlier ages, when officials used their rods to put down disruptive elements.[53] Incidents of spectator violence have continued down to the present, although America's do not approach the destructiveness of soccer riots in Europe and Latin America.

Not every society has had such issues because not every society has exalted spectacular productions. Before we were spectators, we were participants, a developmental pattern often recapitulated in one's life. The ancient Greeks generally limited participation in athletic contests to citizens, leaving it up to slaves to watch. Inhabitants of Rome, the first society of the spectacle, turned this around, watching slaves—also criminals, prisoners of war, and professional fighters—risk their lives and disreputable actors commit lewd and outrageous acts.[54] The earliest version of the football game pitted the inhabitants of one village against those of another.[55] Not so long ago, a few generations back, a man—an average American adult male, say—might seize such opportunities as came his way to play baseball or some other team sport.[56] Such men of our grandfathers' and earlier generations were like the citizen-athletes of ancient Greece compared to the Roman spectators that most of us have become.

However long people have gathered in crowds to watch or listen to others, they have had to develop a cultural capacity for the passivity required of members of an audience. This meant learning to draw a line between dramatic fantasy and social reality so as not to climb onto the stage to participate in battle scenes or to attack an actor who had played the villain when encountering him on the street, as Americans of the nineteenth century sometimes did. Working-class moviegoers of the early twentieth century would engage in conversations in the aisles and throw things at the villain on the silver screen.[57] Rock-and-roll concert-goers of the 1960s also refused to sit still, prompting struggles with the police before authorities became receptive to the more relaxed standards of audience participation now considered appropriate for that musical genre.[58] One can scream watching a horror movie but not at the opera. Indeed, it seems that every kind of entertainment capable of drawing a crowd has its own standards of deportment on the part of viewers or listeners. Guy Debord could not have had a football game or boxing match in mind in writing that the spectacle demands an attitude of "passive acceptance . . . already obtained by its manner of appearance without reply."[59] Only when we contrast the act of playing the game or performing the piece with watching or hearing it played does such a characterization make sense. Watching a performance is also passive in the sense conveyed by Barbara Ehrenreich's distinction between an audience and a crowd:[60] the audience can become a crowd only by taking action—for example, stomping and clapping to protest the failure of a performer to appear as scheduled.[61] In short, being a member of an audience or a crowd of spectators requires a degree of self-control, making truncheons and whips redundant. The performance will normally control the crowd, though not necessarily to everyone's satisfaction.

A miracle, as many Renaissance works of art suggest, requires a crowd of awestruck witnesses.[62] Roman rulers learned that the object of the crowd's collective gaze need not be miraculous to be sufficiently compelling to preoccupy the crowd and channel collective passion into harmless outbursts of excitement. The theater was popular for a reason, offering the descendants of plebeian rioters sexual titillation, shocking tragedy, on-stage torture, and—woven into the plot—the occasional death of a condemned criminal.[63] Meanwhile, at the amphitheater, were decorated animals, exotic gladiatorial match-ups such as combat between a woman and a male dwarf, live castration, reenactment of the myth of Pasiphaë and the bull. "Every effort was made to meet the expectations of a crowd which was accustomed to the bizarre, monstrous, and exciting, and most seem to have been unconcerned" regarding the agony of their entertainment's victims.[64]

The spectacle controlled the crowd, especially those attending the most violent of entertainments, the gladiatorial contest. Demobilizing the mob was the point of making admission to such shows free for those eligible for the allotments of free grain or bread. And unlike the Greeks and spectators of the early Republic, Roman viewers did not have to stand to watch, as the authorities were no longer concerned that they might spend their days in idleness if they were allowed to sit.[65] Their apolitical idleness was the object. Were it not for near-universal access to televised sports, at least in the United States, authorities might have to modify market allocations that put the price of admission to major live events beyond the reach of many Americans.

Allen Guttmann thinks that in watching team sports we achieve a collective identity: the game pits *us* against *them*.[66] This fails to take the fan phenomenon fully into account. Unlike the morality play of a crime drama or the mounting tension of a horror movie, the game may divide the crowd instead of helping it cohere, unless the visiting team has failed to attract many of its own partisans. In short, instead of controlling the crowd as the spectacular production generally does, the team sports event may incite it. Allegiance to the Roman Empire's major chariot teams, the Blues and the Greens, lasted for centuries, dividing regions, cities, even families. Rival fans sometimes burned down the stadium in battling one another. In Constantinople in 532 CE this rivalry came unglued in events known as the Nika Riots. On this occasion, rival racing fans joined forces to rescue condemned prisoners, oust unpopular officials, and proclaim a new emperor. The military regained control only by slaughtering thirty thousand of them.[67] "They have created a world of their own," concluded Procopius, the Byzantine historian, in his postmortem attempt to understand the fan phenomenon.[68] Nothing seemed to matter to them but their team's performance in the hippodrome. But clearly some other things *had* mattered to them, things of far more concern to the authorities than sports riots.

Fan violence, usually fueled by alcohol consumption, goes much further back than that. A prohibition on bringing wine into the stadium for the Pythian Games followed incidents of "rowdy drunkenness."[69] Management of the New York Jets banned alcohol for a game in 2005, following off-field violence and injuries.[70] But Nika's revolutionary spectators appear to have had no successors. Thus today's sports fan has some fans of his or her own. Norbert Elias thought that the civilizing process included not only the enjoyment of books, theater, and film but "the imaginary identification with a small number of combatants to whom moderate and precisely regulated scope is granted for the release of such affects" as aggression and belligerence.[71] The fan in the stadium represents the current endpoint of an evolutionary process that began with "constant wars between neighbors" and evolved through the football games between rival villages mentioned above.[72] That bouncing ball we watch could have been somebody's head at certain times and places of the past. Well over 700,000 fans watched live Major League baseball games one Saturday in July 2007, more than ever before in a single day.[73] Suppose we could have joined them at a local game. What might our experience have been? At Oakland's Major League baseball stadium, gatekeepers check backpacks for weapons and bottles as the crowd filters in. For good reason. Fistfights were a common sight at games not many years ago, especially with the home team losing over a long afternoon. Then management stopped selling alcohol in the stands and letting people bring in their own. Rarely heard now is the kind of fan who bawls obscenities in the later innings. What we hear instead is a pregame announcement: "Fans using foul language are subject to ejection." At least the Oakland fan is not subjected to a pat-down search on entering the stadium, as are 49er football fans across the bay. The courts have upheld the right of National Football League teams to conduct these searches. Entering fans tacitly consent to such physical screening by attending games, said the majority in a recent ruling.[74] At the stadium, the mall, and other crowd habitats of the consumer society, the airport screening we now take for granted may well become the "template" for increased video surveillance, face-recognition technology, and the like.[75]

Inside the stadium at last and now we have to find our seats. Though baseball is known as the American pastime, there are many Americans who are not much represented in this crowd, which appears to consist mainly of white middle-class couples, many trailing kids, all wearing shorts or jeans and T-shirts, everyone with a baseball cap. Big league baseball's fan "demographic" has followed a projectile from elite beginnings to the working-class fans of the early twentieth century (when the upstart American League introduced beer sales to expand its attendance base) through a long series of efforts to refine the crowd—for example, by offering free or reduced admission to women on Ladies Days—culminating in management's present efforts to make the ball park family-friendly.[76]

The game itself must compete with the stadium management's efforts to dazzle and preoccupy the crowd. Large electronic scoreboards and strategically placed smaller screens fill gaps in activities on the field by providing replays of what has just taken place, highlights of previous games, chances for fans to show (by applause) which of three other sporting events they would like to see on the screen, awards of gift certificates or free, brand-name pizza to the lucky fans sitting in some randomly selected seats, and so forth and so on. If the game lacks luster, the corporate-sponsored Dot Race or the equivalent, displayed on the scoreboard, may get a louder response than anything happening on the field. The big oil company's ad, disguised as a variant on the old shell game, also rouses the fans. On cue, people wave aloft the "door prize" (typically, a cheap bag) given to the first ten thousand or so fans to enter the stadium, thus participating in a massive promo for the company whose name appears on the "prize." Clearly, the managers of these heavily managed events view the crowd as both a market and a giant infant requiring the nourishment of constant entertainment. The game is simply not enough.

Most troubling are the electronic commands. Fans by the tens of thousands cheer and stomp in response to the message on the scoreboard to "MAKE SOME NOISE!" Have freeway driving, ATMs, computer usage, instructional manuals, etc., so habituated us to interacting with texts? Elsewhere loudspeakers may assault the ears of fans throughout a college football game, exhorting them to scream their lungs out for the local team. Ushers block aisles with chains while police and security guards stop people from moving in the stands of New York's Yankee Stadium during "The Star-Spangled Banner" and "God Bless America," both of which are played at every game. A representative of the organization says that the Yankees have heard no complaints about this enforcement of the franchise owner's idea of patriotism.[77] Could truncheons and whips achieve greater conformity? Perhaps the perennial popularity of "the wave" (successive sections of spectators raising their arms to create a wave-like effect that undulates around the stadium) originates in the fact that the crowd, acting entirely on its own, creates this phenomenon. But some stadiums, or representatives of the franchise owners who call the shots, even tell fans when to do the wave, leaving nothing to chance.[78]

Whatever the outcome of the game, the fans have probably been good-natured and well-behaved. If the home team has won dramatically, they have experienced a collective thrill that may sustain them on the trip home, maybe even make them feel a little sorry for the fans who wore the caps of the opposing team, or even the entire uniform. Some may even purchase one of the products of the corporate sponsor of the Dot Races. But just by being in attendance, they have helped market this spectacular production to its far more numerous television viewers. Some will even have been included in the close-up shots.

This is what is new in attending major live events. Like a studio audience, the crowd participates in what is, at bottom, an extended ad for branded commodities. For this there are no ancient analogues. Today's sports spectators are the patrons of the team's franchise, a market for the stadium's ad buyers, and the source of marketable images for a media network. Crowd control in the traditional sense has almost become a non-issue. Members of this massive studio audience may face other hazards, however. For major sports events, the television networks may scramble customary starting times to accommodate prime-time viewing in remote markets. The distant viewer may then be treated to the spectacle of shivering fans watching a game that goes on well past midnight, local time.

After all the cheering and without any electronic clues except the final score, the stadium offers up another crowd that has no choice but to regulate itself. I mean the crowd that fills the stadium's corridors at the end of the game, everyone trying to exit at the same time and every exit becoming a bottleneck. This crowd is really on its own. Outside at last, the crush of bodies turns into a massive traffic jam, as everyone tries to get out of the stadium's parking lot as quickly as possible. For those who use the public transit alternative, there are the packed escalators and crowded train platforms. It would take very little for disaster to occur: somebody shouting "fire," somebody brandishing a weapon, somebody falling on the stairs, a fight. Under the circumstances, the crowd exiting the sports spectacle tends to perform quite well.

SCREENINGS

Many of our fellow fans will go home to watch the highlights of the game on television. Many others will seldom venture far enough away from their screens to attend a live game. Viewed historically, the dispersal of spectators that has accompanied popular devotion to electronically mediated entertainment can be seen as a kind of crowd control. This is not to deny the advantages of watching at home, especially watching a sports contest. Leaving aside differences in the *size* of the screen, TV viewing puts everyone in the same seat, and everyone gets close-ups denied the on-site fan. In contrast to this egalitarian experience, on-site seating roughly reflects the socioeconomic hierarchy. It would be astounding to discover that the CEO of a large company was watching a game from the center field bleachers instead of a luxury box and that a production worker in one of his firm's manufacturing units was watching from ground level behind home plate. Though watching at home precludes the possibility of participating in the experience of the massive and delirious celebration that occurs when the home team wins the game on a "walk-off" home run, last-second field goal, or desperation shot in overtime, it also avoids the expense of buying a ticket, getting stuck in traffic, etc. In fact, the only thing easier than pushing a button to bring the game and the entire televised world into the home is doing so via "the remote" from an easy chair.

Such convenience is seductive and, for many, irresistible. Its price—repeated exposure to a barrage of sales efforts, many of which are charmingly disguised—seems almost negligible. And there is no one-to-one correlation between such sales efforts and the viewer's behavior. Indeed, the viewer may have long since realized that for the producers of her favorite sitcom, the object is to get her to watch the commercials, which she may silence with the remote control or channel-surf when they come on. But what will she see then? More commercials, perhaps even the same commercials on another channel. To "monitor [one's] co-optation" does not eliminate it.[79] At some level, televised spectacle orients the viewer toward the mall, auto row, insurance office, or other consumer-spending site. Should the stay-at-home fan venture out and wander into one of the advertised sites, she may encounter screens there as well. A Massachusetts furniture store offers the "shoppertainment" of a 262-seat Imax theater with a giant screen, vibrating seats, 12,000-watt digital sound, and 3-D viewing. Admission is not free.[80] Advertisers are currently placing TV screens in places where watching them is practically unavoidable—grocery stores, office buildings, doctors' offices, on gas pumps, in office building elevators, in health clubs, along the corridors of shopping malls. . . . Wal-Mart and other retail giants want the ad-makers "to think of their real estate as an advertising medium and their shoppers as viewers."[81] Shoppers interviewed at a Connecticut mall had no objection to the screens. "You reach a very targeted audience," says an ad executive of the screens her company has installed in over ten thousand medical offices.[82] I mentioned the many screens at the stadium. But we can shut our eyes, of course.

Devotion to televised entertainment of a certain kind evidently reinforces the dispersal of isolated viewers. Back in the 1970s, George Gerbner and Larry Gross conducted a long-term study of television, its viewers, and its "symbolic content."[83] They found that regular exposure to media violence left a "critical residue" of fear. Whether TV programming consisted of cartoons, professional wrestling, the news, or the nocturnal drama of police patrols, the world depicted was a dangerous place, more dangerous by far than that represented by actual crime statistics and the real-life experience of intimidated TV viewers. Gerbner and Gross concluded that the "heightened sense of risk and insecurity" produced by a steady diet of TV viewing was "likely to increase acquiescence to and dependence upon established authority, and to legitimate its use of force."[84] An unrealistic fear of others may also confine us to a familiar circuit of home, car, workplace, and perhaps the mall, assuming we are willing to go outside at all. Certainly, no one should expect to spot us in a downtown crowd.

The significance of such findings is uncertain today. For example, Gerbner and Gross concluded that TV violence demonstrated the existing order's rules of the game by dramatically showing the consequences of "symbolic violations."[85] The bad guy always gets what he deserves. Recent video games defy such rules. Crime *does* pay in *Postal* (now *Postal II)*, for instance. The player who undertakes the role of Postal Dude garners points for shooting anyone who appears, including people coming out of church, members of the school band, and other innocents. The Dude's programmed defense: "Only my gun understands me."[86] Since he started playing *Grand Theft Auto* a few weeks earlier, a sixteen-year-old says that he has run over and killed so many (virtual) pedestrians that he has lost count: "With this game, you know you're doing something bad, but you still want to do it."[87] If such play is serving the system, it can only be doing so as pre-military training. Members of an Oakland street gang called the Nut Cases used the game as a blueprint for actual crimes. They amused themselves by getting high, playing *Grand Theft Auto,* then going out to commit the robberies and killings they had just rehearsed.[88] Nevertheless, in striking down a California law that would have banned the sale or rental of violent video games to anyone under eighteen, a federal judge has determined that, at least on the basis of the evidence presented, such games are no more harmful than violent TV shows, movies, and the like.[89]

It appears that from the point of view of the powerful, the occasional disruption of the social order by illegal imitations of media violence like those of the Nut Cases is a small price to pay for mass support. Copycat killings in ancient Egypt sometimes followed a reenactment of the murder of Osiris.[90]

POLICING NON-CONSUMING CROWDS

Official crowd control today is largely reserved for public gatherings that take place outside such private or quasi-private zones of mass consumption as shopping malls, entertainment venues, and airports. Large outdoor celebrations will draw a heavy police presence, but this will not necessarily result in heightened public safety. The boisterous event may prompt an overreaction by the police, such as occurred in Los Angeles in 1986 when 150 helmeted cops and a unit of mounted police staged a riotous assault on a downtown festival.[91] Two years later, members of the L.A.P.D. attacked a peaceful crowd on Halloween. A "non-lethal" projectile shot into a crowd of celebrating baseball fans by Boston police killed a twenty-one-year-old college student in 2004.[92] When festivity builds solidarity among social subordinates, "the elite calls out its troops," writes Barbara Ehrenreich, but sometimes its troops show up when people are merely having a good time.[93]

The gathering of non-consumers (or minimal consumers) is generally identifiable by its free admission. Such non-spending crowds are expendable because of their economic irrelevance. Given half a chance, officials will cancel a massive celebration of this kind in advance. San Francisco's Castro district was declared a no-party zone for Halloween in 2007, following violence among the hundreds of thousands of revelers who attended the event the year before. How does one cancel a traditional, unsponsored public event? In this case, parking in the area was banned, public transit diverted, and hundreds of cops walked the neighborhood's streets. It worked, though many would-be partygoers groused and some protested in costume by carrying a cardboard coffin up Market Street, chanting an invitation for one and all to "mourn the death of Castro Halloween."[94]

No one wants to be stabbed or shot, of course, but some degree of violence was always in the mix of drinking, dancing, and singing of traditional carnival.[95] For that matter, some degree of violence will occur in a city of hundreds of thousands any night, though most of it will take place behind closed doors. One need not revert to the slaughter of the Bacchists by Roman authorities in 186 BCE to conclude that fear of collective abandon is nothing new. Representatives of the existing hierarchy tend to see Dionysian spontaneity as a threat—and to act accordingly. Western history includes a long series of efforts to suppress, control, transmute, or co-opt the energy of mass celebrations. By the seventeenth century, religious zealots were attacking every paganish element of popular culture, not just festivals but magic, fortune-telling, short dresses, Morris dancers and their hobby horse, masquerades, and the Satanic maypole.[96] Carnival became the gates of hell in John Bunyan's *Pilgrim's Progress.* Puritan austerity "turned with all its force against one thing: the spontaneous enjoyment of life."[97] Suppression of popular traditions of the kind enjoyed by crowds continued over three centuries (the sixteenth into the nineteenth), affecting almost all of Europe. Even in the Catholic south, festivity was demoted from mass revelry to public processions of holy relics.[98]

The energy behind the effort to drive a stake through carnival and similar celebrations came not only from Calvinists and Counter-Reformationists but from military commanders and the new industrialists. Whether they needed men for firing muskets or members of the entire family to work the factory looms, both wanted a year-round disciplined force, undistracted by numerous holidays. Gunpowder had made the warrior skills of the European nobility obsolete. Nobles became courtiers, discovered manners, and turned into models of gentility and decorum for the burgeoning middle class.[99] At least in public, they stopped taking Dionysus's calls. Festival became "part of the family's private life."[100] All this was part of America's European legacy.

At issue here is something more important than live entertainment in a public place. As historian Rebecca Solnit has written, there is a "continuum between promenades, parades, festivals, and uprisings." All require people "who are at home in their civic space" and not just in their private lairs.[101] At stake is the difference between the possibility of crowds sometimes making history and a consumer society under comprehensive management. San Francisco's latest plan to manage Halloween would replace the spontaneous revelry of the Castro district with a highly organized, multifaceted, and expensive event in a stadium parking lot.[102]

CRACKING DOWN ON DISSIDENTS

Although the demonstration has all but replaced the riot as a means of expressing common grievances in the United States, authorities have often responded to the nonviolent march or rally as though it threatened national security. There was "Coxey's army" of jobless men, denied a Washington, D.C., parade permit and routed by federal troops on May Day, 1894.[103] There were the Oakland police who fired wooden bullets, stinger grenades, and bean bags into a peaceful crowd of antiwar demonstrators on the Oakland docks on 2003. And there were plenty of similar incidents in between. Some have resulted in fatalities. The conflation of collective dissent against the existing order with massive attack upon the existing order becomes especially tempting in time of crisis. Shortly after the September 11 attacks, demonstrators opposing practices of the World Trade Organization (WTO) and International Monetary Fund (IMF) were accused of "seeking to advance their political agenda through intimidation, which is a classic goal of terrorism."[104] Is that what the big anti-WTO demonstration of two years earlier, the so-called Battle of Seattle, had been about? Let's see what massive intimidation looks like at ground level.

Following months of organizing by anti-globalization activists and probably special training by the police, the day of protest arrived with the heavily armed and armored police arraying their forces defensively in front of the WTO meeting site. They were obviously determined to keep demonstrators away from it. They had also closed nearby streets to cars, and local businesses seemed to have taken a holiday. This left the surrounding downtown area to the demonstrators, who responded by taking over several intersections. Each became a crowded world of its own, the mood largely determined by its relationship with the police. Where the latter were drawn up in menacing ranks confronting demonstrators, the atmosphere was tense. Where they were absent, a carnival spirit prevailed, with costumed people banging drums and blowing horns to set up a ruckus.

A large ring of sitters had formed at one of the intersections that was receiving scant attention by the police. WTO delegates were not to be allowed within, and people were dancing in this liberated space to highly amped sounds. Along came a camera crew, explaining to some of the sitters that their cordon would have to be breached to accommodate an interview with the "Belgian Minister," coming up behind them with a well-shod coterie. The sitters refused to budge. The interview would have to be conducted over their heads. A charming man, the minister then interviewed one of the young female sitters.

"Does that hurt?" he asked, pointing to her multiple facial piercings.

"Oh, no," she replied. "Would you like to dance?"

At another intersection, a demonstrator had just been pepper-sprayed. His face was a mass of red blotches, but he seemed to be ecstatic, as if he had just gotten his wings. By and large, the demonstration consisted of thousands of people standing in the street, waiting for something to happen. Many broke for lunch, filling in for the usual noontime crowd in nearby cafes where staff seemed happy to accommodate them. The stand-off continued into the afternoon when large contingents of organized workers marched into the area. Most did not stick around for long. Replacing them in exuberance though certainly not in numbers came the Seattle Antifascist Marching Band.

By four o'clock or so clouds of tear gas were swirling through the streets and police concussion bombs were going off in terrific blasts. Demonstrators were moving out of the area, as the police steadily regained it. Leaving, one heard the sickening crunch of glass, as what became some controversial rocks found plate-glass windows of high-rise representatives of Corporate America. Nobody cheered, except silently perhaps. Someone observed that a little broken glass was necessary to put some fear into the heads of the ruling class. A more extreme version of this position holds that "protest isn't protest if it doesn't threaten the established order."[105] But those broken windows more likely put some joy into the heads of members of the ruling class, for the shattered glass became a media hook defining the event. As Michael Parente has said, "The system makes the protester the issue."[106] In any case, the few who attacked property put everyone at risk of police violence.

That evening, as the police began rounding up anyone they could find on certain streets, a local TV channel showed a WTO delegate punching his way through demonstrators' ranks. Another pulled a pistol on the sitters in his path. Many demonstrators came down with severe flu-like symptoms—attributed by some to the various airborne chemicals used by the police—and so were not among the hundreds arrested and held overnight on buses, without restroom privileges, before being put in cells. But they had succeeded in delaying the start of the WTO proceedings, and many took credit for the subsequent breakdown in negotiations over world trade and investment rules. Their assumption was not that massive "intimidation" had worked but that the demonstration had inspired representatives of poorer nations to refuse to sign on to the trade and investment concessions demanded by the corporate giants and their front men.[107]

The guardians of public order saw the Battle of Seattle as a lesson in crowd control, and they evidently vowed not to be outmaneuvered by protesters again, even for a day. Subsequent WTO meetings were held in remote locations, such as Qatar. The 82nd Airborne Division was on alert at Fort Bragg, North Carolina, during the 2000 Republican convention in Philadelphia.[108] Protesters arriving in Miami to oppose private meetings intended to draw up a Free Trade Area of the Americas (FTAA) in November 2003 were greeted by "a militarized police force . . . sporting tazers [Tasers, the controversial stun-gun], electrified shields, rubber bullets, chemical weapons, and a $9.1 million security budget."[109] At the 2004 Democratic National Convention, Boston police and the Office of Homeland Security tried to confine protesters to a "Free-Speech Zone" consisting of a cage lined with razor wire. Just in case things got out of hand, the security presence included Blackhawk helicopters, military snipers, Coast Guard and Navy gunboats, and more than ten thousand heavily armed cops.[110] National political conventions provide an opportunity "for federal agencies to test their latest and most sophisticated technology," says a *New York Times* report.[111]

As for the Republican National Convention of 2004, which was held in New York, hundreds of thousands of would-be protesters were met by forty thousand police, who arrested over 1,800 of them for assembling in public streets, locked them up in a building that was polluted by toxic chemicals, denied them access to lawyers and medical care, and held them until the convention was over. Police in St. Paul did not even wait for protesters to take to the streets in the days leading up to the Republican National Convention of 2008. Guns drawn, they raided a planning site and the homes of activists, detaining dozens, arresting at least five suspected of conspiring to riot, and confiscating leaflets and equipment. Especially targeted were videographers of police misconduct.[112] Meanwhile, in Los Angeles, police fired rubber bullets into a crowd of immigrant rights demonstrators that included children. They also clubbed demonstrators and journalists, beating a cameraman to the ground.[113] A spokesperson for the L.A.P.D. now concedes that their handling of the situation was "lousy."[114]

When confronted by a large and boisterous crowd, authorities have seldom responded as though handcuffed by people's right to assemble. Impoverished rioters, nonviolent demonstrators, all such en masse manifestations are officially obnoxious when the object is "suppression of the street." As Henry Kissinger wrote of the Tiananmen Square massacre, "No government in the world would have tolerated having the main square of its capital occupied for eight weeks by tens of thousands of demonstrators."[115] What about two weeks? What about an hour? Left to the courts is the task of sorting out any violations of people's rights. In January 2007, a federal jury found that Seattle police had violated the 1999 protesters' constitutional rights by arresting them arbitrarily. The city's insurance company has agreed to settle the claims of 175 people by paying them a million dollars, which means that some veterans of the Battle of Seattle will receive as much as $10,000 each.[116] A year after the Miami protest, none of the 280 people who had been arrested had been convicted of a crime, and only seven cases remained open.[117] (Several busloads of would-be demonstrators had failed to get close enough to the meeting site even to risk arrest. They had been turned away at the Miami city line.) One hundred and twenty demonstrators and pedestrians who were illegally arrested during the massive demonstration against the

World Bank and IMF in September 2002 have settled their claims against Washington for a million dollars.[118] Police Chief Charles Ramsey and other law enforcement officials had conspired to cover up evidence of wrongdoing, such as corralling demonstrators without a warning to disperse.[119] Over 90 percent of the protesters and others swept up by the police and charged with some offense related to the protest of the Republican National Convention of 2004 have had their cases dismissed or received not-guilty verdicts following trials.[120] A judge has found the city guilty of contempt.

Discussing the "formidable" crowds of American cities in the Jacksonian era, Tocqueville had recommended a national police force to keep them under control. But in the Posse Comitatus Act of 1878 and other traditional restraints, the United States government has faced legal limits on the domestic use of military force, limitations that American presidents had sometimes sought to brush aside. Now a little-known amendment to the Defense Authorization Act of 2007 (Section 1042) brings us a big step closer to Tocqueville's idea. Under the amendment, which was buried in the massive bill without discussion or debate, the president may use military troops, including the National Guard, as a domestic police force in the event of a natural disaster, disease outbreak, terrorist attack, or any "other condition" that the executive determines is beyond the capacity of a state to bring under control. Such federal intervention no longer requires the consent of the governor or local authorities. The heading of the *New York Times* lead editorial of February 17, 2007, describes the impact: "Making Martial Law Easier."[121]

But a militarized approach to crowd control has been ongoing. Since the heyday of the racial ghetto riot when the National Guard was used to put down civil disorders hundreds of times, the Department of Defense has arranged an enormous transfer of military weaponry—machine pistols, flash-bang grenades, armored personnel carriers, and much else—to paramilitary units of local police departments, especially SWAT teams. Applying military rules of engagement and overwhelming force, these units play an ever-expanding role in day-to-day policing.[122]

Such new police technology, not to mention the First Amendment of the Constitution, is supposed to provide a humane alternative to the traditional practice of firing live ammunition into an unruly crowd. But more humane does not mean harmless. The Taser has been implicated in so many deaths—280 in the United States since 2001, according to one estimate—that Amnesty International had already urged suspension of its use when a newer and, for crowds, more ominous version of the device was introduced.[123] The eXtended Range Electromuscular Projectile (XREP) uses shotgun shells, enabling police to stun people from a greater distance.[124] The wooden bullets, stinger grenades, etc., fired by police at nonviolent Oakland protesters in 2003 caused over sixty injuries, some of them severe and permanent. Most of the injured were shot in the back while trying to escape the cops.[125] The crowd of protesters had done nothing to provoke the assault, nor (according to many witnesses) had the police even given warning. Police videos and television footage have belied the city's claim that demonstrators threw things at the officers before they opened fire and that they were blocking shipping terminal gates.[126] A United Nations report cited the incident "as one of the most egregious abuses of human rights by any country that year."[127]

While political organizers have been using the Internet, crowd control technologists have been developing a machine that produces 120 decibels of sound.[128] A new military weapon called the Active Denial System or "pain ray" fires millimetric waves that cause the kind of agony one would expect from having a hot iron pressed against the flesh. Charles Heal, an expert on nonlethal weapons, calls it the "Holy Grail of crowd control," although an op-ed piece argues against its deployment, lest it be used someday on American troops or maybe even *by* American troops against American dissidents or unruly crowds.[129] Indeed. With "nonlethal" weapons causing multiple injuries and deaths, a researcher at the University of California, Berkeley—home of the Free Speech Movement—is attempting to develop a truly nonlethal projectile. But there is concern regarding the effectiveness of such a device: "If the shots just bounced off people, they'd backfire as crowd control."[130]

Just as the Pentagon equips our military, at enormous public expense, to fight the conventional warfare of decades past, it appears that our crowd control regime has geared itself to combat the rioters of forty years ago.[131] Not that anyone would dispute that use of crowd control technology which has the potential to cause widespread discomfort and injury without great risk of killing anyone is more humane than firing bullets into a crowd. But there are better ways of dealing with a small number of people throwing rocks and bottles, as some crowd members did in the recent Los Angeles incident, than attacking the entire crowd. Big-city police have shown again and again that they cannot be counted on to deal with dissident or even festive crowds with proper judgment and restraint. Unless we welcome foreclosure of the possibility of massive celebration or mass protest, the proliferation of gadgets for crowd control is nothing to cheer about, nor is legislation that facilitates martial law. Insofar as Americans regard mass protest as an irritating tactic of "protesters," rather than a hard-won citizens' right and occasional necessity, they will respond to these developments with only a shrug. But perhaps the workers' occupation of a Chicago factory to prevent its closure in December 2008 and some recent blockades of residential evictions portend something different. More on this in chapter 8.

CROWDS OF DISASTER

Authorities are chronically suspicious of the spontaneously forming crowd whose members cannot be classed as corporate customers. Such crowds must be dispersed if not controlled. In time of disaster, a regime of crowd control gets in the way of needed help. Whether natural or man-made, a disaster tends to force people out of their homes and into the street. With a militarized response to social chaos, help is the last thing people will get. New Orleans flood victims who went to the Superdome were made to wait outside in the rain for hours while authorities searched them for weapons. Once inside they were trapped by the thousands in the unrelieved heat, wading in sewage amid decomposing bodies. All the things that should have been supplied in advance—food, potable water, sandbags, fuel for generators, satellite phones, portable toilets, buses, boats, and helicopters—were in short supply, and the Federal Emergency Management Agency (FEMA) was not even answering its phones.[132] As for local government, the city's "idea of disaster preparedness [had been] passing out DVDs telling people that if a hurricane came, they should get out of town."[133] No wonder those displaced by the flood waters had to wait for days to get relief.[134]

Outside the sweltering and ill-equipped shelters, hundreds spent a close-pressed night of terror on a freeway overpass. In congressional testimony, a survivor told of going without food or water for days while people nearby died of dehydration. While the poor have often borne the brunt of past disasters, in the case of Katrina military personnel cut off escape routes by training their weapons on members of the desperate crowd.[135] Some police officers allegedly did more than that, firing into a knot of people huddled on a bridge, killing two and wounding four, some severely. Seven New Orleans cops have been charged with first-degree murder or attempted murder.[136]

A Katrina survivor tells of her futile efforts to get drinking water from a fire station and other emergency personnel. "So many army trucks driving past," but none stopped to offer help. The only relief available was in "people helping people . . . to survive."[137] Adds another survivor, "It was more of a security presence than it was 'let's help these residents.'"[138] "People felt they were in an occupied city!" exclaims a Katrina survivor in Spike Lee's *When the Levees Broke.* Private security forces whose company got the first of the federal government's no-bid contracts were allowed to circulate through black neighborhoods, ready to fire their M-16s at anyone suspected of looting.[139] The cost of such private contracts, which a congressional study found were "plagued by waste, fraud, abuse or mismanagement," amounted to $8.75 billion as of August 2006.[140]

A recent lawsuit filed by the son of a ninety-one-year-old woman who died in her wheelchair alleges that police forced the two to join other flood victims at the Convention Center where there was neither food, water, nor medical supplies, as bodies piled up around the inside perimeter. It was not the storm that killed her but the rescue, says her son.[141] Meanwhile, less than half a mile away, staff members and guests of the Royal Sonesta Hotel enjoyed luxurious meals, "eating like kings," as if participating in an allegory of America's maldistribution of goods and burdens.[142] Residents of New Orleans' affluent Audubon Place district hired Instinctive Shooting International, an Israeli firm, to provide guards, brought by helicopter and armed with machine guns, to protect their mansions.[143] To judge by what happened in New Orleans and its sequelae, we can assume that future disaster relief will come first to those with the ability to pay for it. Help Jet of West Palm Beach touts itself as a "hurricane escape plan that turns hurricane evacuation into a jet-setter vacation." With the approach of a major storm, Help Jet will book an upscale getaway for subscribers. "No standing in line," the company promises, "no hassle with crowds, just a first-class experience."[144] A selling point may have been the millions of people in South Florida left standing in enormous lines for basic supplies or sitting in their cars in mile-long buildups for rationed gasoline in their effort to survive Hurricane Wilma, which struck that area a few weeks after Katrina. Absent electric power, many lacked the means to comply with the recommendation of authorities to boil tap water. A photo accompanying the news item shows police officers attempting to shut the gates of the Orange Bowl against the crush of a crowd, desperate to obtain some of the fast-diminishing (or exhausted) supplies of water and ice inside.[145]

A major disaster should provide some lessons in disaster prevention, not just inspire a marketing scheme for privatized relief. However, New Orleans remains "in as much peril [of flooding] as before," despite repair work on the levees.[146] The Superdome has been refurbished, the costs paid for in part by $94 million from FEMA, while garbage continues to clog the streets and a good part of the rest of the city "remains shuttered."[147] In San Francisco, only the absence of a strong wind following the Loma Prieta earthquake of 1989 prevented a disastrous fire. The city is even more flammable now than it was when destroyed by fire in 1906, in the view of some.[148] As for the threat of terrorism, the Department of Homeland Security's list of potential targets of terrorist attacks has grown to eighty thousand, with Indiana having more than any other state, nearly three times as many as California. The DHS had decided that an earlier version of the list had too many large-scale gathering sites like stadiums and arenas, the department's attitude apparently being, let the crowds look out for themselves. The revised list includes petting zoos, doughnut shops, ice cream parlors, and popcorn stands.[149]

7. Safe Crowds

The victims of the kind of crowds that bloodied American history were typically, though certainly not always, members of racial and ethnic minorities. The actual or symbolic descendants of those killer crowds seek residential frontiers that are as far removed as possible from people who are visibly or culturally different than they. The benign crowd spaces of suburban life have accommodated their fears until recently. But now, for shopping and entertainment forays, some venture into made-over urban environments where they can feel almost as secure as they do in the suburban mall. We begin by examining the kind of crowd space from which their forebears fled.

THE LATE DOWNTOWN

When Nietzsche called the nineteenth century "the century of the crowd,"[1] he surely had in mind the central districts of Europe's largest cities. These were so filled with people that some found a new kind of home within the multitude, feeding off its energy and taking refuge in the anonymity to be found there. The urban crowd was addictive, "the newest drug for the solitary" and an "asylum for the reprobate" (this from Baudelaire, emphasis omitted).[2] Such crowds were a drastic departure from most human experience of past centuries. Compared with the social form that characterized all but fairly recent human life, the clan of hunter-gatherers in which everyone had a relationship with everybody else,[3] and compared with the kind of community that could still be found in less populous settings at the end of "the century of the crowd," social contacts in the city were brief and rare.[4] Georg Simmel observed that before they began using buses, trains, and streetcars, people had rarely been in situations where they could look at others without talking to them.[5] Those using such conveyances, as well as people on the city sidewalks, were pretty much all strangers to one another, as we are in such settings today. This made the city exhilarating and perhaps a little frightening. If people's only link to others so often consisted of a monetary transaction, this at least gave them "inner protection . . . against the overcrowded proximity."[6]

Whereas the streets of London served as habitat for Poe's crowd addict,[7] American cities too had their close-pressed multitudes, the United States being "more heavily urbanized than almost any nation on earth."[8] For Walt Whitman, whose poems were intended "to define America" for foreigners, the crowd was a rolling ocean in which one might momentarily glimpse her own true love.[9] The Horatio Alger books were popular not only for their model of individual success through persistent effort, but they also served as "effortless guidebooks" on how to adjust to living in New York.[10] Between 1870 and 1925 (the approximate beginning and end of the second great wave of immigration), Americans came to see themselves as "inhabiting a culture of crowds."[11] Even in Los Angeles, which has gone far to demonstrate that a thriving city does not really need a center, about half the city's residents went downtown every day well into the 1920s.[12] By then, the central area of American cities had long since shed its middle-class residents due to rising real estate values and the easy access to outlying neighborhoods made possible by streetcars and, later, private vehicles. Manufacturers and warehouses had also moved out, lured by cheaper and more plentiful land on the periphery. But residential dispersal soon began presenting downtown merchants with competition, as chain stores moved into outer neighborhoods.[13]

Robert Fogelson exhaustively recounts how, when the American downtown ceased to be a place of residence except for the poorer few, it became a place of horrendous traffic jams, especially when shoppers and workers stopped using crowded streetcars and began driving their own cars downtown.[14] As a Los Angeles planner moaned, "Every possible cure . . . seems to be worse than the original disease."[15] Congestion remedies included widening sidewalks, one-way streets, right-turn only lanes, elevated highways, the list goes on and on with each improvement bringing more and more vehicles downtown where their drivers found diminishing space in which to park. Fearing loss of business, powerful downtown interests consistently opposed any real solution to the problem of downtown congestion, such as a ban on private, non-commercial vehicles. Instead, property owners began replacing buildings with parking lots, and cities sought more turnover of parking opportunities (and more revenue) by installing parking meters. The freeway was intended to answer, once and for all, the problem of access to downtown.[16]

Still, despite the noise, the grit, and the congestion of the typical big-city downtown, many people went there every day to shop and work. They often stayed for nighttime entertainment, too. As late as 1940, one might have joined a three-deep throng that ranged along a block of San Francisco's Market Street to watch the progress of a street-repair crew.[17] Into the 1940s, streetcars connected downtown Los Angeles to outlying locales. In short, until the middle of the twentieth century, people saw the downtown as the heart of the city. Its noise was the city's heartbeat and the flow of cash into its stores and banks its lifeblood. The bustling streets gave political dissidents, street preachers, and anyone else who hoped to win converts without the expense of hiring a hall a ready-made audience. By comparison, the metaphorical crowd reached by a blog or broadcast email tends to be made up of self-selected readers.

On the periphery of downtown was the crowded urban neighborhood. When the narrator of a film shown at the 1939 World's Fair asked whether Americans could continue to afford the disorder of such neighborhoods "where Mr. and Mrs. Zero cannot move until another does," many viewers were no doubt ready to agree that an alternative would be nice, especially the kind of alternative presented by the film. The projected garden city, planned and publicly subsidized, would preserve the conviviality of existing city neighborhoods while avoiding "urban chaos."

"The choice is yours," the narrator offered.[18] But his tone warned fair-going viewers not to make the wrong choice. In fact, the choice was already being made by private investors and developers, with the help of the Federal Housing Authority (FHA). The film was propaganda for what was already in the works. Of course, its viewers could not have foreseen what unpacking the downtown would mean for them as workers, residents, commuters, and shoppers.

The new crowd spaces developed after the Second World War sidestepped both the phantasmagoria of the metropolitan downtown and the kind of place in which the entire white population can conspire to commit murder. They also tended to exclude, at least at first, the kind of people who had served as the mob's victims. One should not look to the spaces of the postwar multitude to find a crowd with a common purpose—for example, protesters, rioters, members of a volunteer project, or the assemblies of self-rule. The crowds of the new crowd space are generally unmotivated, like the crowds of crowded streets: asocial, connected only by physical proximity, and competitive. Their members compete for goods, viewpoints (in the stadium, for example), spatial advantages (on the freeway, etc.), and seating (for airline flights, etc.).

And though these atomized crowd members sometimes collide, they are generally compliant, making such crowds relatively safe.All such new space is characterized by its generic nature, its indifference to local particularities and geography. Much of it displays the brands of large corporations. It tends to be convenient, familiar, and functional, and its domain is spreading throughout the world under American influence.

Easily accessible to anyone with a car and credit card, the new space puts up practical barriers to entry by the very poor. But the poor have their own crowd spaces, to be discussed. At this juncture, many of the denizens of the new crowd spaces seem to long for the bustle of the downtown of ages past. This has created a market for suburban developments with urban touches (the New Urbanism) and resulted in the "bum-proofing" of the most attractive zones of urban public space in order to attract tourists and suburban shoppers.

RESIDENTIAL DISPERSAL

The story of suburbanization in the United States is sufficiently familiar that I will touch on it only lightly here. Americans who could do so had already, in the 1930s and 1940s, begun moving out of the country's urban centers "at a pace unmatched anywhere else in the world."[19] Zoning laws systematically separated living space from commercial space, so that the newly built suburbs to which Americans moved in unprecedented numbers after the Second World War left them far from stores, theaters, and restaurants, as well as from friends and relatives. This process did not happen by chance. Through the National Housing Act of 1949, Veterans Administration home loans, and tax-deductible mortgage interest, the federal government employed taxpayers' dollars to subsidize a landscape of new housing. Suburbanization meant a thinning of residential populations, as the mortgage insurance program was limited to single-family detached homes. Members of a species that had always lived in groups were now isolated as members of nuclear families, each with its father-breadwinner, mother-housewife, and one or more children. In contrast to the traditional farm family, which functioned as a productive unit, the isolated suburban family was susceptible to the commodity culture promoted by major media and became a consuming unit.[20] The woman of the family, usually a mother and housewife with "a psychological compulsion to visit department stores," was especially vulnerable to the promise that the gap between her emotional needs and a family-centered life could "be filled . . . by the acquisition of consumer goods."[21]

Eligible families saw the official bias that made for suburban sprawl as a tremendous boon: nobody wants a noisy neighbor overhead or on the other side of a wall. Much less does anyone wish to live next door to a factory, even if he works there.[22] In 1950, thirty thousand prospective buyers showed up on the first day that homes went on sale in Lakewood, a big Southern California development. Twenty thousand more came every weekend for months, busying the thirty-six salesmen, who worked in shifts.[23] This home-buying frenzy was accompanied by some serious social costs. Besides trapping women inside the suburban home, there was loss of the kind of sociability represented by the neighborhood block party. Residential transformation also meant a loss of potential for social diversity. The FHA did not interpret its 1936 proviso that "properties shall continue to be occupied by the same social and racial classes" as requiring racial integration of the newly built suburban developments. In fact, until 1949 the agency refused mortgage insurance for racially integrated housing; it did not require nondiscrimination pledges from loan applicants until 1962.[24] The Levittown development was typical in presenting buyers with the kind of homeowners clause that read, "No dwelling shall be used or occupied by members of other than the Caucasian Race," domestic servants excepted, of course.[25] Banks and real estate agents also abetted white flight, as did the racial integration of public schools required by *Brown v. Board of Education* (1954). White parents could avoid sending their children to racially mixed schools simply by doing what they were already inclined to do—move to the white suburbs.

A former Lakewood public information officer wrote of that instant city's residents, "They were fairly but not entirely homogenous in their ethnic background."[26] Into the 1990s, a resident could say of the recent Los Angeles riots, "We're far away from that element."[27] Racial fears were only a part of the story, certainly. The postwar baby boom meant more people seeking bigger homes in proximity to the best public schools they could find. For the breadwinners of many of the families that took up residence in Lakewood, the move included a job at nearby McDonnell Douglas or one of the other big military contractors in the area. Residential dispersal and the home ownership that typically came with it deepened the racial divide of the working class and persuaded white workers that they had gained admission to the middle class.[28]

The urban freeways included in the National Interstate and Defense Highway System were intended to shrink some of the distances created by suburbanization. Millions still use them to get to jobs at today's dispersed worksites, of course, but in retrospect it appears that the freeway's basic function has been to take crowds out of cities, scatter their constituents into suburbs, and gather them again in shopping malls and office parks, bypassing all the smaller towns along the older routes. Easy freeway access to proliferating shopping malls eliminated any inducement for the new suburbs to include the hotels and restaurants of the earlier railroad suburbs.[29] Suburbanites had no need of a downtown, or so they thought. Boarded storefronts and the wasteland of empty parking lots display the crowd-dispersing impact of these developments on Main Streets and once-thriving city centers across the land.

The urban poor, especially blacks, were left behind in "chocolate" or "salt and pepper" cities. By 1968, 56 percent of non-white families lived in central cities, two-thirds of them in blighted neighborhoods with substandard housing.[30] New York City experienced a population decline in the 1950s, despite (and, in part, because of) an influx of Puerto Ricans and impoverished blacks from the South.[31] Redevelopment, subsidized by taxpayers under the National Housing Act of 1949, wiped out many poor but often vibrant neighborhoods, replacing them with crime-ridden housing "projects," freeways, corporate office buildings, expensive condos and apartments, and, eventually, entertainment complexes designed to lure suburban spenders back to town, if only for an afternoon.[32] This process has generated much contention. With ongoing "gentrification" and community-destroying private developments (often financed by public dollars), the struggle for control of urban space is in no way confined to the past. As Henri Lefebre wrote, it is "struggle alone which prevents abstract space from taking over the whole planet and papering over all differences."[33]

The dispersive trend continues as today's frontiersmen (and women), the new exurbanites, move so far out into the open spaces of former farmland that they have to drive two or three hours a day to get to work and back, typically behind the wheel of a tank-like SUV. Mike Davis points out that it is probably no coincidence that SUVs came on the market "at the moment when 'carjackings' and freeway shootings dominated prime-time news" and many suburbanites were taking up residence in heavily guarded, gated developments.[34] "I definitely feel safe here," says Lisa Crawford of New River, Florida. "I feel protected."[35] Residents of these crime-free, fast-growing communities voted heavily for the fear-promoting George W. Bush in 2004, whereas voters in the nation's cities, where 13 percent of Americans prefer to live, consistently favor more laid-back Democrats.[36]

Most Americans live in the suburbs, a little closer to an urban core. The advantages of suburbia, like those of exurbia, include the feeling of greater personal safety. "I think community is where people feel safe," opines a pastor in Orange County, California's most suburbanized area.[37] People feel optimally secure, however, in a milieu that tends to exclude the community and makes the world outside appear more threatening than it really is—namely, their own private homes with all the doors and windows locked. Declares the environmentalist son of a major Orange County developer about his father's developments and the like: "These are places that people go to so they don't have to be around whatever they deem undesirable."[38] At this point, the bursting of the housing bubble and the accompanying epidemic of foreclosures has begun to turn some erstwhile residential havens into crime-ridden suburban slums.

One of the consequences of fear of the collective Other is an electoral eagerness to install authorities who will place additional barriers between them and us. The United States now has the largest prison population and the highest rate of incarcerations in the world. Criminal confinements at all levels now stand at over 2.3 million, up from around 330,000 in 1972. Counting the additional five million or so who are on probation or parole, over 3 percent of the American population has gotten caught up in the corrections system. Does this reflect a surge in crime? No, increased crime accounts for only 12 percent of the increase in incarcerations. The remaining 88 percent is attributable to harsher sentencing carried out at the behest of elected officials who have promised to get tough on crime. No doubt the politics of law and order has taken some violent criminals off the streets, but it has also filled our prisons and jails with nonviolent drug offenders and people convicted of nonviolent crimes against property.[39] Because of selective law enforcement, as well as selective drug laws such as those that anathematize crack cocaine, and because of the targeting of urban gangs, the bulk of the prison and jail population consists not only of people of color but of people who come from inner cities where they tended to occupy that part of the public realm often referred to as "the street." In effect, we have jailed a large part of the contemporary version of the city mob (discussed in chapter 1). All too obviously, our mobs lack the patronage of a prince.

CAR COMMUTERS

The typical resident of even the most heavily gated, invitation-only development has to venture out into the world five or so days a week to get to work. This means joining a crowd that people who get around by other means would find unnerving, to say the least—a mobile crowd encased in individual bubbles of steel, plastic, glass, and rubber. In contrast to the social solidarity of, say, the pilgrimage, the daily commute brings travelers together only as numerous drivers, each with a unique destination, taking a common route. The crucial space between one's vehicle and those surrounding it is analogous to the social distance that people of a century ago found they needed to maintain in order to function adequately in the giant metropolis—no friendly greetings and no eye contact.[40] The motor vehicle adds matter to psychic armor: a lapse of attention can result in a collapse of a driver's physical margins, resulting in a freeway pile-up. Thus we are aware of other members of this crowd only as the source of frustrations and hazards. Yet a *New York Times* reporter recently found something like community on the Los Angeles freeways, even comparing the vast transport system to a giant public plaza. The drivers she observed were so polite: they did not honk, they made assiduous use of turn signals, and they maintained proper distance between cars, as if they had all gone to driver finishing school. Los Angelenos were driving scared, at the time, shaken by a series of freeway shootings. No one wanted to risk offending an unknown sniper.[41]

Driving is an asocial act, and not just because while behind the wheel we may call other people names that we might never call them to their face. Eighty-eight percent of those who drive to work drive alone.[42] Huck Finn's determination "to light out for the territory ahead of the rest" has shriveled to the twice-a-day necessity of car commuters to wedge their way into the slowly moving mass of other vehicles. Our experience is the opposite of members of species that have to travel greater distances in search of food because of living in large groups.[43] For refusing to live in large groups, many Americans suffer the long commute. Lewis Mumford said of spatial development in the United States after the Second World War, "The end product is an encapsulated life, spent more and more either in a motor car or within the cabin of darkness before a television set."[44]

Even with gasoline prices climbing above affordable levels, the long-distance commute will seem for many a reasonable price to pay to avoid living in proximity to people they perceive as unlike themselves. Some may while away the miles listening to the fulminations of a hate radio host regarding the "Mexican invasion," which has recently become such an inviting target.[45] Just as for Le Bon the physical gathering was, ultimately, symbolic of what he feared the most, the crowd to be avoided by many American exurbanites has a name and address in the urban ghettos of race, ethnicity, and class. Other crowds, the crowds of America's freeways, shopping malls, airports, and stadiums, may cause irritation, but they do not inspire fear.

SHOPPERS

A shoppers' advocate maintains that "getting and spending has become the most passionate, and often most imaginative, endeavor of modern life."[46] Modern *American* life, that is. Americans spend more time shopping than anyone else, three or four times as much as Europeans. This difference is not a matter of national character. Americans of an earlier age found identity as producers, not consumers. They were farmers, miners, loggers, fishermen, or simply workers. Upward mobility meant owning one's land or tools, maybe even opening a small enterprise. What their descendants mainly got, after the Second World War, was the chance to own their own homes, in the form of title to a mortgaged house. Easy credit and the postwar boom brought a lot of goods within reach, and "people increasingly sought self-realization not through work they controlled but through the things they could buy."[47] As Americans learned that the value of their work was congealed in the goods and services they could buy after work, thrift became "un-American."[48]

Whether or not the consumer society represented a major transformation or merely an extension of the existing system of production [49] (with consumer dreams standing in for the expanding markets formerly provided by imperialism), by the early 1980s the director of New York's South Street Seaport Museum could declare that "shopping is the chief cultural activity in the United States."[50] That he was the head of a museum that doubles as a shopping center does not invalidate his remark. But what could be more natural than what Adam Smith referred to as the human "propensity to truck, barter, and exchange"? Why question an activity that sustains the economy and seems to make people happy?

Let us look at some history. The market was one of the original elements of the city, but traditional markets also occurred periodically, independently of cities.[51] The European marketplace of the Middle Ages and Renaissance was an important site of folk culture, which had its time in feasts and fairs.[52] In Mexican villages today, people come to the market not only to buy and sell but to gossip, be entertained, flirt, and engage in "all the other diversions that make life worth living."[53] Though our local farmers' market may seem a refreshing alternative to the supermarket, a place where one may chat with some of the vendors and run into an acquaintance or two, it hardly compares with the lively milieu of the traditional marketplace, where a shopper might have encountered everyone she knew.

The traditional market and today's typical shopping experience, whose setting is the mall, stand at opposite ends of a social continuum. As Robert Putnam wrote, the mall is not about "connecting with others, but about privately surfing from store to store—in the presence of others."[54] Those other shoppers are our competitors, though this fact may be veiled under ordinary conditions of adequate supplies. The people who camp overnight in line outside a big box store for the post-Thanksgiving rush or begin their "Black Friday" shopping at midnight, when some stores open, are certainly aware of this relationship. Shopping the day after Thanksgiving goes with "being a good American," declares one such camper. He finds "glory" in snapping up a sale item before another shopper can get to it.[55] A photo that accompanied an article on post-Thanksgiving shopping in 2005 showed a pile-up of bodies on the floor of a Wal-Mart in Puyallup, Washington, occasioned by the competition to buy one of thirty-two laptops that went on sale at 5 a.m. Another depiction of retail chaos shows a Sunrise, Florida, woman trying to help a fallen septuagenarian while other people step over and push past this obstacle in their shopping path.[56] In 2006, short supplies of the new PlayStation 3 game system made for long overnight lines when the product finally became available. Some waited outside stores for days; the police fired pepper pellets into one unruly crowd; people were trampled in a parking lot; and in some locations, robbers attacked successful shoppers when they emerged from stores.[57] All just part of being good Americans, it seems. As David Hume wrote two and a half centuries ago, "Throw any considerable goods among men, they instantly fall a quarrelling, while each strives to get possession of what pleases him, without regard to the consequences."[58] With scarce supplies and high demand, the hard-won purchase becomes a trophy for valor in combat.

There are fascinating theories as to why we shop as much as we do and what our purchases mean. For some, shopping is a self-soothing activity, a means of warding off depression or despair,[59] even a way of distracting oneself from existential fears.[60] When people speak glibly of "retail therapy," they acknowledge that consumer needs have come to represent unstated (and perhaps insatiable) desires.[61] One did not really need the new Audi A4 he has just driven home from the dealer. He needed transportation, surely, but what he mainly needed was the sense of identity that the car confers. As advertisers have gotten so many of us to believe, "We are what we drive." Identity implies generally recognizable difference: *in the eyes of others*, we are what we drive. And not everyone can afford such a car. Sipping a martini on a jetliner while seated in a roomy first-class seat, a cartoon character muses, "It's not enough that I fly first class . . . my friends must also fly coach."[62]

Thus, unless one shops with friends or relatives, shopping is a social activity only in the sense that it helps gain position in the social hierarchy, thereby reinforcing it. However crowded the store, the individual shopper communes with an imaginary crowd of absent others, wowing them with the new Versace blouse she wonders if she can afford or defying their judgment by refusing to bend to the winds of fashion. Like the downtown crowd, it would take something bizarre or disastrous to cause such a crowd to act as one. But compared to the downtown crowd, the shopping crowd is homogenous, both in terms of function and (what with market segmentation) socioeconomic class. Considering the problems left for future generations, shoppers are *anti*social. It would take the resources and waste capacity of four more planets to keep up with present levels of consumption by North Americans, says the Earth Council.[63]

If, as Juliet Schor has written, "our sense of social standing and belonging comes from what we consume," this is a problem for many.[64] As Schor points out, shopping is no longer a matter of trying to keep up with the Joneses, who used to live next door. Reference groups have been redefined as women have entered the workplace and developed more important contacts than those of the neighborhood. Additionally, watching television has skewed tastes toward the styles of the rich and famous. Schor argues that the growing concentration of wealth and income (now near levels of the late 1920s) has made "visible status spending the order of the day."[65] "The lives of those who 'make it,'" writes one who did, ". . . are presented as models to inspire us all to consume, consume, consume."[66] Such "upscale emulation" means that desires can outrun incomes. In a poll of a decade ago, over 40 percent of adults earning between $50,000 and $100,000 a year agreed with the statement, "I cannot afford to buy everything I really need."[67] Upscale emulation means that "greater consumption by some people imposes costs on others."[68] Bankruptcies increased sevenfold between 1980 and 1998.[69]

As I write, many Americans have reduced or curtailed credit card spending, and mortgage loans are no longer readily available. Consumer spending actually declined during November and December 2008, the most recent holiday shopping season. For 2008 as a whole, consumer spending was at its lowest level since 1961. However, a closer look reveals that the declines of November and December only amounted to about 1 percent for each month, half of December's loss was due to falling prices, and consumer spending for 2008 actually increased, though only by 3.6 percent.[70] Only in an economic system whose health requires endless accumulation and constant growth, pumped up by consumer spending, would such figures reflect an economic crisis. The crisis is real enough for many people, though, and could even portend large-scale reappearance of the kind of mutual-help crowds of the Depression era. Meanwhile, ours remains a consumer society, with no sign of a shopping letup in prime retail centers such as downtown San Francisco.

The traditional market brought people together, but its sociability was incidental to its economic function of drawing people with something to buy to people with something to sell. The buyer-seller relationship was pivotal. In today's marketplace, the seller seems almost absent, embedded in the multimedia environment of a big-box store or the distracting dazzle of the latest mall. At some stores—Wal-Mart, Home Depot, Kroger—there is no need to interact with even a checkout clerk. We can skip the line and use a self-scan machine. Indeed, "where modern consumerism is concerned, human interaction is becoming passé."[71]

By way of comparison, the traveler in South Asia who is in the market for some semiprecious gems may need to spend several hours, spread over two or three days, in the home of a gem dealer, sipping tea and examining the stones that the dealer will bring to light, a few at a time. With completion of their transaction, the gem dealer may offer to take his customer to his friend the tailor, to have some clothing made. Traditional markets "demand a higher level of attention than is required by most modern shopping" and an emotional commitment to each thing bargained for and bought. Thomas Hine concludes this thought by remarking that "nearly every major retail innovation during the last four centuries has attempted to reduce the fatigue and friction of the marketplace."[72] But it was only in the mid-nineteenth century that merchandise was even marked with a price.[73] Most of the transactional streamlining that has shrunk shopping to a relationship with things has occurred in recent decades.

THE MALL

The United States has almost twice as much shopping space per capita as any other large nation.[74] Here let's take a closer look at the preferred environment of the American shopper. The suburban shopping mall is as familiar to most Americans as the freeway that usually serves as its link. Though malls are more diverse than formerly, such spaces have much in common. For example, every mall is tightly controlled. The management will determine its design, allowable colors, hours of operation, standards of admission for businesses, even store names. Any diversity is part of the plan. With its controlled temperature and lighting, the mall is its own special world. William Kowinski, who may hold the world's record for number of malls visited, compares its parking lot to a moat.[75]

Such a controlled environment was anticipated by the glassed-in arcades of Paris in the nineteenth century. The fabricated comforts that we take for granted were a revelation then. Writing in 1840, Eduard Devrient reported that he avoided a shower by slipping into one, where "in bad weather or after dark, when they are lit up bright as day, they offer promenades . . . past rows of glittering shops."[76] The arcades even inspired a futuristic fantasy in which "a person could stroll through the entire city without ever being exposed to the elements," leaving Parisians with no "desire to set foot on the streets of old—which, they often said, were fit only for dogs."[77] Instead of calling his fantasy "Paris in 2000" (*Paris en l'an 2000)*, he might have called it "America in 2000." The author of a recent opinion piece admits to visiting a local mall for its air conditioning, freedom from pedestrian hazards like cars and bicycles, and the possibilities for watching people. He likes the presence of security guards but complains of the proliferation of small vendors, who clog what was formerly unimpeded walking space.[78] For others, the mall provides a place for "shopping as show," for meeting other singles, or just for something to do.[79]

The element of control so characteristic of the mall makes for a sleek environment that shunts one along its various paths until they narrow into lines to sales counters. Even the man who goes there for the air conditioning will "drop 12 to 15 bucks on a couple of meals . . . buy a book or a CD, or duck into a theater for a movie."[80] Those musical sounds he hears may make him feel like dancing or remind him of a vacation or a past romance, depending on the store. Today's "audio architects" tailor music to their client's marketing needs. Such "audio branding" plays a major role in helping a store put on its own daily version of "retail theater." Like the chemical changes induced by drugs, our "response to musical accompaniment is powerful and involuntary."[81] A writer describes this consumer environment par excellence as "a narcotic made of reality itself!"[82] Its sensory inputs comprise "a veritable commercial symphony."[83] But what Foucault called "control by stimulation" does not necessarily imply a lacuna of physical restraint.[84] For those without antennae for subliminal messages, the security guards in some malls are armed.

For all these elements of control, malls differ. They differ in terms of the nature, quality, and price of goods found in their stores, as well as in customer perceptions of their security. Kowinski found that there were people who visited the Chicago area's newer malls to escape the traffic and crime of older ones.[85] A middle-aged visitor to a mall in a suburb of Washington, D.C., explained, "We come here because it has everything we want and nothing we don't want. There aren't any problems with parking, or crowds, or crime, or . . . well, we don't have to say what the other problems are."[86]

Though some malls evidently let in the wrong crowd, many people will choose the mall over any surroundings in public space. Take Ghirardelli Square in San Francisco and its seasonal throngs. Just outside the square are spread spectacular views of the bay. Inside are only restaurants and shops, with the opportunity to stand in line for a scoop or two of ice cream. The families here appear to be vacationers. Presumably, they could be shopping in a similar, probably much larger mall at home. Why do they spend their time in here? One thinks, albeit uncharitably, of the ghoulish throng that mobs the entrance to the mall in *Dawn of the Dead.* "Why do they come here?" one of the characters asks. "They come here by instinct," her companion replies. "This was an important place in their lives."[87] Do tourists go to malls just to put themselves in a familiar setting? Whatever the answer, vacation shopping leads every other travel activity, "hands down." This from a representative of the travel industry.[88] Even for people who escape into the virtual and heavily branded world of Second Life, an online version of society with 12 million role-playing users, a digitized shopping mall is a favorite destination.[89]

Because the cost and risk of opening a business in a mall will likely exclude any independent, locally owned enterprise, the mall is studded with familiar brands and corporate logos. Still, market segmentation makes for a range of differences, as represented, for example, by the Hilltop Mall in Richmond, California, with its numerous shoe stores, sporting goods stores, cheap jewelry stands, and Playland ("Motherhood—It's Hot," says an ad in the window of a women's clothing shop), and the Stanford Shopping Center, fifty miles away, with its open-air produce market and outlets for Louis Vuitton, Cartier, Tiffany, Armani, Eileen Fisher et al. But nobody will mistake either of these big retail packages for the kind of historic downtown that shopping malls have made almost extinct.

THE COMPLIANT CROWDS OF "GENERICA"

The airport houses many of the same corporate outlets that tenant the mall. Though the crowds of travelers are a somewhat heterogeneous lot, the cost of air travel is such that they are far more representative of the suburbs than the city for which the airport is named. Rybczynski errs in comparing the airport to "the harbor or railroad terminus of old" as a city's "major nucleus."[90] The harbor or railroad terminus may have been the city's seed; a city will not be built around an airport, although various manifestations of Corporate America, such as hotel chains, rental car lots, conference centers, and gas stations, will. The air terminal's prime relationship is with others of its kind, as indicated by the schema of the airline's map included in the information in the seat back in front of you as you settle into your assigned seat.

What the mall is to the downtown, driving on an interstate highway is to the earlier experience of being "on the road."[91] Consider the interstate's predecessor. Route 66 went *through* the towns named in the song.[92] The lyrics take the listener from one day's driving destination to the next along the two-lane route from Chicago to Los Angeles, each one a place to stop, look around, hear the region's twang or drawl in a waitress's voice, and maybe spend the night. By contrast, America's superhighways make it possible to drive across the country without ever exiting the freeway's "Comfort Culture," leaving any local peculiarity behind without its even being glimpsed from the high-speed lanes.[93] Though the interstate itself is free of advertising, off-ramps take one into a familiar, heavily branded zone of gas stations, motels, and restaurants. The geographic feature or defining moment of some local past becomes no more than a theme for the newest outlet for nationally advertised goods and services.

Admittedly, the interstate can be considered a crowd space only by a perilous stretch of definition. But its bland uniformity, its functionality, and the corporate colonization of its exit nodes make it of a piece with the mall, the international airport, the office park, and the stadium, some of which constitute prime crowd habitats of the consumer society. Anthropologist Marc Augé has given a name to the kind of built environment that has proliferated since the Second World War, dubbing it "non-place."[94] Whether we call it that or join filmmaker Jim Jarmusch in calling it "generica," the new spaces are ubiquitous, similar, and highly functional.[95] Each is a copy for which there is no original, as though a family of Platonic forms had died and left their many earthbound representatives to carry on. They constitute a world without center and without immediately noticeable differences within each multi-branded genre. When you are in one of these spaces, whether it is a shopping mall, an international airport, or a stadium, in a sense you are in all of them.

Non-place is also the infrastructure of flows—of people (our focus here), goods, capital, and information. If, as Manuel Castells has written, a place is "a locale whose form, function and meaning are self-contained within the boundaries of physical contiguity" non-place is bounded only by capital investment and individual access. It exists everywhere and nowhere.[96] It synergizes with the sounds and images of a media culture that extends throughout the world to provide a persuasive model of capitalism's apparent comforts. The characters of a popular Chinese film, for example, appear amid apartment buildings, subway stations, coffee bars that could be anywhere in the "developed" world.[97] And everywhere within its growing reach, this meta-process crowds out local variations, products, businesses, and cultures, substituting the consumer commodities which bear its brands.[98] Non-place is corporate capitalism's remake of the natural and human environment,[99] the "smooth space of Empire" that Hardt and Negri wrote about.[100]

Moreover, non-place has altered our experience of time and space. Air travel makes this obvious, but there is more to it than that. Where a church or traditional market would fulfill its function only at certain times, the mall exists in an eternal present: open seven days a week and the lights are always on.[101] Inside the airport, too, there is little difference between night and day. The only time that matters on the interstate is the number of minutes or hours that remain between oneself and one's destination, a calculation that assumes the constant speed made possible by that mode of travel. The pace of this alteration of America's built environment has not been so rapid as to exceed middle-class powers of habituation. But the corporate transplant of an IT park in southern India—"not linked to tradition, context, local resources or people"—gives its neighbors and occupants a "surreal feeling of placelessness."[102]

The branded spaces of specialized crowds—the malls, airports, stadiums, and the like—may resemble public places in their crowd-collecting capacities. However, they exist not to attract the general public but to accommodate various kinds of *customers*, serving as heavily managed spaces of consumption. The members of these customer-crowds are psychologically dispersed. They compete for seats, for goods. Such spaces do not serve as sites of collective action but of astounding levels of individual compliance and forbearance. I have mentioned the baseball fans who cheer by the tens of thousands when electronically directed to "MAKE SOME NOISE." The suburbanites who flocked to San Francisco's new downtown mall on Black Friday 2006 had to wait in line to get their cars into a garage; had to wait for a vacant space once they did; had to stand in line for a chance to buy such items as fish tacos, fruit smoothies, lingerie, and $5,000 watches; and had to stand in another line, for women a long line, to use the big mall's only public restroom. The wait was longest for the latest game consoles and other new items in electronic gadgetry. "It's like a mosh pit you get a receipt for," said one survivor of the shopping crush.[103]

What diplomacy is to international relations, a line is to a crowd of people connected only by competition over spatial or temporal priority. The victims of a suddenly cancelled flight may meekly line up to see what the airline will give them instead.[104] Absent the solidarity traditionally associated with being numerous, each passenger will only ask himself rhetorically, "What can *I* do?" Though urged to circulate throughout the special exhibit, art museum visitors bunch up to view each painting in the sequence prescribed by the audio tour, everyone proceeding at the same crawling pace.[105] Some view video clips on the hand-held devices included in the rented "tour," while standing in front of the paintings they have come to see. Lining up for goods has become so engrained in some that theater-going tourists in Manhattan who already have tickets with assigned seats now form long, unnecessary theater lines that begin an hour and a half before the performance.[106]

I mentioned that customers of some stores now use self-scanning machines. Customers are happier scanning their own purchases, say industry researchers. It takes longer, but because we are participating instead of watching a clerk, "it feels like a shorter time."[107] We can print our own airline tickets now, too, saving the airline as much as $2.86 per check-in. Motel guests at some of the larger chains now get to check themselves in. Fast-food outlets are experimenting with customers placing their own orders. North Americans were expected to spend over a half trillion dollars at self-checkout lanes, ticketing kiosks, and various other self-service machines in 2007. NCR Corporation, a manufacturer of self-service technology, is now eyeing the health care market.[108] Fortunately, patient-activated health care includes only hospital or clinic registration, appointment scheduling, and access to information for now, not diagnosis or surgery. Retrieving things ourselves from storage at the downscale retail warehouse and assembling our purchases at home are additional delights. Several years ago we learned to pump our own gas.

No doubt some consumers gain a sense of empowerment from becoming unpaid participants in the service and even the production process. As for the sellers, now manifest mainly as seductive, or at least abundant, retail spaces, they get to cut labor costs. (The assurance of unnamed analysts that redundant fast-food cashiers will be retained to help customers use the chains' new self-service technology and assist with food preparation is not reassuring.)[109] Even less visible than the corporate beneficiaries of self-serving consumers are the prime producers, the distant masses of workers who make many of the things we buy. In fact, the only clue to their existence is a bit of information on the product's label: Made in ______.

Augé cites the clinic, the hospital, and the refugee camp as additional examples of non-place, stuffing them into the same capacious bag as the freeway, airport, and other kinds of "generica." Such spaces are similarly uniform and bland, but their inclusion suggests what we might think of as a second level of non-place. The people we would expect to encounter in a public hospital, welfare office, or county jail occupy a different social stratum than the typical patron of air travel, suburban mall, or office park. The denizen of this second tier of non-place may be excluded from the mall for no other reason than that city buses do not go that far. There is, admittedly, a stunted kind of progress in that she would not be turned away if she *could* get there. The "lowest orders" were denied entry to Paris's Palais-Royal, the forerunner of the upscale mall, on all but three days a year.[110]

The public spaces of this second-level non-place—the shelters, hallways of government agencies, bus stops, waiting rooms, jail cells, etc.—may draw numerous poor people, waiting for the check, the voucher, the arraignment date, the bed, the overdue bus, the medicine, the work permit, the appointment to be seen. But in contrast to the mall, the airport, or the freeway, such spaces do not necessarily lack for society. From prison gangs to the cliques that will form in a halfway house or ward, the second-tier non-place may contain a rich, even viscid, social stew. Ken Kesey wrote the recipe for such a dish in *One Flew Over the Cuckoo's Nest.*

IMITATION OF SOMEPLACE

Main Street USA, with its mix of shops, restaurants, bars, offices, and a theater or two, was left in the lurch by suburbanization. People who had driven or walked a few blocks to do their downtown errands now lived many miles away. When they needed something from a store or wanted to go out to eat, they would drive to the nearest mall. The prices there were probably lower than in the old downtown, which soon consisted largely of trash-blown parking lots and empty storefronts. The postwar American dream seemed to include everything a middle-class family needed, but it lacked a certain edge. In fact, its blandness has left many people with a taste for something else. The suburban mall caters to this taste with touches of an idealized Main Street—Main Street without cars or dirt or undesirables.[111] Kowinski defends this "Garden of Eden in a box," as he calls it, by pointing out the mall's urban analogues: for the plaza, the court; for the cop on the beat, security guards; for the bag lady, mall rats, etc.[112]

Still, many suburbanites wanted more. They wanted their sprawling houses and suburban conveniences, but they also wanted something of the buzz and cosmopolitan atmosphere that only a major city could provide. Developers lit like flies on this nostalgia for the largely abandoned center. They saw in it a market for urban islands in a sea of shopping malls and detached homes.[113] Forthwith, a downtown was tacked onto a suburb north of San Francisco, complete with condos that were selling for over $300,000 in 2004.[114] Residents of an East Coast suburb tried to improve on that, but their plan for "a market meeting place reminiscent of the Greek agora" evidently got away from them, turning into "a 900,000-square-foot mall."[115] Developers of other Bay Area projects have recently taken to promising "something *real*," but their pricey apartments above stores and their mix of "nostalgic building facades" deliver only "artificial urbanity," in the opinion of an architectural critic.[116] The remake of a Washington, D.C., suburb has included tearing down a twenty-five-year-old mall and replacing it with a new, mixed-use downtown. Planners hope to attract some of the businesses that had been pushed aside by the obsolete mall: "We'll need the presence of homegrown enterprises . . . to retain our unique identity," explains one.[117]

Promoters of this "New Urbanism" are supplanting rundown malls throughout the United States. Replacing an old Lakewood, Colorado, mall, outside of Denver, are twenty-two "city-like" blocks called Belmar. Buildings rise to five stories. Though there are chain-store outlets at sidewalk level, upstairs are offices, apartments, and condominiums. Some units even have artists' studios.[118] Stapleton, another development nearby, blends traditional homes, postage-stamp parks, urban lofts, and a restaurant-crammed "town center."[119] Crocker Park, near Cleveland, will have twelve "city blocks," including a Main Street. In Royal Oak, a Detroit suburb, 18-story towers are under construction. Phoenix has an "urban fantasy" called Keirland Station; Portland, Oregon, has residential units and a town center in Orenco Station; and Glenwood Park outside of Atlanta offers a blend of housing and "stately mixed-use buildings."[120] Other developments also mix features of the city and the suburbs, offering suburbanites something of the flavor of living in an urban center.

Moving shoppers and a few residents further in that direction is super-upscale Santana Row in San Jose. There, cars —expensive cars— pass by on real streets. The visitor can stay in a hotel, eat in fine restaurants, browse in classy shops in showy European-flavored buildings sporting condos on the upper floors, go clubbing, or watch a foreign film. But even though Santana Row provides an urban experience that excludes grit, gridlock, and the poor, underneath the glitter it is "still a mall."[121] A frustrated visitor complains of the difficulty he had in finding a place to park, the crowds "packed cheek by jowl," and Santana Row's detrimental impact on a real downtown—downtown San Jose.[122] A booming downtown San Jose would, of course, include some of the problems he ascribes to Santana Row.

In any event, the kind of people who frequent Santana Row and the toney Stanford Shopping Center a few miles away—people with time and costly jewelry on their hands—make up a narrow market segment. During normal working hours, the cavernous corridors of the more downscale mall may take on the atmosphere of a mausoleum, with security guards outnumbering shoppers. For most of the week and for most of the year, the mall rivals the stadium as the epitome of the built but underutilized environment.

MALLING THE DOWNTOWN

Quickening to the fact that, despite suburbanization, some downtowns were still displaying vital signs in the form of bustling streets, mall developers got a brainstorm: "Suddenly the city made sense for the shopping-mall industry."[123] Maybe mall moguls could lure middle-class shoppers back to the city and, at the same time, skim the cream of shoppers off surviving downtown crowds. By allying themselves with downtown interests, they might even do so under cover of urban revitalization, thereby getting taxpayers to foot a goodly portion of the bill.

Revitalization has given people in Baltimore and Seattle a central city ballpark. Whether this is a good thing depends on how those stadiums were financed and what was there before. For most cities, downtown revitalization has meant a new crowd space within the blank walls of an urban shopping mall, which—with its freeway link and multi-tiered garage, its skyways and atriums—allows suburban shoppers to visit the city without ever setting foot on its streets.

In the Cannery, Ghirardelli Square, and Stonestown, San Francisco already had its share of urban malls. But none was located downtown until recently when 110 stores and a 338,000-square-foot Bloomingdale's were added to an existing complex known as the San Francisco Centre. To get a sense of what urban revitalization looks like up close, we might take an imaginary walk in downtown San Francisco. We begin just south of the San Francisco Centre, where we discover a park-like oasis of fountains, galleries, theaters, and extensive lawn. Into the early 1960s, this was an area where thousands of working-class pensioners and impoverished others lived. After a protracted struggle, they and the forty-eight "mom and pop" hotels they occupied fell victim to eviction notices and the wrecker's ball of urban redevelopment. Besides some counseling that a few of them got, each received $5,000 in settlement of their lawsuit. Most then disappeared for other parts where inexpensive rooms could still be found. Said one displaced former resident, "I miss living in the city. I miss that feeling of clambering down the stairs and going out on the street. You're with a lot of other people doing the same thing. You felt like you were part of the industry of the human effort."[124]

In the Yerba Buena Center for the Arts, the movers and shakers behind the decision to target this area for "slum clearance" got a treasure trove. The center opened as a downtown rejuvenation project whose various exhibitions and entertainment venues would draw tourists and suburbanites into town. Yerba Buena has pretty much lived up to this promise, too. And nobody would deny that it is a lot more attractive than what it replaced. But to measure the full extent of Yerba Buena's success, we would need to do some research, perhaps a survey to determine how many of the hundreds or thousands of people who daily flock to the center's movie multiplex and exhibition halls know that they stand on the site of what was once, for many, a bitter class-war defeat. I suspect that number would approach zero.

Let us hope we don't run into any of those former residents of the area among the homeless people we encounter as we head north toward Market Street. As usual, everyone and his brother is at the foot of Powell Street today—the sketch-a-face lady, the row of paired chess players and the packs of kibitzers they attract, the *Street Sheet* sellers, the man whose sign reminds the passersby that "Jesus Died for Our Sins" and urges all of us fornicators, adulterers, and assorted other sinners listed on his sign to repent before it is too late. The flying feet of Edward Jackson, the self-taught tap dancer, are pounding a sheet of plywood, accompanied by a James Brown hit: "Get up offa that thing / Shake it, you'll feel better." Sweat flies from his bare, well-muscled torso. Street entertainers look for pedestrian flows, a "self-renewing audience."[125] He has that in abundance, in addition to the captive audience of the long line of tourists for the cable car. "Don't you know that God is watching you?" a man with a bullhorn asks the people in the line who watch the dancing man. (It seems the era of the soapbox orator still has a bit of life.) Friends of years ago would complain about having to compete with tourists for space on the cable car when going back and forth between downtown and their Russian Hill home. Nobody would make such regular use of the Powell Street cable car for commuting today. Besides the tourist-level fare, the ever-present lines are just too long.

Powell and Market is like a little slice of Times Square or a remnant of the "Downtown Age," at least in terms of the volume of its pedestrian flows. But if we skirt the women with strollers and squirm through the mass of shoppers, the young couples, the panhandlers and pavement people, we can proceed up Powell Street, passing the "$1.00 Happy Roses" sign, the schlocky shops and fast-food joints, the representatives of clothing and cosmetic chains, the tourist families, and—what's this?—a tight little crowd in front of Tad's Steak House. What are they waiting for? Along comes the answer in the form of a man with a rainbow-striped stick, held erect. They follow him, catching up with us in Union Square.

San Francisco is an exception to John Brinckerhoff Jackson's observation that "the tradition of a central green or square" failed to migrate west.[126] But the recently renovated Union Square is not as green as it used to be. The new plaza of striped granite looks hollowed-out, and not just to me. A generally sympathetic newspaper account of the recent changes describes Union Square as "a sleek void."[127] Gone is the shrubbery which used to divide up the square and make its spaces more intimate. The renovators have also replaced the many wooden benches with a few metal ones whose dividers not only preclude the possibility of anybody stretching out for a snooze but make sitting, even for an average-sized person, a tight fit. There seems to be a lot less grass as well. No place to hide; everybody on view. Which is just what is wanted by the powers that be. The executive director of the Business Improvement District (BID), the private security and maintenance service that the local property owners rent, says that people engaged in illegal activities don't like to be seen: "We're making eye contact and saying hi."[128] One of the BID security guys approaches now, making his rounds, although he does not say hi.

With the shrubbery gone, it is easy to see who is in the Square: a few tourists, baby tourists, and some possible natives basking on the south side's grassy terraces to catch the last few rays of sun. A few people sit on the concrete ledges, too, but the population of the square looks scant compared to what it used to be this time of day. As William H. Whyte pointed out, a "defensive plaza" tends to be empty. The east side of the Square sports a trendy little concession now, with outdoor tables. Il Café, it is called. A big screen flashes ads for the film festival. Renovation looks to have been an elaborate effort to make tourists and suburbanites feel safe. In sum, they have "bum-proofed" the place.[129]

The *Chronicle* article adds historical perspective. By forcing closure of some of the San Francisco's freeway access points and even, for a while, breaching the Bay Bridge, the 1989 Loma Prieta earthquake changed the habits of many suburbanites, who stopped coming to the city to shop. In 1996, Louis Meunier (executive vice president of Macy's West) and other business leaders began to lobby Mayor Willie Brown to redo the square. When he agreed as to the need, the downtown interests financed a competition for a new design, a plan for "courting tourists and suburbanites," for luring "monied masses" away from the suburban malls and into downtown.[130] (Determining who paid what part of the $25 million renovation bill is not for the casual researcher.)

Now, let us admit that the old Union Square had its faults. Many of the wooden benches had broken slats, and the square attracted folks who had no other place to spend their days and nights. A person might not want to share her bench with some of them. But the denizens presented a real mix—tourist families (as now), hustlers, bench lizards, entertainers, sunbathers, shoppers, and miscellaneous others. What that meant was that anything could happen here, though usually not much did. Robert Shields used to please the crowd by miming passers-by, and there was the lady who used to get up on the stage near the soaring monument to Commodore Dewey and lip-synch the lyrics to recorded songs. Well, the Dewey monument is still there, but it is difficult to imagine anything quirky happening in this new, sanitized version of Union Square. Apparently, the planners saw it not as a place where anyone could come and relax and watch the human comedy but as a vista point for the giant ads that now dominate the square's east side.

Like the downtown mall it augments, this is branded space, streamlined and corporatized.

Some argue that instead of making itself over in the image of the suburban mall, a vital area like midtown Manhattan (or, for that matter, downtown San Francisco) should concentrate on attracting tourists and stop competing with the suburbs for shoppers and new office space. How? By "preserving [its] sense of place" to become a kind of outdoor museum for authenticity-starved crowds.[131] As David Harvey has written, "Tradition is now often preserved by being commodified and marketed as such."[132] The problem is that by the time a place's singularity becomes a commodity, the marketers are riding high in the saddle, selling a gentrified version of the original to those who can afford the price. A New Yorker complains that Manhattan today is without a "bohemian frontier." One ambles along the streets of Lower Manhattan meeting "only the same six stores and the same two banks and the same one shopper."[133] The reader might almost think he was describing a mall.

But shopping malls with urban amenities? Downtowns made over to attract suburbanites? Suburban developments that promise homebuyers a (sometimes elusive) patch of downtown?[134] Such phenomena are consistent with upper-income people paying megabucks for condominiums within hiking distance of the urban action and with suburban redevelopment schemes designed to replace parking lots and strip malls with centers where people will not only want to live but to shop and even venture out at night.[135] With the home becoming an outlet for retail merchants via TV shopping channels, online buying, toll-free numbers, and specialized, glossy versions of the old-fashioned mail-order catalog, one might reasonably conclude that retail capital no longer needed the crowd. But to judge by the hundreds of people with shopping bags in hand who fill the sidewalks of San Francisco's downtown shopping district these days and nights, many shoppers are not confining themselves to the security of the home, suburban mall, or familiar big store. They are exposing themselves to the vagaries and mix of city streets, and they seem to enjoy the experience, at least when the crowd consists primarily of people like themselves.

"We just want to be with the crowds," gushes an unnamed Christmas shopper.[136] "CROWDS" heads a half-page ad for a close-out furniture sale.[137] Clearly, people like bustling aisles and streets. Just as they did a hundred years ago, they intensify one's emotional experience with their "swift and continuous shift of external and internal stimuli."[138] Investors, retailers, and developers are trying to catch up. But the number of shoppers in the area these days has changed San Francisco's downtown mix. While dancing for dollars, Edward Jackson has also noticed this. Where he used to see a mixed social bag, everyone now has a shopping bag and is heading for or coming from one of the big new stores.[139] He explains his roughly 50 percent drop in income over recent years by the preponderance of shoppers. Evidently, the heart of downtown San Francisco has become so enticing to them that a well-known busker can no longer make a living there.[140]

BIG BOX CHURCHES

There is one additional component of the infrastructure of consumer crowds that we should acknowledge. Anything that cannot be found at the nearest Wal-Mart or Home Depot will probably be available to members of one of the new megachurches that, for many members of the consumer society, appear to fill both a spiritual and practical void. They offer plenty of room for parking, a friendly greeting and perhaps a free lunch for new "customers," free child care, identity groups, addiction counseling, perhaps an Internet café and food court, a gym, video game kiosks and, to top it off, an entertaining sermon that is likely to include practical advice on the problems of everyday life and to exclude denominational dogma and divisive political pronouncements. These churches are building community where it does not otherwise exist.

The largest of them, Lakewood in Houston, has a congregation of over forty thousand. In a modest version of what critics call "the prosperity gospel,"[141] its pastor tells his enormous flock how faith got him a house, a good marriage, and a parking space.[142] As many as 25,000 routinely attend Sunday services at Saddleback Church in Southern California. Whereas Lakewood occupies an arena that was formerly the home of the Houston Rockets basketball team, the exterior of others may resemble a big box store. With pastors advising parishioners to name what they want and promising that, with sufficient faith in Jesus Christ, they will get it, these big churches are growing individually and in aggregate. There are well over a thousand of them, as I write, mostly concentrated in the Sun Belt.

The business-savvy evangelicals who establish megachurches tend to bank the fires of religious doctrine so as not to turn away potential "customers." Their use of a business model is unabashed. The leader of a megachurch is also its CEO. The head of a firm that designs Web sites and other products for the megachurch market, himself a former big-church minister, describes his services as creating "a brand for churches." He calls the series of sermons that he helps a pastor put together a "marketing blitz."[143] Frances Fitzgerald concludes her report on this phenomenon by saying, "Megachurches are . . . to small churches as corporations are to mom-and-pop stores."[144]

If capital deployed consumerism to head off the possibility of proletarian revolution, as some argue, perhaps the megachurch was needed, too, to sanctify the choice Americans have made and provide the salve of community. An observer notes that "one of the few mechanisms for regular interaction in the suburbs is the church."[145]

8. Who Needs Crowds?

The collapse of IndyMac Bank in Southern California in July 2008 brought hundreds of anxious depositors to its doors, reminding one observer of a scene from the Depression. Police had to restore order to the long line of customers, as tempers flared over accusations that some were cutting in.[1] But the comparison was somewhat inapt. During the Depression, the police might have had to battle the entire crowd to prevent its forcing its way into the bank. The underlying competition that characterizes today's consumer crowds is usually more covert. Americans rarely come together on the basis of a shared determination to act as one, any more than we participate in massive celebrations, except under the dampening influence of official oversight. Our crowds have become no more than the social condition under which certain kinds of individual consumption occur. Crowd control, like the Constitution's hemming in of majorities, is generally besides the point for self-controlled consumers. Is it the goods and spectacles that numb us to the potential for organized numbers to serve as a counterweight to the power of organized money? Or are we just too busy trying to earn enough to pay the bills? One must look to ancient Rome's regime of bread and circuses for a precedent for crowds like these. No wonder analysis of market demographics has taken over the territory formerly occupied by crowd theory.

THE EVOLUTION OF ASSEMBLY RIGHTS

The framers of the Constitution no doubt anticipated a very different world when they wrote, in the First Amendment, that "Congress shall make no law . . . abridging . . . the right of the people peaceably to assemble, and to petition the Government for a redress of grievances." The people's right to assemble, to form crowds to advance shared objectives, had its origin in English common law and statutes that predated the work of the Framers by some centuries. Scholars have traced freedom of assembly to the Magna Carta's recognition of the right—of high nobles, at least—to petition the king.[2] Meeting in October 1774, members of the First Continental Congress declared that Americans, too, had "a right peaceably to assemble, consider their grievances and petition the King."[3] Acting on this right has been vital to the success of American social movements whose gains we now take for granted. For example, no one but a few sympathizers would have heard the suffragists' arguments without their being given public exposure through open-air meetings, soap box lectures, and the like: "The right of assembly provided the foundation for every step of the suffrage campaign."[4]

But the right to collect a crowd in a public place to further political or religious goals, now "nearly absolute" (although somewhat conditioned by the need of public officials to prevent disorder, congestion, and violence), has been hard-won, requiring considerable sacrifice and extensive litigation.[5] Until late in the nineteenth century, judges resolved disputes over assembly rights by deferring to the power of the police to protect the public against the importunities and clamor of dissident street meetings and parades. In *United States v. Cruikshank* (1876), the Supreme Court's majority declared that "the very idea of a government, republican in form, implies a right on the part of its citizens to meet peaceably for consultation in respect to public affairs."[6] But the *Cruikshank* court ruled that the First Amendment only protected assembly rights from congressional interference, not from the limiting effects of state law and local ordinances.[7] In a Massachusetts case, *Commonwealth of Massachusetts v. Davis* (1895), Oliver Wendell Holmes wrote for the majority that, because streets and public parks belonged to the municipality, a legislative ban or restriction on speaking in a street or public park was no more an infringement of basic rights than a homeowner's denial of such activity in his own house.[8] The *Davis* doctrine guided judicial thinking on First Amendment rights for many years.

Given free rein by such rulings, local authorities routinely regulated political gatherings in streets or parks by granting or withholding permits. The first open-air meeting of suffragists in Massachusetts had to be conducted from a parked car because an official had turned down permission for them to speak in a public park. Los Angeles maintained an outright ban on political discussion in public parks, and temperance marchers were convicted of disturbing the peace in Portland, Oregon.[9] Mother Jones and her army of child laborers were initially denied entry to New York City because they were not New York citizens.[10] Suffragists who picketed the White House during the First World War were consistently jailed, and the court refused to entertain objections by their attorneys based on First Amendment grounds.[11] When sailors attacked their peaceful picket line in 1917, a dozen suffragists were arrested for provoking a riot. In fact, speakers were often held responsible for public disturbances occasioned by their actions: local authorities stopped them from speaking, threatened them with arrest, and sometimes arrested them.[12]

Permits to meet were withheld arbitrarily. Suffragists, many of whom were the wives and daughters of prominent members of the political establishment, usually got permission to assemble. Radicals did not. In the early decades of the twentieth century, thousands of members of the Industrial Workers of the World (IWW) were beaten and jailed when trying to get their message across in public.[13] At length, the Supreme Court made a series of rulings that gave the right of assembly the kind of protections it enjoys today. In *Gitlow v. New York* (1925), the Court found that the Fourteenth Amendment guarantees speech rights against abridgement by the states, and *DeJonge v. Oregon* (1937) extended this guarantee to assembly.[14] According to the holding in *DeJonge,* "peaceable assembly for lawful discussion cannot be made a crime," even when it takes the form of a Communist Party rally.[15] This decision supposedly "liberated" the right of assembly "from dependence on the right to petition," making it the coequal, legally, of freedom of speech and of the press.[16] Finally, in *Hague v. C.I.O.* (1939), the Supreme Court struck down a city's permit process, holding that while a city can impose restrictions as to the time, place, and manner of a meeting, it cannot rule out an organization's possibility of holding any meeting at all.[17]

Despite this liberalizing trend, local officials continue to violate our basic assembly rights (as documented in chapter 6). And some gatherings enjoy considerably greater legal protection than others. Writing for the Supreme Court's majority in *City of Chicago v. Morales* (1998), Justice Stevens saw no conflict with First Amendment rights in a Chicago ordinance that barred only purposeless gatherings—namely, loitering by gang members. The First Amendment, Stevens wrote, applies only to "conduct that is apparently intended to convey a message."[18] So much for the right of assembly being "liberated" from the right to petition.

The question in every right-of-assembly case has been, did a gathering have Constitutional protection against government interference? Government obstruction of basic rights must be resisted, of course, but by whom? What happens when the right of assembly withers from disuse? When the only crowds that form consist of shoppers, travelers, and spectators? When civic involvement becomes the specialty of thoroughly marginalized "activists"? What need is there for a right of assembly when corporate lobbyists fill the vacuum left by public apathy and politics is generally viewed with contempt? Does such a right become the exclusive province of religious enthusiasts? But perhaps the more important question is, what kind of society do we get in the United States while the people's right of assembly gathers dust?

For one thing, we get a nation with great disparities of power and wealth. Although we have near-universal suffrage, the formula "one person one vote" is not very meaningful if one person's vote is augmented, for instance, by his control of a television network and a string of newspapers while another person cannot even register to vote because he lives on the streets and has no mailing address. With mass media at his disposal to influence an electoral outcome, the media owner can, in effect, vote many times. Yes, there have always been rich and poor, but certainly not to the present extent. While the economic pie is three times the size it was in 1960, in terms of goods produced, the rewards of economic growth have gone almost entirely to the wealthy since the early 1970s. The income of the top 1 percent of families has tripled to 22 percent of the nation's, the same proportion as prevailed in 1928.[19] At the same time, wage levels for most workers have remained where they were almost forty years ago (allowing for inflation), if they have not declined. In fact, the United States now leads all developed countries in income inequality. In terms of wealth, Americans in the wealthiest 1 percent of the population now own more than a third of the nation's assets; the top 5 percent own almost 60 percent. We have noted the potential effect of such concentration of wealth on American consumers.

But what does all this have to do with the rusting right of assembly? Well, such changes in the distribution of wealth and income are reflected in public policy. Take tax policy. Reductions in what are called marginal tax rates—that is, taxes on the wealthy—have been cut substantially in recent decades, so that rich people now pay taxes at a much lower rate than they did in the 1960s and 1970s. A series of "tax reforms" beginning with the Kennedy-Johnson administrations have turned the idea of a "progressive" income tax into a wink and a nod to the rich.[20] The nation's tax bill for corporations, as a proportion of Gross Domestic Product, is lower than that of almost every other country in the developed world. Tax loopholes have magnified this process. For example, because of one such loophole billionaire private equity fund managers pay taxes at a lower rate than their receptionists.[21] Americans who live off their wealth (capital gains) are generally taxed well below the tax rate for people who live off their labor.[22] Such policies are about what one can expect from elected representatives who depend on Washington lobbyists not only for campaign funding but for information and "talking points" on pending legislation— and never have to face the collective wrath of their constituents.[23] Let's also call attention to the outrageous and increasing amounts that we are required to contribute to a bloated war machine whose primary purpose seems to be the funneling of tax dollars to giant military contractors—this at a time when millions of Americans, both working and unemployed, lack access to adequate health care, food, and affordable housing. We could easily add sufficient grievances to make up a lengthy list. But the point is that our government has become responsive only to a minute but extremely powerful segment of the American public.

This is not to say that we had a golden age of democracy in the nation's past. There have been periods in our history, though, when we seemed to be moving in a democratic direction. That cannot be said for the present. The second Bush administration's tax cuts for the rich significantly contributed to the widening gap between the rich and the poor, but the broadest contours of our political and economic landscape—military empire, de-industrialization, ballooning finance, for-profit health care, and meager social spending—reflect bipartisan engineering. No wonder a growing percentage of people surveyed agree with the statement, "The government is pretty much run by a few big interests looking out for themselves."[24] Surely such skepticism contributes to the fact that about half of potential American voters do not bother to vote. Voting by itself will not ensure that our elected representatives advance or defend popular interests. To drive a wedge through the tight relationship between public officeholders and their corporate sponsors, voting must be supplemented by massive lobbying and the heat of multitudes in the street.

Admittedly, crowds in the street may serve others' needs, may even go horribly wrong. At best they represent a blunt instrument when it comes to effecting political change. But in the absence of dramatic, public, and persistent use of our numbers, plutocracy is sure to grow and to do so at our expense and that of future generations. Then, at some point not of our choosing, we may find that we are members of a crowd that can only wait for help in order to survive.

TOWARD CROWD OBSOLESCENCE?

Perhaps the political crowd, which, through riots, demonstrations, marches, vigils, pickets, sit-ins, and the like, has long served as our ultimate defense against arbitrary and tyrannical rule, has simply been outmoded by technology. Even half a century ago, social observers were beginning to say that "substantial developments in the field of mass communications have largely reduced the need for frequent participation in assemblages."[25] More recently, a historian declares that the Internet has given us "a new style of political communication which is insurgent in its very form." He compares its potential impact on the distribution of power and other key issues to that of the printing press, photography, telegraphy, radio, and television.[26] This revolution in communications heralds "the rise of cyberwar, in which neither mass nor mobility" but superior knowledge will prevail.[27] Combatants in this cyberwar consist of the electronically enhanced opponents of repressive regimes, who now have the means to circumvent the state's monopoly on and control of information.[28]

What comes to mind is the use of cell phones and computers by Chinese activists to organize protests against official abuses of power.[29] But the Chinese government has responded with Internet censorship, provoking indirect criticism in the form of "a new wave of sarcastic—and often subversive—media," including printed matter.[30] The critic may praise the government for eliminating every conceivable social problem. Well, a Mark Twain or Jonathan Swift of the Gutenberg era could have done that. In Vietnam, a blogger declares that he will no longer take his political dissidence into the street, that rebellion now requires only a modem, keyboard, and screen. His government has answered with online censorship.[31] But Asia's virtual police cannot stand guard over the entire blogosphere.[32] In September 2007, images and news of Burmese monks demonstrating against their military rulers reached the outside world where they became Internet postings, inspiring a broadening of street protests in Burma.[33]

In the United States, where the existing regime makes no attempt to monopolize communications but does freeze a growing body of information in its own databases, it is undisputed that Internet activists are using the new electronic media effectively to raise money and to organize massive lobbying campaigns. In December 2002, for instance, as the Bush administration prepared to launch its attack on Iraq, MoveOn.org asked people on its email list to contribute $27,000 toward an antiwar ad in the *New York Times.* The request brought in $400,000 within a few days, enough to pay for TV ads in thirteen cities. MoveOn.org raised $180 million to influence the outcome of the national elections in 2004.[34] But online activists do more than raise money. MoveOn.org members made 77,000 phone calls to help fuel a "voter revolt" in the August 2006 Democratic primary in Connecticut.[35] Of greater significance is the claim that "netroots" organizing secured Barack Obama's victory over Hillary Clinton in the 2008 Democratic primaries and propelled him to the presidency. An organization of liberal bloggers now hopes to present electoral challenges to centrist Democrats and to "push back" when President Obama strays too far to the right.[36]

Besides facilitating fundraising and lobbying, electronic media make it easier to organize physical gatherings under any regime where people enjoy widespread access to the technology, whether the crowds consist of the "cybernegotiated public flocking" of text-messaging adolescents, a "MobMov" of do-it-yourself drive-in movie enthusiasts, or the political "flash mobs" of the Reverend Billy and his anti-shopping brigades.[37] Demonstrations against Bahrain's ruling elite can be announced in advance only on a Web site.[38] By one account, the Battle of Seattle in 1999 was won by "internetworked" clusters of activists using mobile phones, Web sites, laptops, and hand-held computers. Similarly, the massive demonstrations that brought down Philippines president Joseph Estrada in January 2001 were "coordinated by waves of text messages." Electronic communication devices enable people ("smart mobs") "to act in concert even if they don't know each other."[39]

But strangers have been acting together on the basis of shared interests for millennia. The People Power II demonstrations of 2001 were impressive, but what about the original display of People Power in 1986, when fifteen thousand mostly first-time activists showed up at a Manila assembly site late at night in response to radio pleas by Cardinal Jaime Sin and Butz Aquino? With the hundreds of thousands who soon joined them in support of dissident military leaders, they defied a tank battalion and brought down Ferdinand Marcos.[40] Filipinos have long been "networked" by kinship ties. An expert on their text-messaging culture has discovered that "the crowd is a sort of medium . . . the site for the generation of expectations and the circulation of messages." It is not just "an effect of technological devices, but . . . a kind of technology itself."[41] He could as well have been writing about crowds in the French Revolution or those of colonial New England. The mob that provoked the Boston Massacre was largely organized by the city's apprentices, whose communications media were the town's barber shops.[42] The crowd is a medium of communication.

Leaving aside the question of whether either side "won" the Battle of Seattle, some of those present had been participating in nonviolent but highly disruptive demonstrations for twenty years or more, relying on face-to-face meetings and such primitive technology as phone trees, newsletters, flyers, bullhorns, and the public airways. Critics have pointed out the white middle-class bias of reliance on the Internet.[43] In 2004, about 30 percent of American households still had neither a desktop computer nor a mobile phone.[44] "People have to meet one-on-one," says an activist. "There are no shortcuts."[45] Even the organizing director of MoveOn.org acknowledges the political limitations of reliance on information-sharing technology. MoveOn Councils now bring people together in physical gatherings.[46] Free speech requires both uncensored writings and physical assemblies. As a legal scholar writes, "The congregation has distinct advantages over [mass] media when it comes to the tasks of conviction or persuasion . . . and incitement to action."[47] Responding similarly to an email recommendation, numerous individuals who will never meet one another except by chance can create a flood of paper for congressional staffers, but the organizing of disempowered individuals requires physical assemblies.[48]

Although electronic technology may facilitate physical gatherings, its habitual use is more likely to leave us disinclined to enter the public world where such gatherings might have political consequences.[49] The disembodied realm of cyberspace is the very antithesis of a culture of crowds.

CROWDS AND CATASTROPHE REVISITED

In chapter 5 we learned that for the New Orleans victims of Hurricane Katrina the only help available was "people helping people." As John Clark, professor of philosophy and environmental studies at New Orleans' Loyola University has said, "If the forces of human community could have operated, we could have rescued ourselves."[50] Sometimes those forces do come into play. To take a recent example, within hours of the December 2004 tsunami in the Indian Ocean, a "second tsunami" hit devastated areas of Sri Lanka and Thailand. This took the form of an invasion of developers, who had long coveted areas of coastal fishing villages as potential sites of upscale resorts. With the beaches suddenly swept clean of human habitation, they used forceful government support to keep out thousands of Sri Lankans who had lived there for ages and confined them to inland refugee camps. But in Thailand, many villagers combined to engage in "reinvasions," marching past developers' armed guards to rebuild their homes. Naomi Klein reports that a delegation of Hurricane Katrina survivors visited several of these rebuilt Thai villages. Its members "were taken aback by the speed with which rehabilitation had become a reality" —rehabilitation through collective self-help, that is.[51]

Accounts of San Francisco's 1906 earthquake and firestorms are also instructive. Shaken out of their beds and trying to escape the burning city, crowds of survivors were like "a promenade of living specters," a reporter noted. "None spoke."[52] William James, the famous philosopher, who was teaching at Stanford at the time, rushed to San Francisco to observe people's reactions. "Physical fatigue and *seriousness* were the only inner states that one could read," he wrote. "At the place of action, where all are concerned together, healthy animal insensitivity and heartiness take their place."[53] Many of those hearty but insensitive people had already found various roles for themselves amid the advancing flames. Some became members of the private militias that mixed with Army and National Guard troops to shoot people suspected of looting and to dynamite buildings in the fire's path, using the kind of blasting powder that could only make the fires worse. Some tried to suppress the fires by more traditional means, while others watched such efforts from a safe distance. Some served as rescuers and nurses, while others sold scarce goods and services for exorbitant prices—just as in Camus's novel *The Plague*,[54] and just as happened during the great fire in ancient Rome.[55] Most simply tried to save themselves, their loved ones, and whatever they could drag to safety through the smoking streets. In the midst of all this, a small band of Russian Hill homeowners defied the repeated order of soldiers (issued at gunpoint) to abandon their homes. They successfully fought the fire, saving not only their own houses but some of their neighbors'.[56]

Economic disaster, too, may promote collective self-help. During the Depression, radicals organized mutual aid networks of the unemployed in major American cities and many towns. When people's resources became too depleted for bartering to succeed, the focus shifted to mass protest.[57] Before the Detroit rioting of 1967, residents of one 150-square-block area of the ghetto established a neighborhood action committee and block clubs. When the rioting started, they rerouted cars, with youths directing traffic. This area suffered only two small fires.[58] More recently, organizers of City Life/Vida Urbana have been able to mobilize homeowners and tenants to block some foreclosure evictions in Massachusetts.[59] Acorn (the Association of Community Organizations for Reform Now) has launched an anti-eviction campaign in over twenty American cities to connect families facing eviction with volunteers willing to risk arrest.[60] For now, however, foreclosures continue at a record-setting pace, and it appears that deterioration of the economy would have to become much worse for the resistance of some to spark a dissident mass movement. For a recent example of what can happen under more dire circumstances, we might look to Argentina where, in December 2001, the country's economy collapsed, thanks in part to the International Monetary Fund's insistence, as a condition for new loans, that the government cut spending in the midst of a deep recession. When the economic minister poured gasoline on the flames by freezing private bank accounts and raiding pension funds in order to maintain payments to the nation's creditors, people surged into the streets. Some came out to loot food stores, some to bang pots and pans and demand the resignation of President de la Rua, and many to challenge the suspension of constitutional rights and the killing of several protesters by the police. Thousands massed before the presidential palace, where they set bonfires and chanted, "Assassins, assassins, assassins!"[61] Seeking a scapegoat, members of the political class blamed the Buenos Aires governor for "instigating the looting to overthrow the government."[62] Before the protesters were through they forced the resignation of four presidents in three weeks.

Many jobless and impoverished Argentines acted the role traditionally played by the city mob in preindustrial Europe, not rioting but using their numbers to block strategic sections of the nation's highway system to demand that the government meet their needs for paid work, food, and short-term cash. Their leaders reasoned that the government was responsible for their unemployment; therefore, the government should provide relief.[63] Others, many of them middle-class Argentines experiencing economic insecurity for the first time in their lives, went from living "behind closed doors" with their sudden poverty to collective alternatives—for example, by becoming members of the barter clubs that had begun to form as early as 1995. By the time the economic slump became a crisis, these clubs had around a half million members, each of whom had been issued fifty credits of social money on joining and then allowed to attend weekly or semi-weekly fairs at which they could exchange whatever goods or services they could provide for something they could otherwise ill afford. The clubs existed through these fairs, which members "anxiously awaited."[64] Unfortunately, the "explosion" of new participants ignited by the economy's full collapse at the end of 2001 swamped the clubs' capacity to control the barter credits. Also, ingredients for prepared food, a major item of exchange, became too expensive for club members to buy.[65]

With the crisis, neighborhood assemblies also formed. These had their birth in the crowds that collected at intersections throughout the capital on December 19 and 20. Out of one of these crowds of thousands, hundreds might continue to meet, engaging in deliberations, reestablishing badly damaged social ties, and forming committees to address issues of health care, politics, outreach, and unemployment. The assemblies brought together members of the middle class, many of them first-time activists; radical youths; professionals; and the *cartoneros* (cardboard collectors) who, like the people who collect aluminum cans in American cities, were the poorest of the poor.[66] Such encounters often led to strains and splits. As a member of one assembly complained in response to the question of whether the group was open to others or closed, "people run to us from everywhere in a disorderly way to impose on us where we ought to be going. . . . It is difficult [to make decisions] because we are all equal among ourselves, quite unlike the political parties."[67] Say researchers, "What to do was at the center of all assembly experiences."[68]

The question is what will *we* do? Unless we are ready to assume that the United States has had its final experience of major disaster, the hour of the self-generated crowd cannot be consigned to the leaky lifeboat of history. Imagine: all businesses are closed, the freeways are so clogged with cars that nobody is going anywhere except on foot, the power is off, and radio broadcasts are reaching only those who had the foresight to store batteries. Will we hunker down behind the triple-locked doors of our private homes, nursing our drinks, and preparing our arsenals for the dangerous crowds that we imagine will soon be rampaging through the streets?

In *The Road,* Cormac McCarthy's fictional dystopia, a father and son who have managed to survive an unidentified global catastrophe trudge the roads of a blighted America, ever vigilant for the bands of killer cannibals who also roam the land. Why only the worst of humankind have leveraged their numbers to enhance their chances of survival goes unexplained. But clearly an American bias favors the individual, whose successful struggle to rise "above the crowd" always wins applause. This notwithstanding the fact that isolation leaves us vulnerable to organized others and the additional fact that the fully realized individual acts in solidarity with others. As we discovered in earlier chapters, our ancestors knew enough to respond to chaotic events by joining their neighbors in the lane or street. With fast-moving climate change and an economic crisis at hand, we are all living in New Orleans now. Ultimately, the crowd may be our brightest hope.

Beyond individual survival, the ideal of American democracy is under increasing threat. Many Americans, including the author, believe that "democracy" should not be a code word for a plutocratic system with regular elections. Many Americans, including the author, believe that another world—one offering better prospects for social justice, peace, and material security than presently exist—is both possible and desirable. The existing order is unsustainable, but its defenders are powerful and will not relinquish control without a formidable fight. For the long and necessary struggle ahead to succeed, we will have to overcome the dispersive impulses of consumerism. Among other things, we will need to rehabilitate a tradition in which the physical assembly—again, the crowd—is not just an obstacle to the pursuit of private objectives but an agency of protest and much-needed change.

As I write, the executives of huge financial institutions have imperiled the domestic and perhaps the global economy with what amounts to an enormous pyramid scheme of "toxic" loan packages and manic speculation. Their bipartisan representatives call on the rest of us to spend hundreds of billions to bail out these billionaires in order to stabilize financial markets. A few of us, not nearly enough to make a difference, have gathered in financial districts and elsewhere to protest these developments. The fact that we, the potential victims of this crisis, are many and they, its authors, are few is worth very little to the extent that we, the many, have forgotten what crowds are for.

Three months have elapsed since I wrote the above. In Iceland, Latvia, Spain, Ukraine, and elsewhere the global financial crisis has ignited major demonstrations. The mere threat of people in the street has French president Sarkozy "thinking twice" about the kind of changes he would like to make in public education.[69] In the United States, the financial institutions, which have received hundreds of billions of taxpayers' dollars under the Troubled Asset Relief Program (TARP), appear to have used some of their windfall to pad year-end bonuses and the like.[70] Little if any of it has been used for loans, as intended by TARP. Paradoxically, as the economy continues to sink, with more and more Americans losing homes, jobs, and savings, the nation's mood (pollsters report) is one of optimism.[71] An estimated two million joyous people braved freezing temperatures to attend Barack Obama's presidential inauguration. The docility of the crowd was reflected in the fact that despite its great size, there was not a single arrest. Think of it: two million celebrants and not a single one sufficiently disorderly to be hauled off by the police! The new president surely bears the hopes of the nation on his back—or are they on his wings? Snatches of "When the Saints Go Marching In" marched through the mind of this viewer as he watched the inaugural spectacle.

The importance of the fact that an enthusiastic majority of the voting electorate has handed the nation's highest office to a man with an African father can hardly be overstated. But I suspect that for many who attended the inauguration or watched it on a screen, this may serve as change enough. Thus, despite the hoary adage that a political regime is at its most vulnerable with the arousal of widespread hope for change, the new administration will probably be given broad latitude by the kind of people who might otherwise be most inclined to bring mass protest to the halls of power and the streets of America. In his selections for top posts in his administration and his apparent deference to powerful public and private interests, Obama has already signaled that, campaign slogans and stylistic changes to the contrary, he does not intend a major break with the past. Yet the credit crunch and the massive layoffs under way could significantly thin the crowds of the consumer society. Will the absent shoppers, commuters, vacationers, and spectators become members of the kind of crowds that flourished in America's more distant past? Might they physically combine with like-minded others to advance demands for real change? President Obama has repeatedly declared that change comes from the bottom up. As usual with such questions, only time will tell.

Notes

INTRODUCTION

1. Joe Klein, "The Talk of the Town—Comment: Public Life," *The New Yorker* 11 November 2002: 67.
2. Cf. William H. Whyte, *City: Rediscovering the Center* (New York: Doubleday, 1988) 172–3.
3. Glenn McKenzie, "50 Nigerians killed in Miss World protest: Muslim groups don't want nation to host pageant," *San Francisco Chronicle* 22 November 2002: A12.
4. Misha Dzhindzhikhashvili (AP), "Georgians protest election win," *San Francisco Chronicle* 14 January 2008: A19.
5. Elias Canetti, *Crowds and Power,* trans. Carol Stewart (New York: Farrar, Straus & Giroux, 1962.
6. Naomi Klein, *The Shock Doctrine: The Rise of Disaster Capitalism* (New York: Metropolitan Books, 2007) 105.
7. Margaret Bayard Smith, qtd. in Jill Lepore, "Vast Designs: How America came of age," rev. of *What Hath God Wrought: The Transformation of America, 1815-1848* by Daniel Walker Howe, *The New Yorker,* October 29, 2007: 98.
8. Mary Esteve, *The Aesthetics and Politics of the Crowd in American Literature* (New York: Cambridge UP, 2003) 1–2.
9. George P. Smith II, "The Development of the Right of Assembly—A Current Socio-Legal Investigation," *William and Mary Law Review* 9 (Fall 1967) 375.
10. Ehrenreich, *Dancing in the Streets: A History of Collective Joy* (New York: Metropolitan Books, 2007) 187–8.
11. Esteve 3.

12. In Thomas A. Gullason, ed., *The Complete Short Stories & Sketches of Stephen Crane* (Garden City, NY: Doubleday, 1963) 201–4.

1. WHAT CROWDS ARE FOR

1. Eric Partridge, *Origins: A Short Etymological Dictionary of Modern English* (New York: Greenwich House, 1983) 132.
2. Livy, *The Early History of Rome: Books I-V of The History of Rome from Its Foundation,* trans. Aubrey de Sélincourt (New York: Penguin, 1971) 140–1, 153 ff., 170, 172, 195, 198, 232.
3. P. A. Brunt, "The Roman Mob," *Studies in Ancient Society,* ed. M. I. Finley (Boston: Routledge & Kegan Paul, 1974) 96.
4. Robin Dunbar, *Grooming, Gossip, and the Evolution of Language* (Cambridge, Mass.: Harvard UP, 1996) 39, 62–64, and passim.
5. Tacitus, *Annals* 14.45 in *Complete Works of Tacitus,* trans. Alfred J. Church and William Jackson Brodribb (New York: The Modern Library, 1942) 344–5.
6. Ma Jian, *Biejing Coma,* trans. Flora Drew (New York: Farrar, Straus & Giroux, 2008) 97, 279, 305.
7. Suetonius, *Vitellius* 14, *Lives of the Caesars,* trans. Catharine Edwards (New York: Oxford UP, 2000) 256.
8. E. P. Thompson, "The Moral Economy of the Crowd in the Eighteenth Century" in *The Essential E. P. Thompson* (New York: The New Press, 2001) 365.
9. Eric Hobsbawm, *Primitive Rebels: Studies in Archaic Forms of Social Movement in the 19th and 20th Centuries* (New York: W. W. Norton, 1959) 113.
10. Hobsbawm, *Primitive* 115; cf. Suetonius, *Ortho* 7, *Lives* 244.
11. Arlette Farge, *Fragile Lives: Violence, Power and Solidarity in Eighteenth-Century Paris,* trans. Carol Shelton (Cambridge, Mass.: Harvard UP, 1993) 171 ff.
12. Colin Lucas, "The Crowd and Politics," *The Political Culture of the French Revolution,* C. Lucas, ed., vol. 2 of *The French Revolution and the Creation of Modern Political Culture* (New York: Pergamon Press, 1988) 271.
13. George Rudé, *The Crowd in History: A Study of Popular Disturbances in France and England 1730–1848* (London: Serif, 1981) 47.
14. Hobsbawm, *Primitive* 115–16.
15. Wayne E. Lee, *Crowds and Soldiers in Revolutionary North Carolina: The Culture of Violence in Riot and War* (Gainesville, FL: UP of Florida, 2001) 3; cf. Farge.
16. Qtd. in Ronald Takaki, *A Different Mirror: A History of Multicultural America* (Boston: Back Bay Books, 1993) 423.

17. Farge 171.
18. Farge 184.
19. David Andress, *The Terror: Civil War in the French Revolution* (London: Little, Brown, 2005) 103.
20. Mark Steel, *Vive la Revolution* (Chicago: Haymarket Books, 2006) 48.
21. Charles Tilly, "Reflections on the Revolution of Paris: A Review of Recent Historical Writing," *Social Problems* 12 (Summer 1964) 114, qtd. in Frances Fox Piven and Richard A. Cloward, *Poor People's Movements: Why They Succeed, How They Fail* (New York: Vintage Books, 1977) 20.
22. Rudé 98.
23. Dixon Wector, *The Age of the Great Depression* (New York: Macmillan, 1948) 39.
24. Howard Zinn, *A People's History of the United States: 1492–Present* (New York: HarperPerennial, 2003) 389; T. H. Watkins, *The Great Depression: America in the 1930s* (Boston: Little, Brown, 1993) 78, 80.
25. Piven and Cloward 49.
26. Irving Bernstein, *The Lean Years: A History of the American Worker, 1920–1933* (Baltimore: Penguin Books, 1970), qtd. in Piven and Cloward 49.
27. Steve Babson, *The Unfinished Struggle: Turning Points in American Labor, 1877–Present* (Lanham, MD: Rowman & Littlefield, 1999) 60–1; Piven and Cloward 49–51.
28. Zinn 389.
29. Qtd. in Piven and Cloward 53.
30. Babson 65; Zinn 391–2.
31. Qtd. in Piven and Cloward 55; cf. 54.
32. Jeremy Brecher, *Strike!*, rev. ed. (Cambridge, MA: South End Press, 1997) 160.
33. Piven and Cloward 66.
34. Piven and Cloward 66–7.
35. Charles R. Walker, "Relief and Revolution," *The Forum* September 1932: 156, qtd. in Brecher 164.
36. Linda J. Lumsden, *Rampant Women: Suffragists and the Right of Assembly* (Knoxville, TN: U. of Tennessee Press, 1997) 70.
37. Harriot Stanton Blatch and Alma Lutz, *Challenging Years: The Memoirs of Harriot Stanton Blatch* (New York: G. P. Putnam's Sons, 1940) 180.
38. Rudé 239.
39. Qtd. in Peter Burke, *Popular Culture in Early Modern Europe* (New York: New York UP, 1978) 263.
40. Mabel Vernon, White House picket organizer, qtd. in Lumsden 142.
41. Taylor Branch, *Pillar of Fire: America in the King Years, 1963–1965* (New York: Touchstone, 1998) 62; Piven and Cloward 238.
42. William Brink and Louis Harris, *The Negro Revolution in America* (New York: Simon & Schuster, 1964) 44.

43. Barrington Moore, Jr., *Social Origins of Dictatorship and Democracy: Lord and Peasant in the Making of the Modern World* (Boston: Beacon Press, 1966) 212.
44. Walter Rodney, *How Europe Underdeveloped Africa* (Washington, DC: Howard UP, 1982) 34; Graham Greene, *Journey Without Maps* (New York: Penguin Books, 1978) 182–4.
45. Burke 182.
46. James G. Frazer, *The Golden Bough: A Study in Magic and Religion,* abr. ed. (New York: The Macmillan Co., 1950) 157; cf. Robert Graves, *The White Goddess: A Historical Grammar of Poetic Myth,* amended ed. (New York: Farrar, Straus & Giroux, 1948) 357.
47. Mikhail Bakhtin, *Rabelais and His World,* trans. Helene Iswolsky (Bloomington, IN: Indiana UP, 1984) 7.
48. Burke 188 ff.; Frazer 676.
49. Bakhtin 10; cf. Ehrenreich, *Dancing in the Streets: A History of Collective Joy* (New York: Metropolitan Books, 2007) 88.
50. Burke 182 ff.
51. "Manha do Carnaval," by Luiz Bonfiá, sound track of *Black Orpheus* (*Orfeu Negro*), film, dir. Marcel Camus, Lopert Films Release, 1959.
52. Cf. Ehrenreich 37.
53. Frazer 452.
54. Ehrenreich 64, 74, 77.
55. Friedrich Nietzsche, *The Birth of Tragedy* in *The Birth of Tragedy and the Genealogy of Morals,* trans. Francis Golffing (Garden City, NY: Doubleday, 1956) 22.
56. Nietzsche 23.
57. Cf. Bakhtin 278 ff.
58. Bakhtin 48.
59. Cf. Christopher Hill, *The World Turned Upside Down: Radical Ideas during the English Revolution* (New York: Penguin Books, 1975) 132 and passim.
60. "100 Held in May Day Unrest in 2 German Cities," *New York Times* 2 May 2005: A5.
61. See http://www.conference-board.org/utilities/pressPrintFriendly.cfm?pressID=2582; cf. Juliet B. Schor, *The Overworked American: The Unexpected Decline of Leisure* (New York: Basic Books, 1992); Schor, *Do Americans Shop Too Much?* (Boston: Beacon Press, 2000).
62. *Adams Family Correspondence,* vol. 2, L. H. Butterfield, ed. (Cambridge, MA: Belknap Press, 1963) 30.
63. Gary B. Nash, *The Unknown American Revolution: The Unruly Birth of Democracy and the Struggle to Create America* (New York: Penguin Books, 2005) 208.
64. Black and white photo in Harry J. Williams, Richard N. Current, & Frank

Freidel, *A History of the United States [to 1876]* (New York: Alfred A. Knopf, 1961) 318.

65. Susan G. Davis, *Parades and Power: Street Theatre in Nineteenth-Century Philadelphia* (Philadelphia: Temple UP, 1986) 40–44.
66. Anthony F. C. Wallace, *Rockdale* (New York: Knopf, 1980) 312; Cf. John Bodnar, *Remaking America: Public Memory, Commemoration, and Patriotism in the Twentieth Century* (Princeton, NJ: Princeton UP, 1992) 26 ff.
67. Eric Monkonnen, *Murder in New York City* (Berkeley: UC Press, 2001) 130–1.
68. Roy Rosenzweig, *Eight Hours for What We Will: Workers and Leisure in an Industrial City, 1870–1920* (New York: Cambridge UP, 1983) 67–8.
69. Rosenzweig 72.
70. Rosenzweig 73.
71. S. Davis 103.
72. Rosenzweig 77, 80.
73. Rosenzweig 81–84.
74. Burke 180–1.
75. Rosenzweig 86.
76. Rosenzweig 167 and passim.
77. Saul Bellow, *The Adventures of Augie March* in *Novels 1944–1953* (New York: The Library of America, 2003) 451.
78. Gary S. Cross and John K. Walton, *The Playful Crowd: Pleasure Places in the Twentieth Century* (New York: Columbia UP, 2005) 59, 63.
79. Cross and Walton 6, 17, 36.
80. Qtd. in Cross and Walton 77; cf. 39, 59.
81. Cross and Walton 121.
82. *New York Sun* 16 July 1877, qtd. in Cross and Walton 67; cf. 54, 60.
83 J. P. Toner, *Leisure and Ancient Rome* (Cambridge, UK: Polity Press, 1995) 57.
84. Cross and Walton 40, 61, 63, 81.
85. "Sixth of October," *The San Francisco Oracle 2: Youth Quake!*, Allen Cohen, ed., *The San Franisco Oracle Facsimile Edition: The Psychedelic Newspaper of the Haight-Ashbury 1966–1968* (Berkeley: Regent Press, 1991) 33.
86. "Sixth of October" 33.
87. Mari Lanham, now a minister in Washington State, qtd. in Ben Fong-Torres, "What a Time It Was It Was a Time: Forty years later, the Summer of Love's unrequited romance," *California* 118.4 (July/August 2007) 48.
88. James Miller, *Flowers in the Dustbin: The Rise of Rock and Roll, 1947–1977* (New York: Simon and Schuster, 1999) 265, describing the world evoked by *Monterey Pop*, D. A. Pennebaker's documentary film (1969).
89. Ehrenreich 220–1.
90. Kristin Lawler, "High Times: Revisiting the New Left," rev. of *The New Left Revisited*, John McMillan and Paul Buhle, eds., *New Politics* IX.4 (Winter 2004) 172.

91. Cf. Mona Ozouf, *Festivals and the French Revolution,* trans. Alan Sheridan, (Cambridge, MA: Harvard UP, 1988) 10.
92. Max Weber, *The Protestant Ethic and the Spirit of Capitalism,* trans. Talcott Parsons (New York: Chas. Scribner's Sons, 1958) 157.
93. David Grimsted, *American Mobbing, 1828–1861: Toward Civil War* (New York: Oxford UP, 1998) 9.
94. Grimsted, "Rioting in Its Jacksonian Setting," *The American Historical Review* 77.2 (April 1972) 380.
95. Zinn 222–3; Grimsted, "Rioting" 367–7. The latter cites much lower figures for killed and wounded.
96. Grimsted, "Rioting" 384–5.
97. Robert M. Fogelson, "White on Black: A Critique of the McCone Commission Report," in Anthony Platt, ed., *The Politics of Riot Commissions 1917–1970: A Collection of Official Reports and Critical Essays* (New York: Macmillan, 1971) 318.
98. *Report of the National Advisory Commission on Civil Disorders* [aka the Kerner Report] (New York: Bantam Books, 1968) 91; cf. 88.
99. Unnamed observer, qtd. in *Report* [Kerner] 91.
100. Jeffrey Eugenides, *Middlesex* (New York: Picador, 2002) 240.
101. See, e.g., Ehrenreich 23.
102. Blatch and Lutz 180.

2. WHEN CROWDS RULED

1. J. S. McClelland, *The Crowd and the Mob: From Plato to Canetti* (Boston: Unwin Hyman, 1989) 37.
2. John Thorley, *Athenian Democracy* (New York: Lancaster Pamphlets/Routledge, 1996) 33.
3. Thorley 33, 80, and passim; Mogens Herman Hansen, *The Athenian Democracy in the Age of Demosthenes: Structure, Principles and Ideology,* trans. J. A. Crook (Cambridge, Mass: Basil Blackwell, 1991) 97–137.
4. Hansen 178–80.
5. Thorley 31; cf. 27 ff.; Hansen 230–49.
6. Hansen 125.
7. M. I. Finley, *Democracy Ancient and Modern,* 2d ed. (London: Hogarth Press, 1985) 22.
8. Hansen 105.
9. Thucydides, *The Complete Writings of Thucydides: The Peloponnesian War,* II.40, trans. Crawley (New York: The Modern Library, 1951) 105.
10. Paul Woodruff, *First Democracy: The Challenge of an Ancient Idea* (New York:

Oxford UP, 2005) 23–4, 53–4, 122 and passim.

11. Sheldon S. Wolin, *Politics and Vision: Continuity and Innovation in Western Political Thought* (Boston: Little, Brown, 1960) 41.
12. McClelland 314; cf. Wolin 28–58.
13. David Andress, *The Terror: Civil War in the French Revolution* (London: Little, Brown, 2005) 6.
14. Qtd. in Andress 142.
15. Eric Hobsbawm, *The Age of Revolution: 1789–1848* (New York: Mentor, 1962) 85.
16. Louis-Sébastien Mercier, qtd. in Barbara Ehrenreich, *Dancing in the Streets: A History of Collective Joy* (New York: Metropolitan Books) 189.
17. Qtd. in George Rudé, *The Crowd in History: A Study of Popular Disturbances in France and England 1730–1848* (London: Serif, 1981) 106; cf. 93 ff.
18. Albert Soboul, *The French Revolution 1787-1799: From the Storming of the Bastille to Napoleon,* trans. Alan Forrest and Colin Jones (New York: Vintage Books, 1975) 143.
19. Barrington Moore, Jr., *Social Origins of Dictatorship and Democracy: Lord and Peasant in the Making of the Modern World* (Boston: Beacon Press, 1966) 65, 69, 73, 92.
20. Rudé 103–4; 110 ff.
21. E. P. Thompson, "The Moral Economy of the Crowd in the Eighteenth Century" in *The Essential E. P. Thompson* (New York: The New Press, 2001) 316–377.
22. Andress 151.
23. Rudé 119.
24. Mark Steel, *Vive la Revolution* (Chicago: Haymarket Books, 2006) 79.
25. Daniel Mendelsohn, "Lost in Versailles," rev. of *Marie Antoinette,* dir. Sofia Coppola, *New York Review of Books* LIII.19 (November 30, 2006) 22.
26. Steel 148.
27. Gary B. Nash, *The Unknown American Revolution: The Unruly Birth of Democracy and the Struggle to Create America* (New York: Penguin Books, 2005) 45–7.
28. Dirk Hoerder, *Crowd Action in Revolutionary Massachusetts, 1765–1780* (New York: Academic Press, 1977) 100.
29. Cf. Richard L. Bushman, *The Refinement of America: Persons, Houses, Cities* (New York: Alfred A. Knopf, 1992) 402 ff.
30. Howard Zinn, *A People's History of the United States: 1492–Present* (New York: Harper Perennial, 2003) 94.
31. Qtd. in Nash 53.
32. Elias Canetti, *Crowds and Power,* Carol Stewart, trans. (New York: Farrar, Straus & Giroux, 1962) 19.

33. Nash 50–1.
34. Nash 54.
35. Nash 55.
36. Nash 56.
37. Nash 59.
38. Gary J. Kornblith and John M. Murrin, "The Making and Unmaking of an American Ruling Class," in *Beyond the American Revolution: Explorations in the History of American Radicalism,* Alfred F. Young, ed. (DeKalb, IL: N. Illinois UP, 1993) 46.
39. Nash 99.
40. Hugh Brogan, *The Pelican History of the United States of America* (New York: Penguin Books, 1985) 156; cf. 153.
41. A. J. Langguth, *Patriots: The Men Who Started the American Revolution* (New York: Simon & Schuster, 1988) 125 ff.; Hoerder 216 ff.
42. Brogan 156.
43. Qtd. in Brogan 156.
44. Hoerder 220.
45. Langguth 130 ff.; Hoerder 223 ff.
46. Langguth 138.
47. In *The Crowd: A Study of the Popular Mind* (Mineola, NY: Dover Pub., 2002).
48. Qtd. in Hoerder 231; cf. Langguth 138 ff.
49. Nash 192.
50. Nash 26.
51. Nash 52.
52. Nash 78, 104–7.
53. Unnamed New Yorker, qtd. in Nash 48.
54. Nash 340, 388.
55. Daniel Lazare, "Patriotic Bore," rev. of *The Unknown American Revolution* by Gary B. Nash, *Thomas Paine and the Promise of America* by Harvey J. Kaye, and *1776* by David McCullough, *The Nation* 281.7 (12 September 2005) 32-3.
56. Nash 373–4.
57. Nash 232.
58. Nash 236; cf. 237–8.
59. Qtd. in Nash 311.
60. Hoerder 42–45, 48, 58, 60, 66; Brogan 129.
61. Nash 135.
62. Nash 2–3.
63. Zinn 181.
64. David Grimsted, *American Mobbing, 1828–1861: Toward Civil War* (New York: Oxford UP, 1998) 34, 74–80.

65. Grimsted, *Mobbing* 76.
66. Grimsted, "Rioting in Its Jacksonian Setting," *The American Historical Review* 77.2 (April 1972) 392.
67. Grimsted, *Mobbing* 220.
68. Grimsted, *Mobbing* 218.
69. Grimsted, *Mobbing* 226.
70. Grimsted, *Mobbing* 227.
71. Grimsted, *Mobbing* 230–1.
72. Grimsted, *Mobbing* 239–41.
73. Grimsted, *Mobbing* 238.
74. Grimsted, *Mobbing* 227–8.
75. William Hogeland, *The Whiskey Rebellion: George Washington, Alexander Hamilton, and the Frontier Rebels Who Challenged America's Newfound Sovereignty* (New York: Scribner, 2006) 66.
76. Jill Lepore, "Vast Designs: How America Came of Age," rev. of *What Hath God Wrought: The Transformation of America, 1815–1848* by Daniel Walker Howe, *The New Yorker,* Oct. 29, 2007: 91.
77. Cf. Norbert Elias, *The History of Manners, The Civilizing Process,* Vol. 1, trans. Edmund Jephcott (New York: Pantheon Books, 1978) 200.
78. Grimsted, *Mobbing* 222.
79. Cf. Charley Richardson, "Working Alone: The Erosion of Solidarity in Today's Workplace," *New Labor Forum* 17(3), Fall 2008: 69–78.
80. Michael Steinberg, *The Fiction of a Thinkable World: Body, Meaning, and the Culture of Capitalism* (New York: Monthly Review Press, 2005) 143.
81. See, for example, Jim Herron Zamora, "Fight over parking spot ends in slaying: Father, 33, shot after friend takes neighbor's space," *San Francisco Chronicle* 11 January 2007: B3; cf. Kate Zernike, "Violent Crime Rising Sharply in Some Cities: An Increase in Killings Over Petty Disputes," *New York Times* 12 February 2006: I-1, 28.
82. Eric H. Monkkonen, *Murder in New York City* (Berkeley: UC Press, 2001) 20.
83. David T. Burbank, *Reign of the Rabble: The St. Louis General Strike of 1877* (New York: Augustus M. Kelley, 1966) 17, 19, 31.
84. Qtd. in Burbank 53.
85. Burbank 43.
86. St. Louis *Republican,* qtd. in Burbank 75.
87. *Daily Market Reporter,* qtd. in Burbank 95.
88. Qtd. Burbank 61.
89. Qtd. in Burbank 56. Whether or not Hillquit was a direct participant is unclear.
90. Burbank 112, 101–2, 118.
91. Burbank 86.
92. Burbank 75.

93. Jeremy Brecher, *Strike!* Rev. ed. (Cambridge, MA: South End Press, 1997) 33–4.
94. Burbank 148; cf. 76 and passim.
95. Burbank 106–7, 110, 135.
96. Ash, *The Magic Lantern: The Revolution of '89 Witnessed in Warsaw, Budapest, Berlin and Prague* (New York: Vintage Books, 1999) 84 ff.
97. Frances Fox Piven and Richard A. Cloward, *Poor People's Movements: Why They Succeed, How They Fail* (New York: Vintage Books, 1977) 36.
98. Burbank 109, 141, 143.
99. *Martinsburg Independent* 21 July 1877, qtd. in Brecher 16.
100. Brecher 36.
101. Brecher 19–20.
102. Brecher 26; Steve Babson, *The Unfinished Struggle: Turning Points in American Labor, 1877–Present* (Lanham, MD: Rowman & Littlefield, 1999) 1.
103. Canetti 56.
104. Babson 74.
105. Brecher 163–4.
106. Brecher 176-8; Piven and Cloward 121–2.
107. *New York Times* 5 September 1934, qtd. in Brecher 186.
108. Brecher 184–92; Babson 82–4.
109. Brecher 227; Piven and Cloward 140.
110. Brecher 221.
111. Jean Baudrillard, *Selected Writings,* 2d ed., Mark Poster, ed. (Stanford, CA: Stanford UP, 2001) 53.
112. Baudrillard, *Selected* 49, 56.
113. "Mayor's Commission on Conditions in Harlem: A Report on Social and Economic Conditions Responsible for the Outbreak of March 19, 1935," in Anthony Platt, ed., *The Politics of Riot Commissions 1917–1970: A Collection of Official Reports and Critical Essays* (New York: Macmillan, 1971) 167.
114. "Mayor's Commission," in A. Platt 170.
115. Canetti 19.
116. "Mayor's Commission," in A. Platt 170.
117. Ronald Takaki, *A Different Mirror: A History of Multicultural America* (Boston: Back Bay Books, 1993) 409 ff.; Brogan 662; Marilynn S. Johnson, *The Second Gold Rush: Oakland and the East Bay in World War II* (Berkeley: U. of Calif. Press, 1993); Piven and Cloward 12.
118. Piven and Cloward 192.
119. Taylor Branch, *Pillar of Fire: America in the King Years, 1963–1965* (New York: Touchstone, 1998) 296, paraphrasing Bob Moses, Stanford University speech of April 24, 1964.
120. Qtd. in Takaki 410.
121. Zinn 458.

122. Brogan 648, 652–3.
123. Branch 418.
124. Zinn 458; Piven and Cloward 248.
125. Branch 420–1.
126. *Report of the National Advisory Commission on Civil Disorders* [The Kerner Report] (New York: Bantam Books, 1968) 38; Robert Fogelson, "White on Black: A Critique of the McCone Commission Report," in A. Platt 307.
127. Brogan 659.
128. Fogelson, "White" in A. Platt 313.
129. Fogelson, "White" in A. Platt 318, 323.
130. Dept. of Labor statistic, cited in Zinn 466.
131. *Report* [Kerner] 6.
132. *Report* [Kerner] 111–12.
133. *Report* [Kerner] 42–47.
134. *Report* [Kerner] 47–52.
135. *Report* [Kerner] 52–56.
136. *Report* [Kerner] 56–59, 100.
137. *Report* [Kerner] 72.
138. Qtd. in *Report* [Kerner] 83.
139. *Report* [Kerner] 84.
140. *Report* [Kerner] 507.
141. *Report* [Kerner] 84–108.
142. *Report* [Kerner] 203, 2.
143. *Report* [Kerner] 23.
144. Zinn 198–9.
145. William D. Carrigan, *The Making of a Lynching Culture: Violence and Vigilantism in Central Texas, 1836–1916* (Chicago: U. of Ill. Press, 2004).
146. Allen Guttman, *Sports Spectators* (New York: Columbia UP, 1986) 119.
147. See, e.g., Darryl Pinckney, "Branding in America," rev. of *Apex Hides the Hurt* by Colson Whitehead, *New York Review of Books* LIII.17 (November 2, 2006) 56.
148. Mike Davis, *Dead Cities and Other Tales* (New York: The New Press, 2002) 228.
149. Richard Rodriguez, "Horizontal City," *This World, San Francisco Chronicle* May 24, 1992: 16.
150. Qtd. in Takaki 422.
151. Qtd. in Zinn 464.
152. See Robin Morgan, *The Word of a Woman* (New York: W. W. Norton, 1992) 21 ff.
153. Jo Freeman, "From Freedom Now! to Free Speech: The FSM's Roots in the Bay Area Civil Rights Movement," in *The Free Speech Movement: Reflections on Berkeley in the 1960s,* Robert Cohen and Reginald E. Zelnik, eds. (Berkeley: UC Press, 2002) 75.

154. Freeman in Cohen and Zelnik 75–6.
155. Branch 494–5.
156. Rossman, "The 'Rossman Report': A Memoir of Making History," in Cohen and Zelnik 192.
157. Margot Adler, "My Life in the FSM: Memories of a Freshman," in Cohen and Zelnik 116.
158. Rossman in Cohen and Zelnik 195.
159. "Riot Erupts at UC: Sproul Hall Battle—Police in Retreat," *San Francisco Chronicle* 2 October 1964: 1.
160. Branch 505; Robert Cohen, "The Many Meanings of the FSM: In Lieu of an Introduction," in Cohen and Zelnik 5.

3. KILLER CROWDS

1. Iver Bernstein, *The New York Draft Riots: Their Significance for American Society and Politics in the Age of the Civil War* (New York: Oxford UP, 1990); Howard Zinn, *A People's History of the United States: 1492–Present* (New York: HarperPerennial, 2003) 198–99; William D. Carrigan, *The Making of a Lynching Culture: Violence and Vigilantism in Central Texas, 1836–1916* (Chicago: U. of Illinois Press, 2004) 1–2, 173, 191–7; Tony Platt, "Reign of Terror Against Chinese: Professor Traces Deadly Campaigns that Aimed to Drive Them Out of the West," rev. of *Driven Out: The Forgotten War Against Chinese Americans* by Jean Pfaelzer, *San Francisco Chronicle* 3 June 2007: M5.
2. Cf. J. S. McClelland, *The Crowd and the Mob: From Plato to Canetti* (Boston: Unwin Hyman, 1989) 5–6.
3. Qtd. in David Andress, *The Terror: Civil War in the French Revolution* (London: Little, Brown, 2005) 82–3.
4. Andress 108.
5. Andress 95.
6. Andress 95.
7. George Orwell, summarizing a description of the Paris mob in Charles Dickens, *A Tale of Two Cities.* See Orwell, "Charles Dickens," *A Collection of Essays* (Garden City, NY: Doubleday Anchor, 1954) 65.
8. Colin Lucas, "Revolutionary Violence, the People and the Terror," *The Terror*, Keith Michael Baker, ed., vol. 4 of *The French Revolution and the Creation of Modern Political Culture* (Tarrytown, NY: Pergamon Press, 1994) 73.
9. Lucas, "Revolutionary Violence" 73. Lucas attributed this analysis to Soboul; cf. Barbara Ehrenreich, *Dancing in the Streets: A History of Collective Joy* (New York: Metropolitan Books, 2007) 175.
10. Lucas, "Revolutionary Violence," in Baker 73.

11. Judith Thurman, "Dressed for Excess: Marie Antoinette, out of the closet," *The New Yorker,* 25 September 2006: 136.
12. Eric Hobsbawm, *The Age of Revolution: 1789–1848* (New York: Mentor, 1962) 91.
13. Hobsbawm, *Age of Revolution* 87.
14. Moore, "Thoughts on Violence and Democracy," *Urban Riots: Violence and Social Change,* ed. Robert H. Connery (New York: The Academy of Political Science, Columbia U., 1968) 4.
15. Guy Debord, *Society of the Spectacle* (Detroit: Black & Red, 1983) 172.
16. Qtd. in George Rudé, *The Crowd in History: A Study of Popular Disturbances in France and England 1730–1848* (London: Serif, 1981) 8.
17. Gustave Le Bon, *The Crowd: A Study of the Popular Mind* (Mineola, NY: Dover Pub., 2002) 42.
18. Le Bon 4.
19. Le Bon 6.
20. Le Bon iv.
21. Le Bon 15–16.
22. Aristotle, *The Politics* 1281b, ed. and trans. Ernest Barker (New York: Oxford UP, 1962) 123–5.
23. Le Bon 14.
24. Le Bon 8.
25. Le Bon 7.
26. Max Brooks, qtd. in Warren St. John, "Market for Zombies? It's Undead (Aaahhh!)," *New York Times* 26 March 2006: Sec. 9, 13.
27. Le Bon 72.
28. Le Bon 104; cf. 11, 15–16, and passim.
29. Le Bon 25.
30. Le Bon 27–8.
31. Susanna Barrows, *Distorting Mirrors: Visions of the Crowd in Late Nineteenth-Century France* (New Haven: Yale UP, 1981) 168.
32. Qtd. in Ehrenreich 185. Original source unclear.
33. Sigmund Freud, *Group Psychology and the Analysis of the Ego,* trans. James Strachey (New York: W. W. Norton, 1959) 13 and passim.
34. Freud 49.
35. Qtd. in Peter Hayes, *The People and the Mob: The Ideology of Civil Conflict in Modern Europe* (Westport, Conn: Praeger, 1992) 65.
36. C. G. Jung, *The Archetypes and the Collective Unconscious,* vol. 9, part 1 of *The Collected Works,* trans. R. F. C. Hull (New York: Bollingen Foundation/Pantheon Books, 1959) 125.
37. Jung, *Civilization in Transition,* vol. 10 of *The Collected Works,* trans. Hull (New York: Bollingen Foundation/Pantheon Books, 1964) 238–9.

38. Cf. Ernest Becker, *The Denial of Death* (New York: The Free Press, 1973) 135–6.
39. In Robert Coover, *The Public Burning* (New York: Grove Press, 1977) 207.
40. See http://en.wikipedia.org/wiki/Group_polarization; http://changingminds.org/explanations/theories/ risky_shift.htm.
41. AP photo accompanying Sheryl Gay Stolberg, "The Senate Apologizes, Mostly," *New York Times* 19 June 2005: sec. 4, 3.
42. Cynthia Carr, *Our Town: A Heartland Lynching, a Haunted Town, and the Hidden History of White America* (New York: Crown Pub., 2006) 32, 97.
43. Qtd. in Carr 101.
44. James Cameron, qtd. in Carr 18, apparently from Cameron's *A Time of Terror: A Survivor's Story* (Baltimore: Black Classics Press, 1994).
45. Betty Beitler, qtd. in Carr 32.
46. Carr 29.
47. David Grimsted, *American Mobbing, 1828–1861: Toward Civil War* (New York: Oxford UP, 1998) 104.
48. Carr 29.
49. Carr 13, 25.
50. Carr 46, 115, 99, 119, 101.
51. Qtd. in Lerone Bennett, Jr., *Before the Mayflower: A History of the Negro in America, 1619–1964*, Rev. ed. (New York: Penguin, 1964) 236.
52. Le Bon 6.
53. Qtd. in Hannah Arendt, *Eichmann in Jerusalem: A Report on the Banality of Evil,* rev. & enlarged ed. (New York: Penguin Books, 1992) 246–7.
54. Philip Zimbardo, *The Lucifer Effect: Understanding How Good People Turn Evil* (New York: Random House, 2007) 25.
55. Zimbardo 299–300.
56. Zimbardo 299–300.
57. Zimbardo 240.
58. Zimbardo 307.
59. Jean Hatzfeld, *Machete Season: The Killers in Rwanda Speak* (New York: Farrar, Straus & Giroux, 2005) 47.
60. Arendt 126.
61. Carrigan 187; cf. 12–14, 30, 106–7.
62. Carr 14, 60.
63. Carr 56.
64. Carr 340.
65. Carr 99, 17.
66. Carr 124, 98.
67. Qtd. in Carr 142.
68. Zimbardo 197.

69. Le Bon xi, xiii.
70. Marc Cooper, "L. A.'s State of Siege: City of Angels, Cops from Hell," *Inside the L. A. Riots: What really happened—and why it will happen again* (Institute for Alternative Journalism, 1992) 12.
71. Arlette Farge, *Fragile Lives Violence, Power and Solidarity in Eighteenth-Century Paris,* trans. Carol Shelton (Cambridge, MA: Harvard UP, 1993) 259.
72. Jim Dwyer and Christopher Drew, "Fear Exceeded Crime's Reality in New Orleans," *New York Times* 29 September 2005: A1, A22.
73. Cf. David Kadlecek, "Reviewing disasters: San Francisco 1906, New Orleans 2005," *The Partisan* 22 (1st quarter, 2007) 7.
74. Liz Austin Peterson (AP), "Police: Texas man killed by a few, not a mob," *San Francisco Chronicle* 22 June 2007: A5.
75. Philip L. Fradkin, *The Great Earthquake and Firestorms of 1906: How San Francisco Nearly Destroyed Itself* (Berkeley: U. of Calif. Press, 2005) xiii.
76. Cited in Iver Bernstein 263.
77. "Thousands of Quake Refugees Find Shelter on Campus: Relief Efforts, Berkeley seismology highlighted in library exhibits," *Bene Legere* 70 (Summer 2006) 1.
78. Fradkin xiv, 15, 80.
79. Fradkin xiii, 15, 20.
80. Anon., Letter to Buddy, "Hardly a window remains intact"; "Peace at a price: 12 dead, 1,000 hurt"; and Josette Dermody Wingo, "It made the bricks vibrate," *San Francisco Examiner* 11 August 1995: A19. Also, Carl Nolte, "S.F. Welcomed Peace With a Riot," *San Francisco Chronicle* 14 August 1985: A6. Accompanying photo shows a crowd around a woman who has evidently been stripped of her clothes from the waist down.

4. CROWD AS OPPORTUNITY

1. Matthew 3: 3–5; cf. Pieter Brueghel the Elder, *The Sermon of Saint John the Baptist* (1566).
2. Jérôme Carcopino, *Daily Life in Ancient Rome,* 2d ed., trans. E. O. Lorimer (New Haven: Yale UP, 2003) 214–5.
3. Ross King, *Brunelleschi's Dome: How a Renaissance Genius Reinvented Architecture* (New York: Penguin Books, 2000) 137.
4. Zonaras, *Epitome* 7.21, qtd. in G. I. F. Tingay and J. Badcock, *These Were the Romans,* 2d ed. (Chester Springs, PA: Dufour, 1989) 89.
5. Qtd. in Lewis Mumford, *The City in History: Its Origins, Its Transformations, and Its Prospects* (New York: Harcourt, Brace & World, 1961) 279–80.
6. J. Huizinga, *The Waning of the Middle Ages: A Study of the Forms of Life,*

Thought, and Art in France and the Netherlands in the Fourteenth and Fifteenth Centuries (Montréal: Penguin Books, 1955) 58.

7. Fernand Braudel, *The Perspective of the World,* trans. Siân Reynolds, Vol. 3 of *Civilization and Capitalism, 15th–18th Century* (New York: Harper & Row, 1984) 148–54.
8. Guy Debord, *Society of the Spectacle* (Detroit: Black and Red, 1983) 23.
9. Richard L. Bushman, *The Refinement of America: Persons, Houses, Cities* (New York: Alfred A. Knopf, 1992) 154.
10. Roberta Gratz and Stephen A. Goldsmith, "In the Park With Christo," *The Nation* 280.12 (28 March 2005) 25.
11. Susan G. Davis, *Parades and Power: Street Theatre in Nineteenth-Century Philadelphia* (Philadelphia: Temple UP, 1986) 3, 14, 27, 28.
12. Gary B. Nash, *The Unknown American Revolution: The Unruly Birth of Democracy and the Struggle to Create America* (New York: Penguin Books, 2005) 145–6.
13. Alfred F. Young, "Afterward: How Radical Was the American Revolution?" in ed. Young, *Beyond the American Revolution: Explorations in the History of American Radicalism* (DeKalb, IL: N. Illinois UP, 1993) 332.
14. S. Davis 15.
15. John Bodnar, *Remaking America: Public Memory, Commemoration, and Patriotism in the Twentieth Century* (Princeton, NJ: Princeton UP, 1992) 24.
16. Charles C. Mann, "The Founding Sachems," op. ed., *New York Times* 4 July 2005: A17.
17. Hawthorne, *The House of the Seven Gables* (New York: Bantam, 1981) 126.
18. Bodnar 25.
19. S. Davis 29, 30.
20. Philippe Ariès, *Centuries of Childhood: A Social History of Family Life,* trans. Robert Baldick (New York: Vintage, 1962) 341.
21. Barbara Tuchman, *A Distant Mirror: The Calamitous 14th Century* (New York: Ballantine Books, 1978) 32–3; Barbara Ehrenreich, *Dancing in the Streets: A History of Collective Joy* (New York: Metropolitan Books, 2007) 90.
22. Nash 315, 318.
23. S. Davis 8, 82, 98–9, 156, 161.
24. S. Davis 32, 34.
25. S. Davis 13 and passim.
26. Philip S. Foner, *May Day: A Short History of the International Workers' Holiday, 1886–1986* (New York: International Pub., 1986) 8; Eric Chase, "The Brief Origins of May Day," http://www.iww.org/projects/mayday/origins.shtml. Half a century later, workers at some locales were still struggling for a ten-hour workday. See Jeremy Brecher, *Strike!* Rev. ed. (Cambridge, MA: South End Press, 1997) 47.

27. Thomas M. Spencer, *The St. Louis Veiled Prophet Celebration: Power on Parade, 1877–1995* (Columbia, MO: U. of Missouri Press, 2000) 2.
28. David Harvey, *The New Imperialism* (New York: Oxford UP, 2003) 70.
29. Spencer 169.
30. Bodnar 96, 135, 147.
31. Bodnar 160–1.
32. Bodnar 90.
33. William Hogeland, *The Whiskey Rebellion: George Washington, Alexander Hamilton, and the Frontier Rebels Who Challenged America's Newfound Sovereignty* (New York: Scribner, 2006) 235–6.
34. Sharon Smith, *Subterranean Fire: A History of Working-Class Radicalism in the United States* (Chicago: Haymarket Books, 2006) 95.
35. From *In re Frazee,* 63 Michigan 396,407 (1886), qtd. in Linda J. Lumsden, *Rampant Women: Suffragists and the Right of Assembly* (Knoxville, TN: U. of Tennessee Press, 1997) xvii; cf. M. Glenn Abernathy, *The Right of Assembly and Association,* 2d ed., rev. (Columbia, SC: U. of South Carolina Press, 1981) 85–6.
36. Abernathy 94, 98.
37. Abernathy 83; cf. 94, 98, 106.
38. Irma Santana, qtd. in Richard Fausset (*L.A. Times),* "Few Hispanics march in Deep South: Area is home to fastest-growing Latino population," *San Francisco Chronicle* 31 March 2006: A4.
39. Spencer 18.
40. Spencer 18, 3 ff.
41. Spencer 19.
42. Spencer 131.
43. Spencer 4, 59.
44. Spencer 77.
45. Spencer 61–62, 94, 96.
46. Spencer 75.
47. Qtd. in Spencer 79.
48. Spencer 131–32.
49. Spencer 151, 153.
50. Ronald Henges, qtd. in Spencer 166.
51. Lumsden xxxi.
52. Lumsden 79–80.
53. *Cleveland Plain Dealer* 2 and 3 May 1919, cited in http://Publications.ohiohistory.org/ohstemplate.cfm?action=detail&Page=0081202.html&S.
54. Qtd. in Taylor Branch, *Pillar of Fire: America in the King Years, 1963–1965* (New York: Touchstone, 1998) 331; cf. 335.
55. Martin Roysher, "Recollections of the Free Speech Movement," in Robert

Cohen and Reginald E. Zelnik, eds. *The Free Speech Movement: Reflections on Berkeley in the 1960s* (Berkeley: UC Press, 2002) 154.

56. *What's Going On?—California and the Vietnam Era,* Exhibit, Oakland Museum of California, 2004.
57. Abernathy 49.
58. Frances Fox Piven and Richard A. Cloward, *Poor People's Movements: Why They Succeed, How They Fail* (New York: Vintage Books, 1977) 29.
59. One of the convicted men had died in his cell, the governor commuted the sentences of two others to life imprisonment, and one received a long prison sentence. See Foner 34–38; Howard Zinn, *A People's History of the United States: 1492–Present* (New York: Harper Perennial, 2003) 265.
60. Most of the policemen died of bullet wounds rather than bomb shrapnel, meaning that they were probably killed by "friendly fire" when fellow officers fired on the crowd assembled there. See Paul Arvich, *The Haymarket Tragedy* (Princeton, NJ: 1984), cited in Foner 31; cf. Caleb Crain, "The Terror Last Time: What Happened at Haymarket," *The New Yorker* 13 March 2006: 84.
61. Crain 82.
62. Foner 41–42; 44–45.
63. Qtd. in Foner 52.
64. Paul Buhle, "Words & Pictures: Nicole Schulman," *New Politics* X.2 (Winter 2005) 191.
65. Qtd. in Foner 79.
66. *New York Times* 2 May 1914, qtd. in Foner 80.
67. Foner 86.
68. Foner 88.
69. Editor of *Masses*, qtd. in Lumsden 116.
70. Foner 103.
71. *New York Times* 2 May 1930, qtd. in Foner 110.
72. *New York Times* 2 May 1937, qtd. in Foner 119.
73. S. Smith, cover.
74. Foner 130.
75. Foner 75; 3–4.
76. Foner 136.
77. *New York Times* 2 May 1951, qtd. in Foner 137.
78. Foner 137–39.
79. *The Partisan* 24 (4th Quarter 2007) 4.
80. Novelist William Kennedy, reminiscing about Albany, New York; qtd. in Fogelson, *Downtown: Its Rise and Fall, 1880–1950* (New Haven: Yale UP, 2001) 7.
81. *American Architect and Building News,* probably August 20, 1892:10, but citation unclear. Qtd. in Fogelson, *Downtown* 16.

82. Fogelson, *Downtown* 192.
83. *New York: The Power and the People: Episode Four: 1898–1918,* videotape, dir. Ric Burns, Steeplechase Films & WGBH Boston/Thirteen, WNET & The New York Historical Society (Warner Home Video, 1999).
84. Lumsden 29.
85. Anon. regarding Seattle c. 1915, qtd. in Harvey O'Connor, *Revolution in Seattle: A Memoir* (New York: Monthly Review Press, 1964) 243.
86. Miriam Allen DeFord, Boston suffragist, qtd. in Sherna Gluck, ed., *From Parlor to Prison* (New York: Vintage Books, 1976), cited in Lumsden 29.
87. Lumsden 13, 23, 24, 33, 51.
88. Lumsden 47–9.
89. Maud Malone, qtd. in Lumsden 33, citing *New York Times* 27 March 1908: 4.
90. Lumsden 74.
91. Lumsden 85.
92. Qtd. in Lumsden 76.
93. Lumsden 25, 70.
94. Lumsden 49.
95. Mother Mary Jones, Chap. X: "March of the Mill Children," *The Autobiography of Mother Jones,* http//womenshistory.about.com/ library/etext /mj/bl_mj10.htm.
96. Simone Sebastian and Dermian Bulwa, "36th S.F. Gay Pride Parade: Huge Celebration of pride: Hundreds of thousands fill Market Street with 'incredible' color," *San Francisco Chronicle* 26 June 2006, at http://sfgate.com/cgi-bin/article.cgi? f=/c/a/2006/06/25/Mnpride25.DTL.
97. Beth Greenfield, "A Month of Coming-Out Parties," *New York Times* 25 May 2007: D2.
98. http://castroonline.com/spectrum/0604/DykeMarch.html.
99. Gary S. Cross and John K. Walton, *The Playful Crowd: Pleasure Places in the Twentieth Century* (New York: Columbia UP, 2005) 3.
100. http://www.chapelhill.indymedia.org/print.php?id=11451.
101. Kevin Bracken, flash mob organizer, qtd. in Justin Berton, "Urban stunts get right in your face," *San Francisco Chronicle* 10 November 2007: A4.
102. E.g., in the California Supreme Court's 1979 ruling, *Robins v. Pruneyard Shopping Center.* Cf. Bob Egelko, "California: Malls cannot bar protestors from leafleting stores," *San Francisco Chronicle* 25 December 2007: B1–2, which describes the more recent case of *Fashion Valley Mall v. Labor Relations Board,* S144753.
103. Abernathy 55.
104. Branch 487.
105. See for example, Branch 218.
106. Mike Fennelly, Letter, *San Francisco Chronicle* 3 January 2007: B8.
107. Matthew Smucker, "What is to be done? Assessing the antiwar movement,"

RESIST Newsletter 17.3 (May–June 2008): 10.

108. Rick Lyman (*NYT*), "Fervant vigil kept at hospice," *San Francisco Chronicle* 26 March 2005: A8.
109. Robert D. Putnam, *Bowling Alone: The Collapse and Revival of American Community* (New York: Simon & Schuster, 2000) 162.
110. Putnam 44–5.
111. Qtd. in Robert Schlesinger, "Foes of a War in Iraq Spread Their Message," *Boston Globe* 16 January 2003, excerpted in Parisher, "Our TV ads launch today," MoveOn.org email, 16 January 2003.
112. Cross and Walton 174.
113. Cf. Sewell Chan (*NYT*), "Balloon mishap mars Macy's parade: Giant contraption crashes into light pole—2 sisters injured," *San Francisco Chronicle* 25 November 2005: A2.
114. Cf. "The Parade Lineup 2004" at http://www.nytourist.com/macys_news_lineup.htm with Macy's ad, *New York Times* 22 November 2006: A7.
115. Cross and Walton 128, 245–6.
116. Cross and Walton 248.
117. Chalmers Johnson, *The Sorrows of Empire: Militarism, Secrecy, and the End of the Republic* (New York: Henry Holt & Co., 2004) 188, 154, and passim; Lewis Seiler and Dan Hamburg, "Why there was no exit plan," op-ed, *San Francisco Chronicle* 30 April 2007: B7.
118. John Zerzan, *Twilight of the Machines* (Port Townsend, WA: Feral House, 2008) 22.
119. Stockholm International Peace Research Institute (SPIRI)'s 2006 Year Book, summarized at http://www.globalissues.org/Geopolitics/ArmsTrade/Spending.asp; Ana Marte and Winslow T. Wheeler, "The U.S. Military: By the Numbers," *The Defense Monitor: The Newsletter of the Center for Defense Information* XXXVI.6 (November/December 2007) 7.

5. WHO OWNS THE CROWD?

1. Sheldon S. Wolin, *Politics and Vision: Continuity and Innovation in Western Political Thought* (Boston: Little, Brown, 1960) 78.
2. Fergus Millar, *The Crowd in Rome in the Late Republic* (Ann Arbor: U. of Michigan Press, 1998) 215.
3. Florence Dupont, *Daily Life in Ancient Rome,* trans. Christopher Woodall (Cambridge, Mass.: Blackwell, 1992) 165.
4. Juvenal, Sat. *X* 75–80, *The Sixteen* Satires, 3d ed., trans. Peter Green (New York: Penguin, 1998) 78.
5. Millar 224, 82.

6. Millar 4, 25, 37, 47, 111, 135, 161–2, 211–12, 219.
7. See Mark Jewell (AP), "Cable giant Comcast hires 'seat-warmers' to pack FCC hearing," *San Francisco Chronicle* 27 February 2008: C3.
8. The Economic Policy Institute, *The State of Working America, 2008–2009,* p. 357. See at www.stateofworkingamerica.org/excerpt.html.
9. Michael E. McGerr, *The Decline of Popular Politics: The American North, 1865–1928* (New York: Oxford UP, 1986) 37.
10. Alexis de Tocqueville, *Democracy in America,* Vol. I (New York: Vintage Books, 1959) 180.
11. Tocqueville, *Democracy* II, 110.
12. McGerr 26 ff.
13. Linda J. Lumsden, *Rampant Women: Suffragists and the Right of Assembly* (Knoxville, TN: U. of Tennessee Press, 1997) 71.
14. David Grimsted, *American Mobbing, 1828–1861: Toward Civil War* (New York: Oxford UP, 1998) 187.
15. Grimsted, *Mobbing* 198; cf. 185 ff.
16. McGerr 26, 28, 35, 37.
17. McGerr 31.
18. McGerr 33; cf. 31–2.
19. McGerr 214–15.
20. McGerr 216; his quote is from the *Topeka Advocate* 13 May 1891: 4.
21. Qtd. in Lumsden xxxi, but rev. ed. of source cited, Susan Dye Lee, "Trampling Out the Vintage," in *Women in American Theatre,* ed. Helen K. Chinoy and Linda W. Jenkins (New York: Theatre Communications Group, 1987) 19, includes nothing on the WTC.
22. Grimsted, *Mobbing* 181–4.
23. Grimsted, *Mobbing* 36 and 17–18; cf. "Rioting" 375–6.
24. Grimsted, *Mobbing* 9.
25. Grimsted, *Mobbing* 26, 30.
26. Grimsted, *Mobbing* 35.
27. Grimsted, *Mobbing* 16.
28. Iver Bernstein, *The New York City Draft Riots: Their Significance for American Society and Politics in the Age of the Civil War* (New York: Oxford UP, 1990) 6.
29. Iver Bernstein 11–12, 19, 35.
30. Grimsted, *Mobbing* 49.
31. Cf. William D. Carrigan, *The Making of a Lynching Culture: Violence and Vigilantism in Central Texas, 1836–1916* (Chicago: U. of Illinois Press, 2004) 49, 74.
32. John Townsend, *The Doom of Slavery in the Union: Its Safety Out of It* (Charleston: Evans & Cogswell, 1860) 35–6, qtd. in Carrigan 79.
33. Carrigan 90.

34. Grimsted, *Mobbing* 106, 110.
35. Grimsted, *Mobbing* 104; cf. 16.
36. Carrigan 164–5.
37. James G. Frazer, *The Golden Bough: A Study in Magic and Religion,* abridged ed. (New York: Macmillan, 1950) 678.
38. Seneca, qtd. without additional reference in F. R. Cowell, *Life in Ancient Rome* (New York: Perigee, 1961) 186.
39. Publius Papius Statius, *Silvae* 1, vi, in *Statius,* vol. 1, trans. J. H. Mozley (New York: G. P. Putnam's Sons, 1928) 69.
40. Qtd. in Mikhail Bakhtin, *Rabelais and His World,* trans. Helene Iswolsky (Bloomington, IN: Indiana UP, 1984) 75.
41. Max Gluckman, qtd. in Peter Burke, *Popular Culture in Early Modern Europe* (New York: New York UP, 1978) 201.
42. Mona Ozouf, *Festivals and the French Revolution,* trans. Alan Sheridan (Cambridge, MA: Harvard UP, 1988) 1, 3.
43. Ozouf 37.
44. Ozouf 37.
45. Mark Steel, *Vive la Revolution* (Chicago: Haymarket Books, 2006) 121.
46. Barbara Ehrenreich, *Dancing in the Streets: A History of Collective Joy* (New York: Metropolitan Books, 2007) 147.
47. Ozouf 20.
48. Ozouf 39 ff., 86 ff.
49. Ehrenreich 191.
50. Ozouf 91.
51. Georges Bataille, *Literature and Evil: Essays by Georges Bataille,* trans. Alastair Hamilton (New York: Mario Boyars, 1993) 107.
52. Gary S. Cross and John K. Walton, *The Playful Crowd: Pleasure Places in the Twentieth Century* (New York: Columbia UP, 2005) 6, 27, 99, 106.
53. Cross and Walton 32; cf. 62.
54. *Public Ledger* 10 May 1836, qtd. in Susan G. Davis, *Parades and Power: Street Theatre in Nineteenth-Century Philadelphia* (Philadelphia: Temple UP, 1986) 40.
55. *Worcester Telegram* 4 July 1907, qtd. in Roy Rosenzweig, *Eight Hours for What We Will: Workers and Leisure in an Industrial City, 1870–1920* (New York: Cambridge UP, 1983) 156.
56. Rosenzweig 155.
57. Rosenzweig 154, 157–58.
58. Warren I. Susman, *Culture as History: The Transformation of American Society in the Twentieth Century* (New York: Pantheon Books, 1984) 77.
59. John Bodnar, *Remaking America: Public Memory, Commemoration, and Patriotism in the Twentieth Century* (Princeton, NJ: Princeton UP, 1992) 94–5.

60. Rosenzweig 160–1.
61. Qtd. in Harvey O'Connor, *Revolution in Seattle: A Memoir* (New York: Monthly Review Press, 1964) 124.
62. Rosenzweig 157–59.
63. Rosenzweig 162; cf. 160–61.
64. Jim Herron Zamora, "Fireworks display cancelled: Decision will allow more cops on street," *San Francisco Chronicle* 27 June 2007: B2.
65. Eric H. Monkkonen, *Murder in New York City* (Berkeley: UC Press, 2001) 132.
66. Maribeth Mellin, "Protests, passion part of Mexican culture," *San Francisco Chronicle* 1 October 2006: H6.
67. S. Davis 170.
68. Bodnar 30.
69. Bodnar 30.
70. *New York Times* 5 May 1939. Qtd. by Susman 216.
71. Kenneth Chang, "Enlisting Science's Lessons to Entice More Shoppers to Spend More," *New York Times* 19 September 2006: D3.
72. Walter Benjamin, *The Arcades Project,* trans. Howard Eiland and Kevin McLaughlin (Cambridge, MA: Belknap Press, 1999) 7.
73. Susman 218-223. Cf. Ozouf, *L'Ecole de la France* (Paris, 1985) 295, on the value of festival in eighteenth-century France: ". . . the community had the opportunity to contemplate itself and rejoice in one another." Qtd. in Arlette Farge, *Fragile Lives: Violence, Power and Solidarity in Eighteenth-Century Paris,* trans. Carol Shelton (Cambridge, MA: Harvard UP, 1993) 227.
74. Richard Heinberg, "Morning Show," KPFA 94.1 FM, 14 June 2005; Sam Roberts, "Sports and the Wide World of Tomorrow," *New York Times* 27 April 2005: A20.
75. Eric Hobsbawm, *The Age of Extremes: A History of the World, 1914–1991* (New York: Vintage Books, 1996) 306.
76. Rosenzweig 182; 177 ff.
77. Cross and Walton 201; cf. 185, 243.
78. Cross and Walton 255; cf. 171, 246.
79. Frederic Thompson, qtd. in Cross and Walton 76.
80. Philippe Ariès, *Centuries of Childhood: A Social History of Family Life,* trans. Robert Baldick (New York: Vintage Books, 1962) 369.
81. Cross and Walton 169.
82. Cross and Walton 249.
83. Cross and Walton 185; cf. 180 ff.
84. "Fair Opens, Rights Stall-in Fails; Protestors Drown Out Johnson; 300 Arrested in Demonstrations," *New York Times* 23 April 1964: 1, 26.
85. Taylor Branch, *Pillar of Fire: America in the King Years, 1963–1965* (New York: Touchstone, 1998) 296.

86. Bodnar 87–92, 106–7, 156.
87. Niccolò Machiavelli, *The Prince,* trans. Luigi Ricci, *The Prince and The Discourses* (New York: Modern Library, 1950) 85.
88. Cf. S. Davis 17; Thomas M. Spencer, *The St. Louis Veiled Prophet Celebration: Power on Parade, 1877–1995* (Columbia, MO: U. of Missouri Press, 2000) 163–64; McGerr 148.
89. Cross and Walton 253–4.
90. Cf. Timothy K. Beal, "Roadside Religion: A Right at Righteous, A Left at Licentious," *New York Times* 17 July 2005: 1–17; "Minnesota: Mall of America gets new theme park" (AP), *San Francisco Chronicle* 16 March 2008: E2.
91. See http://www.scottware.com.au/theme/feature/attendance _ nav.htm.
92. Cross and Walton 199; cf. 191–8.
93. Ehrenreich 192.
94. Jules Michelet, *History of the French Revolution,* trans. Charles Cocks (Chicago: U. of Chicago Press, 1967) 445, qtd. in Ehrenreich 193.
95. Qtd. in Jérôme Carcopino, *Daily Life in Ancient Rome,* 2d ed., trans. E. O. Lorimer (New Haven: Yale UP, 2003) 219.
96. Allen Guttmann, *Sports Spectators* (New York: Columbia UP, 1986) 29.
97. Carcopino 219.
98. Juvenal, *Satire VII 243,* 61.
99. J. S. McClelland, *The Crowd and the Mob: From Plato to Canetti* (Boston: Unwin Hyman, 1989) 57.
100. Qtd. in Thomas C. O'Guinn, "Touching Greatness: The Central Midwest Barry Manilow Fan Club," in Juliet B. Schor and Douglas B. Holt, *The Consumer Society Reader* (New York: The New Press, 2000) 159.
101. *The Day of the Locust,* dir. John Schlesinger, Paramount Pictures/Long Road Productions, 1974.
102. See, e.g., David M. Halbfinger and Allison Hope Weiner, "Eye vs. Eye: Inside the Photo Wars: Hollywood paparazzi face tough new rivals. And no one plays by the rules," *New York Times* 17 July 2005: Sec. 2–1, 12, 20.
103. David Samuels, "Shooting Britney," *The Atlantic* 301.3, April 2008: 36.
104. Robert J. Thompson of Syracuse University, qtd. in Louise Story, "Forget About Milk and Bread. Give Me Gossip!" *New York Times* 13 June 2005: C8.
105. Steve Rubenstein, "Jerry Garcia's toilet could be yours: Headed for eBay to benefit nonprofit Sophia Foundation," *San Francisco Chronicle* 39 November 2005: B2.
106. Dave Curtis, "Arenas Is Giving Fans More than Thrills," *New York Times* 2 May 2005: D2.
107. Cf. Guy Debord, *Society of the Spectacle* (Detroit: Black & Red, 1983) 20.
108. Demian Bulwa and Steve Rubenstein, "Mayhem ends, ball in hands of Mets fan," *San Francisco Chronicle* 8 August 2007: A7.

109. Henry Schulman, "Bonds' Ecko: 'stupid,'" *San Francisco Chronicle* 19 September 2007: D1.
110. See David Krauss, review of the televised revival, 11 January 2005, at http://www.digitallyobsessed.com /scenescolumns.php3.
111. George Gerbner and Larry Gross, "Living ith Television: The Violence Profile," *Journal of Communication* 26.2 (Spring 1976) 176.
112. Robert D. Putnam, *Bowling Alone: The Collapse and Revival of American Community* (New York; Simon & Schuster, 2000) 242; cf. 223–4.
113. Putnam 222–3.
114. The Associated Press, September 21, 2006, cited in Rick Moranis, "My Days Are Numbered," op. ed., *New York Times* 22 November 2006: A27.
115. Economic Policy Institute, *The State of Working America*, p. 363.
116. Lynette Clemetson, "Parents Making Use of TV Despite Risks," *New York Times* 25 May 2006: A16.
117. Ashley Parker, "Skipping the Grand Canyon for a Town Hall Meeting," *New York Times* 8 January 2008: A12.
118. Qtd. in Parker.
119. Jon Becker, Letter, *Sierra* (May/June 2005) 8.
120. Cf. Gerald Nachman, "I blab, therefore I am: Media puffs up our inflated sense of importance," op-ed, *San Francisco Chronicle* 29 July 2007: E2.
121. Charlotte Holt, phone interview, 31 January 2008.
122. Qtd. in Dirk Hoerder, *Crowd Action in Revolutionary Massachusetts, 1765–1780* (New York: Academic Press, 1977) 231.
123. Alan Brinkley, *American History: A Survey, Vol. 1: To 1877,* 10th ed. (Boston: McGraw-Hill College, 1999) 136, illustration on 116.
124. Charles Burress, "Berkeley: Free speech returns to Sproul: 3,000 pack UC plaza to celebrate 40th anniversary of historic student movement," *San Francisco Chronicle* 9 October 2004: B1.
125. Davis Jacobs, "California: The Late Great Golden State," *New Politics* X.2 (Winter 2005) 12.
126. Andrew Rosenthal, "There Is Silence in the Streets; Where Have All the Protesters Gone?" editorial, *New York Times* 31 August 2006: A26.
127. Russell Morse, "Things to do in Denver when your cause is dead," op-ed, *San Francisco Chronicle* 27 August 2008: B9.
128. Cf. Shaun Hargreaves Heap, "Living in an affluent society: it is so 'more-ish,'" *post-autistic economics review* 26: 2 August 2004, http://www.paecon.net /PAEReview/issue26/Heap26.htm.
129. Douglas B. Holt, "Postmodern Markets," in Schor, *Do Americans Shop Too Much?* Forum with Robert Frank, Michelle Lamont, et al. (Boston: Beacon Press, 2000) 65.
130. Schor in Schor, *Do Americans Shop* 93.

131. Heap.
132. Cf. Anastasios Korkotsides, *Consumer Capitalism* (New York: Routledge, 2007) 21.
133. Lawrence Mishel, Jared Bernstein and John Schmitt, "Leisure for All," in Schor, *Do Americans Shop* 82–3.

6. REGIMES OF CROWD CONTROL

1. William Hogeland, *The Whiskey Rebellion: George Washington, Alexander Hamilton, and the Frontier Rebels Who Challenged America's Newfound Sovereignty* (New York: Scribner, 2006) 53.
2. Howard Zinn, *A People's History of the United States: 1492–Present* (New York: HarperPerennial, 2003) 92.
3. Gary B. Nash, *The Unknown American Revolution: The Unruly Birth of Democracy and the Struggle to Create America* (New York: Penguin Books, 2005) 400.
4. Zinn 92–3.
5. Nash 391; Zinn 92.
6. Gary J. Kornblith and John M. Murrin, "The Making and Unmaking of an American Ruling Class," *Beyond the American Revolution: Explorations in the History of American Radicalism,* ed. Alfred F. Young (DeKalb, IL: N. Illinois UP, 1993) 54.
7. Zinn 93–5.
8. Young, "Afterward: How Radical Was the American Revolution?" in Young 332.
9. Nash 292.
10. Samuel Miller, qtd. in Nash 266.
11. Qtd. in Nash 279.
12. Madison, *The Federalist* No. 10, lines 136–7, J. R. Pole, ed., *The Federalist* (Indianapolis: Hackett Pub. Co., 2005) 52.
13. Madison, *The Federalist* no. 10, lines 149–51, in Pole 52.
14. Madison, *The Federalist* no. 10, lines 188–203, Pole 53.
15. Richard Henry Lee, *Letters from the Federal Farmer to a Republican,* excerpted in Vernon L. Parrington, *The Colonial Mind,* Vol. One of *Main Currents in American Thought* (New York: Harcourt, Brace & World, 1954) 295.
16. Qtd. in Kornblith and Murrin 55.
17. *Federalist,* No. 10, lines 221–3: 54.
18. *Federalist,* No. 6, lines 63–5; cf. l. 5: 24, 21.
19. At *Federalist,* No. 10, line 112: 51.
20. *Federalist,* No. 10, lines 3–4: 48.

21. Hogeland 132, 168, and passim.
22. Eric H. Monkkonen, *Police in Urban America: 1860–1920* (New York: Cambridge UP, 1981) 37–38.
23. Christine Stansell, *City of Women* (Urbana, IL: U. of Illinois Press, 1987) 197.
24. Alexis de Tocqueville, *Democracy in America,* vol. 1 (New York: Vintage Books, 1959) 299. The quote appears in a lengthy footnote to Chapter XVII, which he seems to have written after he learned of the riotous attacks on blacks and abolitionist properties in New York and Philadelphia in 1834.
25. Richard L. Bushman, *The Refinement of America: Persons, Houses, Cities* (New York: Alfred A. Knopf, 1992) 366; cf. 166.
26. Monkkonen, *Police* 151, 160.
27. Monkkonen, *Police* 39ff.
28. Susan G. Davis, *Parades and Power: Street Theatre in Nineteenth-Century Philadelphia* (Philadelphia: Temple UP, 1986) 30–31, 164, 167.
29. Monkkonen, *Police* 103.
30. Staff, Center on Juvenile and Criminal Justice, letter, *San Francisco Chronicle* 11 December 2004: B8.
31. Dave Zirin, *Welcome to the Terrordome: The Pain, Politics, and Promise of Sports* (Chicago: Haymarket Books, 2007) 16–17.
32. Michael Cabanatuan, "Mall expands—parking doesn't: Shoppers are urged to take public transit to Bloomingdale's," *San Francisco Chronicle* 28 September 2006: A1, A14; Victoria Colliver, Marni Leff, and Wyatt Buchanan, "Long-awaited grand opening draws huge crowds downtown: Urban mall's gala celebrates arrival of shopping mecca," *San Francisco Chronicle* 29 September 2006: C1, C6.
33. Colliver, Kottle, and Buchanan C6.
34. Steve Rubenstein, "Homeless feel unwelcome: Police deny rousting panhandlers near new Westfield Mall," *San Francisco Chronicle* 29 September 2006: B7.
35. Pia Sarkar, "Bringing the shoppers back to downtowns," *San Francisco Chronicle* 26 September 2006: E4.
36. Cf. Monkkonen, *Police* 191, note 20.
37. Hugh Brogan, *The Pelican History of the United States of America* (New York: Penguin Books, 1985) 414–5.
38. Steve Babson, *The Unfinished Struggle: Turning Points in American Labor, 1877–Present* (Lanham, MD: Rowman & Littlefield, 1999) 3, 6.
39. "Workday World: A Brief Timeline of U.S. Labor History," *American Writer* (Summer 2002) 18; Zinn 276–7, 355–7.
40. Russell Baker, "The Wealth of Loneliness," rev. of *Mellon: An American Life* by David Cannadine, *The New York Review of Books* LIII.17 (November 2, 2006) 12.
41. See http://www.bls.gov/oes/current/oes_nat.htm#b33–0000.

42. Adrianne Aron, *Social Autism: An Analysis of the Hippie Movement*, diss., U. of Calif., Santa Cruz, 1978, 213; cf. 204ff.
43. Aron 215.
44. Aron 216.
45. Aron 207, 220.
46. Aron 230.
47. Aron 231.
48. See Lewis Yablonsky, *The Hippie Trip* (New York: Pegasus, 1968) 307; Nicholas Von Hoffman, *We Are the People Our Parents Warned Us Against* (New York: Fawcett World Library, 1968) 97, 101.
49. Aron 220.
50. Hunter Thompson, *Fear and Loathing in Las Vegas: A Savage Journey to the Heart of the American Dream* (New York: Popular Library, 1971) 202.
51. http://www.burningman.com.
52. Allen Guttmann, *Sports Spectators* (New York: Columbia UP, 1986) 17.
53. Plato, *The Laws 700d,* trans. A. E. Taylor in Edith Hamilton and Huntington Cairns, eds., *The Collected Dialogues of Plato, Including the Letters* (New York: Bollingen Foundation, 1961) 1294.
54. Guttmann 22.
55. Barbara Ehrenreich, *Dancing in the Streets: A History of Collective Joy* (New York: Metropolitan Books, 2007) 228.
56. Russell Baker, "Glimpses," rev. of *Let Me Finish* by Roger Angell, *The New York Review of Books* L111.13 (August 10, 2006) 17.
57. Alan Brinkley, *American History: A Survey, Volume 1: To 1877,* 10th ed. (Boston: McGraw-Hill College, 1999) 361; Roy Rosenzweig, *Eight Hours for What We Will: Workers and Leisure in an Industrial City* (New York: Cambridge UP, 1983) 199 ff.; Ehrenreich 138–9.
58. Ehrenreich 207 ff.
59. Guy Debord, *Society of the Spectacle* (Detroit: Black & Red, 1983) 12.
60. Ehrenreich 187.
61. Note the mounting tension at the end of Henry James's *The Bostonians* when the protagonist decides that she cannot go on stage as advertised.
62. See, for example, the panel on Ghiberti's famous doors in Florence that shows Moses on the mountain receiving the tablets from God, Titian's painting of the Assumption in the Basilica of the Frari in Venice, or Donatello's bronze reliefs in the Church of St. Anthony in Padua. All such depictions of miracles are packed with witnesses.
63. Jérôme Carcopino, *Daily Life in Ancient Rome,* 2d ed., trans. E. O. Lorimer (New Haven: Yale UP, 2003) 231.
64. J. P. Toner, *Leisure and Ancient Rome* (Cambridge, UK: Polity Press, 1995) 37.
65. Cf. Tacitus, *Annals 14.20* in *Complete Works of Tacitus,* trans. Alfred J. Church

and William Jackson Brodribb (New York: The Modern Library: 1942) 331.

66. Guttmann 182–3.

67. Guttmann 32.

68. Qtd. in J. S. McClelland, *The Crowd and the Mob: From Plato to Canetti* (Boston: Unwin Hyman, 1989) 56.

69. Guttmann 17.

70. "Jets ban alcohol sales for Patriots game" (AP), *San Francisco Chronicle* 21 December 2005: D5. This same management is considering a more lasting ban following discovery that, for years, hundreds of men have been congregating at a certain gate at halftime to harass any female fans who came their way, chanting for them to bare their breasts. The president of the National Organization for Women acknowledges that such mass behavior will be hard to stop. See David Picker, "Measures Considered to Curtail Fan Behavior," *New York Times* 11 December 2007: C14.

71. Norbert Elias, *The History of Manners, The Civilizing Process,* Vol. 1, trans. Edmund Jephcott (New York: Pantheon Books, 1978) 202.

72. A. Luchaire, *La Societé Française au temps de Philippe-Auguste* (Paris, 1909), 278 ff., qtd. in Elias 201.

73. Steven Winn, "We may look down on athletes, but we don't stop watching," *San Francisco Chronicle* 1 August 2007: E1.

74. Bob Egelko, "Court upholds pat-down searches at 49er games," *San Francisco Chronicle* 18 July 2007: B1.

75. Cf. Mike Davis, *Dead Cities and Other Tales* (New York: The New Press, 2002) 12.

76. Guttmann 111–14.

77. Michael S. Schmidt, "Yanks Define Patriotism, and Then They Enforce It," *New York Times* 10 May 2007: C16.

78. Ehrenreich 238.

79. Thomas McLaughlin, *Street Smarts and Critical Theory: Listening to the Vernacular* (Madison, WI: U. of Wisconsin Press, 1996) 74; cf. 57 ff.

80. *Wall Street Journal* article, date not cited in National City Mortgage, "Trend Talk: Shoppertainment," *The Mortgage Update* (February 2003 flyer).

81. Louise Story, "Away from Home, TV Ads Are Inescapable," *New York Times* 2 March 2007: C6.

82. Edith Hodkinson, sr. vice president of sales and marketing for AccentHealth, qtd. in Story, "Away."

83. George Gerbner and Larry Gross, "Living with Television: The Violence Profile," *Journal of Communication* 26.2 (Spring 1976) 172–199.

84. Gerbner and Gross 194.

85. Gerbner and Gross 177.

86. Media Awareness Network, "Violence in Media," http://www. media-aware-

ness.ca/english/issues/violence/violence_entertainment.cfm; cf. Lynda Gledhill, "Judge blocks ban on sale of violent video games to minors," *San Francisco Chronicle* 23 December 2005: A1, A12.

87. Qtd. in Steve Rubenstein, "Shoppers call judge's video ruling irrelevant: Minors say they'll get the games they want, legal or not," *San Francisco Chronicle* 23 December 2005: A12.
88. Marisa Lagos, "Alleged gang founder sentenced to 75 years in man's 2004 killing," *San Francisco Chronicle* 24 March 2007: B3.
89. Matthew Yi, "Judge rejects law to limit sale of violent games," *San Francisco Chronicle* 7 August 2007: D2.
90. Media Awareness Network, "Violence in Media."
91. Mike Davis, *City of Quartz: Excavating the Future in Los Angeles* (New York: Vintage, 1990) 258.
92. *San Francisco Chronicle* 22 October 2004: D3.
93. Ehrenreich 252.
94. Wyatt Buchanan, Heather Knight, and Robert Selna, "This Party's Dead: Castro district is quiet as many bars and restaurants close early in response to city's campaign to put a damper on the annual raucous Halloween revelry," *San Francisco Chronicle* 1 November 2007: A1, A13.
95. Peter Burke, *Popular Culture in Early Modern Europe* (New York UP, 1978) 183.
96. Burke 209 ff., 270 ff.; cf. Keith Thomas, *Religion and the Decline of Magic: Studies in Popular Beliefs in Sixteenth and Seventeenth Century England* (New York: Oxford UP, 1971) 66.
97. Max Weber, *The Protestant Ethic and the Spirit of Capitalism,* trans. Talcott Parsons (New York: Chas. Scribner's Sons, 1958) 166.
98. Ehrenreich 97–9.
99. Ehrenreich 100–1, 111–12, 116, 126; cf. Bushman 410 ff.
100. Mikhail Bakhtin, *Rabelais and His World,* trans. Helene Iswolsky (Bloomington, IN: Indiana UP, 1984) 33.
101. Rebecca Solnit, "Democracy Should Be Exercised Regularly, on Foot," *The Guardian* 6 July 2006, available at Common Dreams News Center, http://www.commondreams.org/ views06/0706-35.htm.
102. Marisa Lagos, "S.F.'s new Halloween party plan—bash at AT&T Park lot, not Castro," *San Francisco Chronicle* 5 September 2008: A1, A12.
103. Zinn 260.
104. Reginald Dale, "Terrorists Exploit Anti-Globalization," *International Herald Tribune* 22–23 September 2001.
105. Web site posting on eve of a big antiwar demonstration, qtd. in Tom Abate, "Technology creates a new form of activism," *San Francisco Chronicle* 14 February 2003: A17.

106. Michael Parente, "Flashpoints," KPFA-94.1FM, February 23, 2005.
107. Cf. Naomi Klein, *The Shock Doctrine: The Rise of Disaster Capitalism* (New York: Metropolitan Books, 2007) 279.
108. Chalmers Johnson, *The Sorrows of Empire: Militarism, Secrecy, and the End of the Republic* (New York: Henry Holt & Co., 2004) 120.
109. Midnight Special Law Collective newsletter, November 30, 2004.
110. Cynthia Peters, "We're Building Another World," *Resist* 13.7 (September 2004).
111. David Johnston and Eric Schmitt, "Denver Police Brace for Convention," *New York Times* 5 August 2008: A12.
112. Joe Garofoli, "Police raid homes, headquarters of protestors," *San Francisco Chronicle* 31 August 2008: A17; Amy Goodman, Interviews, "Democracy Now," Pacifica Radio, 1 September 2008.
113. Peter Prengaman (AP), "L.A. chief says tactics against crowd were wrong: Officers used force against some at rally for immigrant rights," *San Francisco Chronicle* 3 May 2007: A9.
114. Cmdr. Sandy Jo MacArthur, qtd. in Thomas Watkins (AP), "Police preparing for May Day protest," *San Francisco Chronicle* 30 April 2008: B5.
115. Qtd. in N. Klein 189. (Source not identified.)
116. "Seattle to pay claims by trade protesters," *San Francisco Chronicle* 3 April 2007: A19.
117. Midnight Special.
118. "DC World Bank Demonstrators Get a Million," *Defending Dissent Foundation Letter* (September 2007) 4.
119. This according to DC Council Member Kathy Patterson. Email, February 7, 2005, struggle-and-win@earthlink.net.
120. Andrew Jacobs, "Banner Bearer at Convention Is Acquitted," *New York Times* 24 June 2005: A20.
121. Cf. Peter Phillips, "Immigrants Used to Justify a Homeland Security Police State," *Alert! The Newsletter of Project Censored* 10.2 (Fall 2007) 7–8; Lewis Seiler and Dan Hamburg, "Rule by fear or rule by law?" op-ed, *San Francisco Chronicle* 4 February 2008: B7.
122. Richard Rapaport, "Dying and living in 'COPS' America," op-ed, *San Francisco Chronicle* 7 January 2007: E5.
123. Ian Austen, "After a Death, Use of Taser in Canada Is Debated," *New York Times* 16 November 2007: A16.
124. Amanda Lee Myers (AP), "Taser loading blast of electricity into shotgun shells," *San Francisco Chronicle* 22 February 2006: A3; Mark Sherman (AP), "Report finds increase in Taser use by police: 156 deaths in U.S. tied to shock gun, rights group says," *San Francisco Chronicle* 28 March 2006: D9.
125. Osha Neumann, "Morning Show," KPFA 94.1FM, 6 April 2005.

126. Jack Heyman, "Defending labor's right to protest the war," op-ed., *San Francisco Chronicle* 16 March 2005: B11.
127. Midnight Special.
128. Ellen Simon, "Protestors utilizing technology: Activists go online to organize efforts at GOP convention," *San Francisco Chronicle* 30 August 2004: C6.
129. Brett Wagner, "Why the U.S. should never deploy its latest weapon," op ed., *San Francisco Chronicle* 18 January 2006: B9.
130. Maiannna Voge, "Bang you're alive: In search of a truly non-lethal bullet," *California* 119.3 (May/June 2008) 12.
131. Robert Scheer, "War industry regains command," op-ed, *San Francisco Chronicle* 31 October 2007: B11.
132. Mike Davis, *In Praise of Barbarians: Essays Against Empire* (Chicago: Haymarket Books, 2007) 221.
133. N. Klein 408.
134. Anna Badkhen, "Scarred Inside and Out," *San Francisco Chronicle* 26 August 2006: A9.
135. Alan H. Stein and Gene B. Preuss, "Oral History, Folklore, and Katrina," in Chester Hartman and Gregory D. Squires, eds., *There Is No Such Thing as a Natural Disaster: Race, Class, and Hurricane Katrina* (New York: Routledge, 2006) 38; cf. John Noble Wilford, "Plague: How Cholera Helped Shape New York," *New York Times* 15 April 2008: D4.
136. Shaila Dewan, "Police Officers Charged in Deaths in Hurricane's Aftermath," *New York Times* 29 December 2006: A19.
137. Annette Allison, testimony in *Response to Hurricane Katrina: Before, During and After,* #5 of *The Bush Crimes Commission Hearings,* International Commission of Inquiry on Crimes Against Humanity Committed by the Bush Administration, 2006 (2 DVD set).
138. Aaron Guyton, testimony in *Response to Hurricane Katrina.*
139. Jeremy Scahill, journalist, testimony in *Response to Hurricane Katrina.*
140. Institute for Southern Studies, *Blueprint for Gulf Renewal: The Katrina Crisis and a Community Agenda for Action,* qtd. in "Katrina Index: The State of the Gulf Coast by Numbers," *RESIST Newsletter* 16.5 (September/October 2007) 7.
141. "Louisiana: Suit Over Storm Victim's Death" (AP), *New York Times* 18 August 2006: A14; KPFA-94.1FM *Evening News*, August 17, 2006.
142. Gary Davis, qtd. in Brad Parks (Newhouse News Svc.), "In New Orleans' French Quarter, a tale of two cities," *San Francisco Chronicle* 3 September 2005: A9.
143. Klein 421; M. Davis, *In Praise* 239.
144. Qtd. in N. Klein 415–6. Help Jet's website no longer advertises disaster getaway services.

145. Abby Goodnough and Joseph B. Treaster, "Florida: Millions Are Still Without Power and in Need of Basic Supplies," *New York Times* 26 October 2005: A23.
146. Dan Baum, "Letter From New Orleans: The Lost Year: Behind the Failure to Rebuild," *The New Yorker* August 21, 2006: 59 and passim.
147. Zirin, *Welcome* 253; Jack Wood, Letter to *USA Today*, in Zirin, *Welcome* 257.
148. Philip L. Fradkin, *The Great Earthquake and Firestorms of 1906: How San Francisco Nearly Destroyed Itself* (Berkeley: U. of Calif. Press, 2005) 344.
149. Spencer S. Hsu (*Washington Post*), "Homeland Security slow to ID targets needing protection: Petting zoos, snack stands on list with dams, power plants," *San Francisco Chronicle* 16 July 2006: A7. A further revision of this list is pending with Congress.

7. SAFE CROWDS

1. Qtd. in Mary Esteve, *The Aesthetics and Politics of the Crowd in American Literature* (New York: Cambridge UP, 2003) 2.
2. Walter Benjamin, *The Arcades Project,* trans. Howard Eiland and Kevin McLaughlin (Cambridge, MA: Belknap Press, 1999) 446 (his paraphrasing); cf. 10, 443.
3. Robin Dunbar, *Grooming, Gossip, and the Evolution of Language* (Cambridge, MA: Harvard UP, 1996) 69–71, 77.
4. Georg Simmel, "The Metropolis and Mental Life," *On Individuality and Social Forms,* ed. Donald N. Levine, trans. Edward A. Shils (Chicago: U. of Chicago Press, 1971) 336–7.
5. Benjamin 433.
6. Simmel, qtd. in Benjamin 448.
7. Edgar Allen Poe, "The Man in the Crowd." In the short story "Convicta et Combusta," Joanna Scott has imagined a female counterpart of Poe's crowd man, a woman who lives only through participation in the crowds of Coney Island. See Scott, *Various Antidotes: Stories* (New York: Henry Holt & Co., 1994) 145–62.
8. Warren I. Susman, *Culture as History: The Transformations of American Society in the Twentieth Century* (New York: Pantheon Books, 1984) 237.
9. Walt Whitman, "Out of the Rolling Ocean the Crowd"; cf. "To Foreign Lands" and "Among the Multitude."
10. Susman 244.
11. Esteve 1–2.
12. Mike Davis, *City of Quartz: Excavating the Future in Los Angeles* (New York: Vintage Books, 1990) 226–7; Robert M. Fogelson, *Downtown: Its Rise and Fall, 1880–1950* (New Haven: Yale UP, 2001) 189.

13. Fogelson, *Downtown* 194 ff., 199.
14. Fogelson, *Downtown* 249 ff.
15. George A. Damon, qtd. in Fogelson, *Downtown* 260; cf. Jane Jacobs, *The Death and Life of Great American Cities* (New York: Vintage Books, 1992) 338 ff.
16. Fogelson, *Downtown* 241, 277, 299 ff.
17. See photo at www.sfpl.org>"San Francisco streets after 1940">AAB5101.
18. *The City,* videotape, dir. Willard Van Dyke and Ralph Steiner (Pyramid Media, 1939).
19. Fogelson, *Downtown* 231.
20. Cf. Marty Jezer, *The Dark Ages: Life in the United States 1945–1960* (Boston: South End Press, 1982) 220.
21. From 1957 motivational research surveys, qtd. in Betty Friedan, *The Feminine Mystique* (New York: Dell Pub. Co., 1963) 214, 215.
22. Cf. Jim Straub, "Braddock, Pennsylvania: Out of the Furnace and into the Fire," *Monthly Review* 60.7 (December 2008) 44.
23. Joan Didion, *Where I Was From* (New York: Vintage International, 2003) 105.
24. *Report of the National Advisory Commission on Civil Disorders* [The Kerner Report] (New York: Bantam Books, 1968) 474.
25. Qtd. in Jezer, note, 189.
26. Donald J. Waldie, *Holy Land: A Suburban Memoir,* qtd. in Didion 106.
27. Qtd. in Didion 107.
28. Cf. Didion 115.
29. Witold Rybczynski, *City Life: Urban Expectations in a New World* (Toronto: HarperCollins, 1995) 201.
30. *Report* [Kerner] 467.
31. Jezer 188.
32. James Howard Kunstler, *The Geography of Nowhere: The Rise and Decline of America's Man-Made Landscape* (New York: Simon & Schuster, 1993) 102–3, 212, 229; Jezer, 179 ff.; J. Jacobs.
33. Lefebre, *La Production de l'espace,* trans. and qtd. in David Harvey, *The Condition of Postmodernity: An Enquiry into the Origins of Cultural Change* (Cambridge, MA: Blackwell, 1990) 237.
34. M. Davis, *In Praise of Barbarians: Essays Against Empire* (Chicago: Haymarket Books, 2007) 136–7.
35. Qtd. in Lyman, "Living Large, by Design, in Middle of Nowhere," *New York Times* 15 August 2005: A15.
36. Joel Kotkin, "In Praise of Suburbs: Suburbia often gets a bad rap, but government should accept that people want the picket fence ideal," *San Francisco Chronicle* 29 January 2006: D5.
37. Tim Timmons, qtd. in Joel Garreau, *Edge City: Life on the New Frontier* (New York: Doubleday, 1991) 294.

38. John Nielsen, qtd. in Garreau 297.
39. "Nation's Inmate Population Increased 2.3 Percent Last Year" (AP), *New York Times* 25 April 2005: A14; "Number of Women in Prisons Is on Rise" (AP), *New York Times* 24 October 2005: A18; Marc Mauer, "Don't Throw Away the Key: Lessons from the 'Get Tough on Crime' Initiatives," *Resist* 15.2 (March/April 2006) 1–3; Sitara Nieves, "The 'Policing-to-Prisons' Track: Bay Area Organizers Oppose Operation Impact," *Resist* 15.2 (March/April 2006) 5–6; Richard Rapaport, "Dying and living in 'COPS' America," op. ed., *San Francisco Chronicle* 7 January 2007: E5; N. C. Aizenman (*Washington Post*), "U.S. tops world in prison inmates," *San Francisco Chronicle* 29 February 2008: A7; "Prison Nation," editorial, *New York Times* 10 March 2008: A20.
40. Simmel 331.
41. Verlyn Klinkenborg, "The Psychology of Los Angeles Freeways and the Effect of Recent Shootings," *New York Times* 3 May 2005: A24.
42. Nick Paumgarten, "There and Back Again: The Soul of the Commuter," *The New Yorker,* April 16, 2007: 62.
43. Dunbar 39–40.
44. Lewis Mumford, qtd. in Kunstler 10, without further attribution.
45. M. Davis, *In Praise* 153–4, 179.
46. James B. Twitchell, "Two Cheers for Materialism," in Juliet B. Schor and Doublas B. Holt, eds., *The Consumer Society Reader* (New York: The New Press, 2000) 290.
47. David Moberg, "'Ownership' Swindle," *The Nation* 280.13 (4 April 2005) 6.
48. Attributed to William H. Whyte in Jean Baudrillard, *Selected Writings,* 2d ed., Mark Poster, ed. (Stanford, CA: Stanford UP, 2001) 54.
49. As ad executive Dan Seymour declared in a 1964 speech, "We must expand consumption to match production." Qtd. in Thomas McLaughlin, *Street Smarts and Critical Theory: Listening to the Vernacular* (Madison, WI: U. of Wisconsin Press, 1996) 119.
50. Qtd. in William Severini Kowinski, *The Malling of America: An Inside Look at the Great Consumer Paradise* (New York: Wm. Morrow & Co., 1985) 330, repub. as *The Malling of America: Travels in the United States of Shopping* (Philadelphia: Xlibris, 2002); cf. Schor, *The Overworked American: The Unexpected Decline of Leisure* (New York: Basic Books, 1992) 108.
51. Lewis Mumford, *The City in History: Its Origins, Its Transformations, and Its Prospects* (New York: Harcourt, Brace & World, 1961) 71.
52. Mikhail Bakhtin, *Rabelais and His World,* trans. Helene Iswolsky (Bloomington, IN: Indiana UP, 1984) 154.
53. Bruce Whipperman, *Moon Handbooks: Oaxaca,* 2d ed. (Emeryville, CA: Avalon Travel Pub., 2001) 112.

54. Robert D. Putnam, *Bowling Alone: The Collapse and Revival of American Community* (New York: Simon & Schuster, 2000) 211.
55. Kent Nuckols of San Francisco, qtd. in Jenny Strasburg et al., "Serious Shopping: Bay Area residents cut back on sleep, get out early to find bargains before someone else snaps them up—welcome to Black Friday," *San Francisco Chronicle* 27 November 2004: A19; cf. Hanna DeBare, Kelly Zito and Robert Selna, "Black Friday Packs 'Em In," *San Francisco Chronicle* 24 November 2007: Al, A8.
56. David Armstrong, "The Retail Rituals of Predawn Lines and the Frenzied Pursuit of Deals Mark Start of Holiday Shopping," *San Francisco Chronicle* 26 November 2005: A15.
57. Steve Feica (AP), "PlayStation 3 mayhem brings shooting, stabbing: Buyers singled out; men hurt in Indiana and Connecticut," *San Francisco Chronicle* 18 November 2006: A10; Lou Kesten (AP), "Real-life action strikes onscreen game world: PlayStation 3 sales lead to robberies, political scandal," *San Francisco Chronicle* 27 November 2006: D3; cf. "Mayhem at Wal-Mart over Xbox sales," *San Francisco Chronicle* 24 November 2005: A3.
58. David Hume, *A Treatise of Human Nature* (Oxford: Oxford UP, 2000) 236, qtd. in Anastasios S. Korkotsides, *Consumer Capitalism* (New York: Routledge, 2007) 36.
59. See, e.g., Mark Morford, "America—open your wallet and say 'aah,'" *San Francisco Chronicle* 15 February 2008: E6.
60. Korkotsides 101 and passim.
61. Cf. Baudrillard, *Selected* 48.
62. Leo Cullum, cartoon, *The New Yorker* 11 and 18 February 2008: 133.
63. Betsy Taylor, "The Personal Level," in Schor, *Do Americans Shop Too Much?,* forum with Robert Frank, Michelle Lamont, et al. (Boston: Beacon Press, 2000) 58.
64. Schor, *Do Americans Shop* 6.
65. Schor, *Do Americans Shop* 9.
66. John Perkins, *Confessions of an Economic Hit Man* (New York: Plume, 2004) xv.
67. Schor, *Do Americans Shop* 28.
68. Robert H. Frank, "Market Failures," in Schor, *Do Americans Shop* 40.
69. Schor, *Do Americans Shop* 11.
70. http://money.cnn.com/2009/02/02/news/economy/ personal_income_ spending/.
71. Marlon Manuel (Cox News Svc.), "Scan-it-yourself part, parcel of life: Customers at stores across U.S. can now check themselves out," *San Francisco Chronicle* 30 January 2005: E3.
72. Thomas Hine, *I Want That! How We All Became Shoppers* (New York: Harper Collins, 2002) 48.

73. Benjamin 189.
74. Jeff Milchen, "The Retail Bubble: After Economic Quake, a Shop-Space Tsunami," *San Francisco Chronicle* 4 January 2009: *Insight* 2.
75. Kowinski 60; cf. 53–63, 317.
76. Eduard Devrient, *Briefe aus Paris,* qtd. in Benjamin 42.
77. Tony Moilin, *Paris en l'an 2000,* qtd. in Benjamin 53.
78. Kevin Mims, "Cluttered malls lose potential customers: Kiosks, sales pitches will often backfire," *San Francisco Chronicle* 15 July 2007: D5.
79. Kowinski 159, 188, 199, 201, 218, 259.
80. Mims.
81. David Owen, "The Soundtrack of Your Life: Muzak in the realm of retail theatre," *The New Yorker,* April 10, 2006: 67, 69–71.
82. Susan Buck-Morss, "Aesthetics and anaesthetics: Walter Benjamin's artwork essay reconsidered," *October* 62 (1992): 22, qtd. in Kevin Robins, *Into the Image: Culture and Politics in the Field of Vision* (New York: Routledge, 1996) 119.
83. M. Davis, *City of Quartz* 457
84. Michel Foucault, "Prison Talk," trans. Colin Gordon in Gordon ed., *Power/Knowledge: Selected Interviews & Other Writings 1972–1977* (New York: Pantheon, 1980) 57.
85. Kowinski 108.
86. Interview by Lynn Darling, *The Washingtonian,* qtd. in Kowinski without additional attribution, 158.
87. *Dawn of the Dead,* dir. George A. Romero, Dawn Assoc., 1978.
88. Cathy Keefe of Travel Industry Assoc. of America, qtd. in Korky Vann, "If you haven't shopped there, you haven't been there," *San Francisco Chronicle* 17 October 2004: D3.
89. Cherilyn Parsons, "Virtual Vacation," *San Francisco Chronicle* 9 March 2008: D4; Hubert L. Dreyfus, "Faking it," *California* 119.2 (March/April 2008): 50–4.
90. Rybczynski 228.
91. Cf. Louis Menand, "Drive, He Wrote: What the Beats Were About," *The New Yorker,* October 1, 2007: 91.
92. "Get Your Kicks on Route 66" (Bobby Troupe), most famously recorded by the Nat King Cole Trio in 1946.
93. Kowinski 51; cf. Arrol Gellner, "Freeway to nowhere: Roads of convenience translate to roads of monotony," *San Francisco Chronicle* 26 November 2005: F2.
94. Marc Augé, *Non-places: Introduction to an Anthropology of Supermodernity,* trans. John Howe (New York: Verso, 1995).
95. A. O. Scott, "Jarmusch: Funny and Tender," *International Herald Tribune* 20 May 2005: 11.

96. Manuel Castells, *The Rise of the Network Society,* vol. 1 of *The Information Age: Economy, Society and Culture* (Cambridge, Mass.: Blackwell Pub., 1996) 423.
97. Michael Steinberg, *The Fiction of a Thinkable World: Body, Meaning, and the Culture of Capitalism* (New York: Monthly Review Press, 2005) 158.
98. See, e.g., Juan Forero, "Venezuelan Strongman's New Gig: National Disc Jockey," *New York Times* 3 October 2005: A4; Keith Bradsher, "Read the Tea Leaves: China Will Be Top Exporter," *New York Times* 11 October 2005: A1, C4; Mike McPhate, "India's liberalized children embrace lap of luxury: Boom had middle-class zippies spending freely, living high life," *San Francisco Chronicle* 13 November 2005: E5; Alan Scher Zagier, "Alone among Istanbul's throngs: West seeks city's soul in East," *San Francisco Chronicle* 13 November 2005: F7.
99. Cf. Guy Debord, *Society of the Spectacle* (Detroit: Black & Red, 1983) ¶169.
100. Michael Hardt and Antonio Negri, *Empire* (Cambridge, Mass.: Harvard UP, 2000).
101. Augé 94, 59.
102. MAGNET, *Non-place* (London: Institute of International Visual Arts, 2001) 31.
103. Andrew Bower, qtd. in Pia Sarkar, John Coté and Marni Leff Kottle, "Shoppers Flock to Answer the Siren Song of Savings: Early birds snap up best deals before sunrise in traditional post-holiday buying frenzy," *San Francisco Chronicle* 25 November 2006: A1, A11.
104. Richard Rapaport, "Unfriendly skies cloud our American horizons," *San Francisco Chronicle* 23 July 2007: D5.
105. *Frida Kahlo,* exhibition, San Francisco Museum of Modern Art, June 14-September 28, 2008.
106. Richard Schickel, "Avenue Queue," op-ed, *New York Times* 20 July 2005: A25.
107. Manual E3.
108. Dan Caterinicchia (AP), "Self-service kiosks gaining acceptance," *San Francisco Chronicle* 3 August 2007: D3.
109. Caterinicchia D3.
110. Rybczynski 211–12.
111. Cf. Kowinski 64–68.
112. Kowinski 22, 26–37; cf. Ryzczynski 230.
113. John King, "New Urban Centers Take on a Stage-Set Feel in Bay Area," *San Francisco Chronicle* 9 April 2007: A1.
114. King, "Downtown grows in . . . Windsor?" *San Francisco Chronicle* 3 March 2004: E1; cf. Pia Sarkar, "The new face of retail: Mimicked Main Streets, mall makeovers seek to lure shoppers," *San Francisco Chronicle* 3 May 2005: D1, D5.
115. Garreau 42–3.

116. King, "Main Street Mirage: Retail complexes mimic quaint urban districts," *San Francisco Chronicle* 29 December 2002: A29.
117. Elsa Brenner, "A Piazza for a Maryland Suburb: Rockville's New Mixed-Use Downtown Aims to Avoid the 'Anyplace, U.S.A.' Look," *New York Times* 22 November 2006: C7.
118. King, "Citified Suburbs Becoming New Model for the Bay Area," *San Francisco Chronicle* 8 April 2007: A1, A12.
119. King, "Citified Suburbs," A12.
120. King, "Citified Suburbs," A12.
121. Christine Delsol, "The amazing two-day trip abroad: Santana Row inspires comparisons to anywhere but San Jose," *San Francisco Chronicle* 20 August 2006: G8.
122. Shayne W. Watson, Letter, *San Francisco Chronicle* 11 April 2007: B8.
123. Kowinski 306; cf. 270 ff.; William H. Whyte, *City: Rediscovering the Center* (New York: Doubleday, 1988) 222 ff.
124. Connie Hatch, photographer, qtd. in Rebecca Solnit and Susan Schwartzenberg, *Hollow City: The Siege of San Francisco and the Crisis of American Urbanism* (New York: Verso, 2000) 73.
125. Whyte 34.
126. Jackson, *A Sense of Place, A Sense of Time* (New Haven, CT: Yale UP, 1994) 156.
127. King, "15 seconds that changed San Francisco: Union Square overcomes a psychological jolt," *San Francisco Chronicle* 19 October 2004: A11.
128. Leigh Ann Braughman, qtd. in King, "15 seconds" A11.
129. Cf. M. Davis, *City of Quartz* 235. Regarding "bum-proofing" across the bay in Berkeley, see http://www.berkeleydailyplanet.com/article.Cfm?issue=11-23-07&storyID=28537.
130. King, "15 seconds" A10–11.
131. Garreau 60–1, citing the opinion expressed in a *New Yorker* article by Tony Hiss.
132. Harvey 303.
133. Adam Gopnik, "The Talk of the Town: Comment: Gothamitis," *The New Yorker*, January 8, 2007: 22.
134. Paul Kilduff, "A Long Way to a Latte: Four years on, residents of Hercules' New Urbanist neighborhoods are still driving to the mall," *San Francisco Chronicle* 17 February 2007: G1, G4.
135. See, e.g., Kayla Webley, "Downtown 'renaissance' under way," *Seattle Times* 24 May 2006.
136. Jenny Strasberg et al., "Many say they plan to spend less this year," *San Francisco Chronicle* 30 November 2002: A17.
137. Thomasville ad, *San Francisco Chronicle* 17 November 2007: A5.

138. Simmel 325.
139. Edward Guthmann, "Taking His Show on the Road," *San Francisco Chronicle* 11 February 2007: B8. Jackson has now moved on, and the downtown area described continues to undergo rapid change.
140. Jackson has subsequently moved on.
141. Jeff Keilholtz, "The Megachurch Juggernaut: The Making of McChurch," *Z Magazine* 21.3 (March 2008) 35.
142. John Leland, "A Church That Packs them In, 16,000 at a Time," *New York Times* 18 July 2005: A15; cf. Frances Fitzgerald, "Come One, Come All: Building a megachurch in New England," *The New Yorker*, December 3, 2007: 46–48, 51–56.
143. Maurilio Amorin, church-growth consultant, qtd. in Fitzgerald 53.
144. Fitzgerald 54.
145. Thomas Nuypauer, Letter, *The Economist* 385.8557 (December 1, 2007): 22.

8. WHO NEEDS CROWDS?

1. Jacob Adelman (AP), "Mood is angry and bitter as IndyMac customers line up," *San Francisco Chronicle* 16 July 2008: C6.
2. See, e.g., Jethro K. Lieberman, *A Practical Companion to the Constitution: How the Supreme Court Has Ruled on Issues from Abortion to Zoning* (Berkeley: UC Press, 1999) 196.
3. Qtd. in George P. Smith II, "The Development of the Right of Assembly—A Current Socio-Legal Investigation," *William and Mary Law Review* (Fall 1967) 9:366.
4. Linda J. Lumsden, *Rampant Women: Suffragists and the Right of Assembly* (Knoxville, TN: U. of Tennessee Press, 1997) xiv.
5. Lieberman 196.
6. Qtd. in Lieberman 196.
7. Abernathy 14.
8. Abernathy 53.
9. Lumsden xvi, 36.
10. Mother Mary Jones, Chap. X: "March of the Mill Children," *The Autobiography of Mother Jones*, http//womenshistory. about.com/library/etext/mj/bl_mj10.htm.
11. Lumsden 135.
12. Lumsden 125, 36.
13. Lumsden 33–4.
14. M. Glenn Abernathy, *The Right of Assembly and Association*, 2d ed.—rev., (Columbia, SC: U. of South Carolina Press, 1981) 14, 16.

15. Lieberman 196.
16. Milton R. Konvitz, *First Amendment Freedoms: Selected Cases on Freedom of Religion, Speech, Press, Assembly* (Ithaca, NY: Cornell UP, 1963) 154.
17. Lieberman 196.
18. Qtd. in Howard Schweber, *Speech, Conduct, and the First Amendment* (New York: Peter Lang, 2003) 344.
19. Jack Rasmus, "From Global Financial Crisis to Global Recession, Part I: Precipitating a major recession," *Z Magazine* 21.3 (March 2008): 39.
20. Howard Zinn, *A People's History of the United States: 1492–Present* (New York: HarperPerennial, 2003) 580.
21. They would lose this tax break under President Obama's proposed budget. See Edmund L. Andrews, "Taxes: Upper-Income Pinch," *New York Times* 27 February 2009: A16.
22. Steve Wamhoff, "America's Populism Deficit," *Just Taxes: The CTJ & ITEP Newsletter* (September 2007) 1, 3.
23. Cf. William Greider, *Who Will Tell the People: The betrayal of American democracy* (New York: Simon & Schuster, 1992) 45.
24. Greider 23.
25. Abernathy 6.
26. Michael Y. Dartnell, *Insurgency Online: Web Activism and Global Conflict* (Toronto: U. of Toronto Press, 2006) x, 5.
27. John Arquila and David Ronfeldt, "Cyberwar Is Coming!" *Comparative Strategy* 12.2 (Spring 1993) 141, qtd. in Dartnell 19.
28. Dartnell 6, 9, 25.
29. Howard W. French, "China's New Frontiers: Tests of Democracy and Dissent," *New York Times* 19 June 2006: 6.
30. Craig Simons (Cox News Svc.), "Chinese Evade Big Brother: Internet culture gives birth to *egao,* using sarcastic humor and parody to mask criticism and avoid censorship," *San Francisco Chronicle* 8 March 2007: A9.
31. Geoffrey Cain, "Bloggers are the new rebels in Vietnam," *San Francisco Chronicle* 14 December 2008: A19, A22.
32. Xiao Qiang, "Great Firewall: Site bans prevail, and cartoon cops spy on 137 million users," *San Francisco Chronicle* 23 September 2007: E1, E3; cf. Andres Jacobs, "Chinese Learn Limits of Online Freedom as the Filter Tightens," *New York Times* 5 February 2009: A8.
33. George Packer, "Letter from Rangoon: Drowning," *The New Yorker* August 25, 2008: 51.
34. Qtd. in Robert Schlesinger, "Foes of a War in Iraq Spread Their Message," *Boston Globe* 16 January 2003, excerpted in Parisher, "Our TV ads launch today," MoveOn.org email, 16 January 2003; Tom Hayden, speech, Peace Strategies Forum, Oakland: March 1, 2008.

35. "Victory!" Email, August 9, 2006, moveon-help@list.moveon.org; cf. Joe Garofoli, "Rise of the 'Net-roots': Upset hints at impact of online activists," *San Francisco Chronicle* 9 August 2006: A1, A7.
36. Jim Rutenberg, "Bloggers Seek Candidates to Push Democrats to Left," *New York Times* 27 February 2009: A19.
37. Howard Rheingold, *Smart Mobs: The Next Social Revolution* (Cambridge, MA: Perseus Pub., 2002) 13; Karen Solomon, "MobMov creates a new guerrilla theater while reviving drive-in culture," *San Francisco Chronicle* 39 July 2007: E1, E3; Ellen Simon, "Protestors utilizing technology: Activists go online to organize efforts at GOP convention," *San Francisco Chronicle* 30 August 2004: C1, C6.
38. Neil MacFarquhar, "In Tiny Arab State, Web Takes on Ruling Elite," *New York Times* 15 January 2005: Sec. 1, 1 and 11.
39. Rheingold xii; cf. 157–61.
40. Bryan Johnson, *The Four Days of Courage: The Untold Story of the People Who Brought Marcos Down* (New York: The Free Press, 1987).
41. Vicente Rafael, qtd. in Rheingold 160.
42. Dirk Hoerder, *Crowd Action in Revolutionary Massachusetts, 1765-1780* (New York: Academic Press, 1977) 374.
43. Arif Mamdani and Mark Sherman, Letter, *The Nation* 280.1: (January 3, 2005) 2, 19; Jim Driscoll, Letter, same source, 19.
44. Dylan Loeb McClain, "It's a Gadget, Gadget, Gadget World," *New York Times* 8 August 2005: C5.
45. Anonymous attendee of the World Social Forum of 2001, qtd. in "Porto Alegre and Beyond: Following up on the World Social Forum," Interhemispheric Resource Center Report (November 22, 2002).
46. Christopher Hayes, "MoveOn @ Ten," *The Nation* 287.4 (August 4/11, 2008) 17.
47. Abernathy 8.
48. Cf. Lumsden xvii.
49. Cf. John Zerzan, *Twilight of the Machines* (Port Townsend, WA: Feral House, 2008) 65; also James Polk, *The Triumph of Ignorance and Bliss: Pathologies of Public America* (Tonawanda, NY: Black Rose, 2008) 297–8.
50. Testimony in *Response to Hurricane Katrina: Before, During and After,* #5 of *The Bush Crimes Commission Hearings*, 2006, DVD.
51. Naomi Klein, *The Shock Doctrine: The Rise of Disaster Capitalism* (New York: Metropolitan Books, 2007) 465; cf. 385–402, 463–4; cf. "Thailand Land Tenure," "Tsunami-hit communities with shaky land status get busy . . . ," and "Thailand: the toughest foes," *Tsunami Update* (June 2006) 2, 4, at http://www.achr.net/ 000ACHRTsunami.
52. James Hopper, qtd. in Philip L. Fradkin, *The Great Earthquake and Firestorms of 1906: How San Francisco Nearly Destroyed Itself* (Berkeley: U. of Calif. Press, 2005) 87; cf. 55.

53. Qtd. in Fradkin 146–7.
54. Albert Camus, *The Plague.*
55. Tacitus, *Annals* 15.38 in *Complete Works of Tacitus,* trans. Alfred J. Church and William Jackson Brodribb (New York: The Modern Library, 1942) 377.
56. Fradkin 164 ff.
57. Steve Babson, *The Unfinished Struggle: Turning Points in American Labor, 1877–Present* (Lanham, MD: Rowman & Littlefield, 1999) 62.
58. *Report of the National Advisory Commission on Civil Disorders* [The Kerner Report] (New York: Bantam Books, 1968) 96.
59. Soledad Lawrence, "A Way to Stop Foreclosures: Using direct action to confront the subprime mortgage crisis," *Resist* 17:4 (July-August 2008) 1, 3, 6.
60. Fernanda Santos, "A Bid to Link Arms Against Eviction: Grass-Roots Effort Takes Shape to Support Families Facing Foreclosure," *New York Times* 18 February 2009: A20.
61. Clifford Krauss, "Argentine Leader, His Nation Frayed, Abruptly Resigns," *New York Times* 21 December 2001: A1, A6; Joseph Kahn, "Argentina's Chaos Raises New Doubts on Monetary Fund: Critics Left and Right," *New York Times* 22 December 2001: A1, A10.
62. Krauss A6.
63. Edward Epstein, "The Piquetero Movement in Greater Buenos Aires: Political Protests by the Unemployed Poor during the Crisis," in Epstein and David Pion-Berlin, eds., *Broken Promises? The Argentine Crisis and Argentine Democracy* (Boulder, CO: Lexington Books, 2006) 107.
64. Inés González Bombal and Mariana Luzzi, "Middle-Class Use of Barter Clubs: A Real Alternative or Just Survivor?" trans. Epstein, in Epstein and Pion-Berlin 151.
65. González Bombal and Luzzi 149.
66. Maristella Svampa and Damián Corral, "Political Mobilization in Neighborhood Assemblies: The Cases of Villa Crespo and Palermo," trans. Epstein, in Epstein and Pion-Berlin 118–22.
67. Unnamed member of the Palermo Assembly, qtd. in Svampa and Corral 128.
68. Svampa and Corral 133.
69. Judy Dempsey, "Iceland Government Collapse Reflects European Troubles," *New York Times* 27 January 2009: A8.
70. Dave Krasne, "Money for Nothing," op-ed, *New York Times* 27 January 2009: A29.
71. Adam Nagourney and Marjorie Connelly (*NYT*), "Poll finds high hopes for Obama, tempered by patience," *San Francisco Chronicle* 18 January 2009: A11.

INDEX